D0641701

JAPANESE FOR COLLEGE STUDENTS

JAPANESE FOR COLLEGE STUDENTS

Basic

International Christian University

KODANSHA INTERNATIONAL
Tokyo • New York • London

International Christian University staff who participated in the writing of *Japanese for College Students: Basic* (in alphabetical order with an asterisk indicating the coordinator for this edition)

George D. Bedell
Marie J. Bedell
Rebecca L. Copeland
Yoshifumi Hida
Izumi Hirata
Masayoshi Hirose
Shigeko Inagaki
Mayumi Yuki Johnson
Ryoko Murano
Ichiro Nakamura
Taeko Nakamura
*Machiko Netsu
Takashi Ogawa
Kumiko Osaki
Yoko Suzuki
Mari Tanaka
Sayoko Yamashita

Illustrations by Midori Murasaki

Distributed in the United States by Kodansha America, Inc., 114 Fifth Avenue, New York N.Y. 10011, and in the United Kingdom and continental Europe by Kodansha Europe Ltd., 95 Aldwych, London WC2B 4JF. Published by Kodansha International Ltd., 17-14 Otowa 1-chome, Bunkyo-ku, Tokyo 112, and Kodansha America, Inc.

First edition, 1996
98 99 10 9 8 7 6 5 4 3 2

ISBN 4-7700-1997-1

CONTENTS

PREFACE

Japanese for College Students: Basic is a comprehensive beginner's textbook of Japanese for university students, including sentence patterns, idiomatic expressions, conversations, kanji, vocabulary, reading, and writing. The vocabulary, expressions, grammar, and kanji have all been carefully selected on the basis of a close observation of the life-styles and activities of contemporary students; they assume situations and settings which foreigners would be likely to encounter in everyday life as university students in Japan. The textbook has been structured so that students not only acquire the language proficiency necessary for daily life, but also gain an ample grounding in basic grammar and kanji for proceeding to higher levels.

Many illustrations, a great number of conversational Japanese expressions, and various roleplays have been included to make the book suitable for teaching with a communicative approach. Special care has been taken to ensure that the points to be learned are presented over several lessons and recur in spiral fashion to facilitate absorption. Detailed English explanations are provided for the study of grammatical points. With a total of thirty lessons (ten per volume), the three volumes are intended to be completed in a program of approximately 300 hours of classroom study, resulting in an acquired vocabulary of some 2,000 words and 400 kanji.

The teaching of Japanese in universities has become more widely spread in recent years. At ICU the regular Japanese language program for foreign students was inaugurated in 1953. In 1963 ICU published *Modern Japanese for University Students, Part I.* This textbook, based on then-current theories of structural linguistics and language teaching pedagogy, enjoyed a life of thirty years at institutions in Japan and abroad. In 1989 it was decided to create a completely new textbook for foreign students based on the latest linguistic theories and teaching methodologies. Since that time, the new textbook has gone through several preliminary versions and two trial printings, and now appears as *Japanese for College Students: Basic.* Although the utmost care was taken with the content, there is still undoubtedly room for improvement. Comments and suggestions would be greatly appreciated.

This book could not have been completed without the assistance of many people. We are particularly indebted to the following people for their efforts during the process of actual publication: Yoko Sakumae, Kumi Noguchi, Nobuko Ikeda, Chika Maruyama, Ikumi Ozawa, Chiaki Hatanaka, and Kenji Nakagawa of the ICU Japanese Language Programs; and to Taku Ogawa and Michael Brase of Kodansha International Ltd. To all we express our sincerest appreciation.

Japanese Language Programs and
The Research Center for Japanese Language Education
International Christian University, 1996

はじめに

本書は、大学生のための、会話、文型、表現、漢字、語彙、読解、書き方を含む総合的な初級教科書である。学生の実際の生活行動を参考に、外国人が大学生として生活していく上で日常出会うと思われる場面を想定し、初級レベルとして必要な語彙、表現、文法項目、漢字を厳選してある。この教科書をマスターすれば、日常生活に必要な日本語力が得られるばかりでなく、さらに上のレベルに進むのに十分な基礎的文法力、漢字力が得られるように構成されている。

本書はコミュニカティブな教授法に合うように、イラストをほどこし、自然な表現を取り入れてある。重要な学習項目はいくつかの課にわたって提示され、学習が繰返しスパイラル式に行なわれ、定着するように配慮されている。文法事項は予習・復習の便をはかり、英語によるくわしい解説をほどこしてある。全体を全3巻30課(各巻10課)で構成し、約300時間のプログラムを考えて作られている。(語彙約2000語、漢字400字)

大学において日本語教育が行なわれるようになってから久しい。ICUにおいては、1953年、外国人学生に対する日本語教育が正規の学科目として始められ、1963年、大学生のための独自の日本語教科書「Modern Japanese for University Students」Part Iを出版した。この教科書は当時の構造言語学、外国語教授法に基づいて作られ、幸い約30年の長きにわたり内外の機関で使用された。1989年、現代の学生のニーズにあった全く新しい外国人学生のための日本語教科書を、最新の言語学、外国語教授理論に基づいて作ることになり、以来幾回にもおよぶ仮印刷版、2回にわたる試用版を経て、今回ようやく「Japanese for College Students:Basic」として上梓のはこびとなった。内容等万全を期したが、なお問題もあろうかと思う。さらなる改善のために皆様のご叱正を請う次第である。

この本ができるまでには多くの方々の献身的な助力があった。出版にあたって特に日本語教育プログラムの作前陽子、野口久美、池田伸子、丸山千歌、小澤伊久美、畑中千晶、中川健司、講談社インターナショナル編集部のマイケル・ブレーズ、小川卓の諸氏に謝意を表したい。

1996年9月

国際基督教大学
日本語教育プログラム・
日本語教育研究センター

HOW TO USE THIS BOOK

This textbook is for college students studying the Japanese language for the first time. The goal of the book is to enable students to function linguistically in everyday situations involving listening, speaking, reading, and writing. All of these aspects of the language, as well as grammar, are studied and practiced in context. By practicing in context, students learn accuracy and appropriateness. In keeping with this objective, the Japanese writing system of kana and kanji is introduced from the very first lesson. Kana and kanji are exclusively used in the "Listening and Speaking" section; the "Grammar Notes" use Japanese script plus selected subscript romanization in Lessons 1-4, but thereafter the romanization is dropped. On the oral side, it is important that the tapes be used for self-study practice in the preview and review of each lesson, and in the classroom the basic underlying assumption concerning the "Listening and Speaking" section is that the class will be conducted orally, and that any oral practice will be done with the book closed.

The text consists of 30 lessons divided into three volumes of ten lessons each. Each volume presents situations and contexts familiar to college students. Volume 1 relates to the students themselves and their immediate circumstances; Volume 2 involves frequently encountered situations; Volume 3 presents social and public situations relevant to college life.

The lessons that follow "Getting Started" are organized as follows:

- Listening and Speaking
- Grammar Notes
- Reading
- Writing

Listening and Speaking

OBJECTIVES: Here the goals of the lesson are given. In order to make the most efficient use of their time, students should have these objectives firmly in mind before beginning the lesson.

POINTS: The major linguistic functions of the lesson are listed here. These functions must be learned in order to achieve the lesson's goals. Students should go over these points before starting the lesson and review them again afterwards.

SENTENCES: Grammatical items to be studied in the lesson are listed in example sentence form and underscored with a dotted line. These sentences are practiced orally one by one in the "Formation" section. Students should go over this list before starting the lesson and refer to it again later for review purposes.

EXPRESSIONS: Expressions that are particularly helpful in making conversation flow smoothly and naturally are listed here. Later they are studied in the "Drills" section, where they are underscored with a dotted line. They include sentence final particles, conjunctions, interjections, and contracted forms. For each expression, English equivalents are provided. When there are no expressions for a particular lesson, the "Expressions" heading does not appear.

The following three oral practice activities should be taken up in the order presented: "Formation," "Drills," and "Roleplay." Each activity has different goals.

「フォーメーション」 FORMATION: Here the grammatical items listed in "Sentences" are practiced orally. The goal is to achieve accuracy in pronunciation and grammar. This basic practice is extremely important in preparing for the "Drills" and "Roleplay" sections. The numbers of the subheadings in "Sentences" and "Formation" correspond for easy reference. Each example in "Formation" indicates how the intended sentence pattern is obtained from the given cues: the word or words to the left of the arrow (→) in the example are the cue and those to the right of the arrow are the sentence to be produced, with the underlined part to the right of the arrow to be replaced with the cues given below. This is a form of substitution practice. Each exercise is limited to a single sentence focusing on a single grammatical point and one sentence pattern; no context is given. New vocabulary, grammatical items, and accurate pronunciation are the focus here. When previewing and reviewing the "Formation" section, the student practices making sentences as directed while listening to the tape. Only examples and cues are given in the book, not intended sentences; however, in the tape the sentences to be produced are also given. These patterns should be practiced repeatedly and indelibly committed to memory. In class, along with reproduction of the patterns and vocabulary, the aim should be for accurate pronunciation.

Study of the "Formation" section cannot be considered complete until the student can participate actively, accurately, and appropriately in the "Drill" and "Roleplay" activities.

「ドリル」 DRILL: Each drill takes the form of a short conversation in a specific context. The underlined words are to be replaced by a vocabulary item or expression selected from the box below. Through this activity the student learns to choose an item appropriate to a given context. New vocabulary and new grammar items from the "Formation" section are intensively drilled here, in context and with appropriate pronunciation and intonation. For self-study the student should practice these drills as much as possible with the tapes. In class the instructor may change the situations given in the book to ones more familiar and relevant to the student, but this does not in any way diminish the importance of studying, as given, the vocabulary and expressions in the drills prior to class.

「ロールプレイ」 ROLEPLAY: Each roleplay presents familiar situations in which the language the student has learned up to that point may be used in real-life situations. Two students perform specific tasks as directed by the role cards, using vocabulary and grammatical items not only from the current lesson but from all the lessons previously studied. Since the roleplay is to be acted out spontaneously, a different conversation should result when the same roleplay is acted out by different students. Model roleplays are provided at the end of the book for students in need of help and encouragement, but it must be remembered that these are only models, representing several of many possibilities; they are not to be seen as restricting the content of the roleplay in any way. Since one of the goals of this textbook is for students to become familiar with usage that is appropriate to specific situations and given interpersonal relationships, the model roleplays are given in both informal and formal speech styles. For the informal styles (following this symbol, ☆★☆), examples of female and male speech are also included. The importance of appropriateness to context is strongly emphasized in this activity. Successful performance of roleplays is a sign that the material covered in the lesson has been mastered.

Grammar Notes

Grammatical items introduced in the "Listening and Speaking" section are explained here. Each grammatical item or pattern offered for discussion is highlighted in a boxed area. Meaning, function, and other relevant points necessary for the creation of accurate sentences are discussed. Japanese examples of usage are followed by English equivalents. Useful linguistic and cultural information is occasionally provided in "Usage Notes." Grammar and usage notes should be carefully read before and after class in order to gain a full appreciation of how the Japanese language is structured. It is of utmost importance that the material in each lesson be thoroughly understood before preceding to the next.

Reading

READING PASSAGE: Each lesson features a commonly encountered type of reading material or category of writing. The type is specified in the beginning of each lesson. Both vertical and horizontal printed materials and handwritten realia are used. The topic of each section is based on the vocabulary, grammatical items, and functions introduced in "Listening and Speaking." Vocabulary whose meaning or Kanji reading were not introduced in "Listening and Speaking" is listed below the reading passage with English equivalents.

Before starting the "Reading" section of Lesson 1, the student must be familiar with the kana script, which is covered in "Getting Started." In addition, since each lesson introduces new kanji, students should study those kanji in the "Writing" section before attempting the reading passage.

「読む前に」 BEFORE READING: Here the topic and the format of the reading passage are introduced. It is best to go through this part before reading the passage.

「質問」 COMPREHENSION CHECK: To confirm their understanding of the passage, students should go over the exercise in the "Comprehension Check" before and after class.

「書きましょう」 WRITING ACTIVITY: This part presents two activities: 1) writing the same type of passage and 2) writing some type of reaction or response in keeping with the content of the reading passage.

「話しましょう」 SPEAKING ACTIVITY: Here the student is encouraged to discuss the topics introduced in the lesson or to conduct interviews of other students.

Writing

This section consists of four parts: "Let's Learn the Readings," "New Kanji," "Writing Practice," and "Reading Practice." The "New Kanji" section introduces 245 kanji (corresponding to the kanji required in the Japanese Language Proficiency Test, Level 3); another 155 kanji are introduced in "Let's Learn the Readings." A total of 400 kanji are thus introduced in the 30 lessons comprising the three volumes.

「読み方を覚えましょう」 LET'S LEARN THE READINGS: A number of words written in kanji are introduced here. The section includes all the vocabulary items using kanji that were introduced in the "New Kanji" section as well as 155 additional kanji. All the words here are needed for reading Japanese at a basic level.

「新しい漢字」 NEW KANJI: 245 kanji and one repetition symbol are introduced in the charts here.

ことば	れんしゅう	日	
1 日 ひ ・ 2 日曜日 にちようび	日 日	くん	おん
		ひ・び・か	にち・に・にっ
		いみ	
		the sun, day(s)	
	かきじゅん		
1 a day 2 Sunday			

1 — **Consecutive Number**

New Kanji

「くん」「おん」 KUN-READING, ON-READING: Kanji can be read in two ways. One is called the kun-reading, which is Japanese in origin, and the other is the On-reading, which is Chinese in origin. Although the chart does not contain every possible reading, it has all the readings necessary for most tasks at a basic level.

「いみ」 MEANING: The meaning of the kanji are given in English.

「かきじゅん」 STROKE ORDER: This part shows the order of the strokes used to write each kanji. The fundamental rule is that stroke order proceeds from left to right and/or from top to bottom.

「れんしゅう」 PRACTICE: Here, the writing of kanji can be practiced, emulating the model and following the correct stroke order.

「ことば」 WORDS: Here are listed some of the words formed with the kanji in question; while some have already appeared in the main text, other words of a very basic nature are given here for the first time. English equivalents are shown at the bottom.

「書く練習」「読む練習」 WRITING PRACTICE, READING PRACTICE: In "Writing Practice," students practice writing the kanji that appear in the "New Kanji" section. In "Reading Practice," students practice reading the kanji introduced both in "New Kanji" and in "Let's Learn the Readings." For the writing exercises, students should make photocopies as needed of the pertinent pages and write on them rather than directly in the book.

Each volume contains an index by reading of all the kanji introduced in the 30 lessons. This book adheres to the current standards for Japanese script. However, in order to facilitate study by non-Japanese students, certain nonstandard but widely used elements have been incorporated.

About Kanji Usage

In principle, single kanji and kanji compounds appear with subscript readings in hiragana (called 'rubi') until they have been introduced for study in a particular lesson; thereafter, the rubi are omitted. In the case of kanji compounds, rubi is given for the whole compound even if one of the characters has already been learned; the rubi are only dispensed with after both kanji in the compound have been studied. Proper nouns and other words which are commonly written in kanji in the real world, but which are not studied in *Japanese for College Students: Basic,* are given in kanji with rubi attached. For the student's benefit, all the kanji in the Grammar Notes appear with rubi.

Romanization and 'Wakachigaki'

For romanization, a modified version of the Hepburn system is used: e.g., [aa] indicates a long vowel, [itte] represents double [t] sounds, [n] is the syllabic nasal. Lessons 1 through 10 are written in 'wakachigaki', that is, with spaces between words and phrases for ease of reading. In normal text, there are usually no such spaces.

Cassette Tapes

Cassette tapes are available for study with *Japanese for College Students: Basic.* These tapes play a crucial role in the learning of Japanese, and students are encouraged to make the utmost use of them. They include the "Listening and Speaking" sections of Lessons 1-30, in addition to the "Getting Started" section in Volume 1. "Getting Started" includes a syllabary of sounds. The aim of this section is to familiarize students with the sounds of the Japanese language and to help students learn some simple phrases and expressions that are extremely useful in everyday life. It is important here to pay particular attention to accent and intonation. While accent and intonation are not indicated in the written text of the book, students may refer for help to the vocabulary lists at the end of the book, where accent is marked over every word.

After "Getting Started," the tapes proceed to the "Formation" and "Drills" sections of each lesson. "Formation" consists of a cue (to the left of the arrow [→]) and an expression to be produced on the basis of the cue (to the right of the arrow in the example). The portion of the example to be replaced by the student (i.e., the object of substitution) is underlined. In the textbook, the expression that is to be produced from the cue is not given, so it is impossible from the text alone for students to know if they have produced the correct expression. In the tapes, however, the correct expression is given so that students can know if the expression they have produced is the correct one. It is best to conduct the "Formation" exercises with the book closed.

The "Drills" consist of dialogues between two parties, A and B. The words or expressions to be provided by the student are chosen from the boxed area below the exercise. There may be more than one correct answer. Although a number of combinations are possible, only one is given in the tape as correct. Other possible substitutions can be given in class, to be checked by the instructor for accuracy. The textbook should be kept closed except for the "Drills" that make use of illustrations, of which there are a good number.

この本を使う人のために

この教科書は、初めて日本語を学ぶ学生のためのものです。学生として日常生活のさまざまな場面で必要な言語活動—聴き、話し、読み、書き—ができるようになることを目指しています。
そのために、文法の規則を学び、それを現実に機能させる練習を行い、正確かつ適切な運用能力を身に付けるように編集してあります。四技能を身につけることを目標としていますから1課からかな・漢字で表記しています。1課を始める前にGETTING STARTEDでひらがな・かたかな表記を紹介しています。
聴き・話しのセクションは日本語表記でなされていますが目標がこの2つの技能の習得なので、自習においては音声テープを、授業においてはオーラルを基本にした練習を行う、つまり、本を開いて読みながら口頭練習をしないことを前提にしています。

この教科書は初級日本語を第1巻、第2巻、第3巻の3つに分け、各巻を10課で構成しています。第1巻では、自分のことや身の回りのこと、第2巻では、他の人と接触する場面を、第3巻では、社会的な場面や公的な場面の中で学生が経験するであろう場面を取り上げています。

各課はLISTENING AND SPEAKING（聴き・話し）、GRAMMAR NOTES（文法）、READING（読み）、WRITING（書き）のセクションから成り、各セクションは次のように構成されています。

LISTENING AND SPEAKING 聴き・話し

OBJECTIVES: その課の目標が書いてあります。学習を始めるに当たって、ここで何ができるようにするのかを理解しておくことは、学習を効果的にします。

POINTS: その課で学習する言語活動を機能別にあげた項目です。課の目標を達成するために、学習しなければならないことがあげてあります。課の学習を始める前に目を通しておきましょう。また課の学習を終えたときに、確認のチェックをしてください。

SENTENCES: その課の文法面での学習項目を点線を付けて提示し、簡単な文の形で示しました。学習を始めるに当たって、目を通して学習の準備をしておきます。また復習するときは、チェック・リストとして使うとよいでしょう。

EXPRESSIONS： フォーメーションで置き換え練習をするSENTENCESの文とは別に、その課のドリルにでてくる表現・終助詞・接続詞・接続助詞・副助詞・間投詞・短縮形などを会話をスムーズに行うために必要な表現としてまとめました。表現には対訳がついています。この項目がない課もあります。

フォーメーション： 文型や語彙を身に付けるための練習で、発音や文法の正確さを目指します。ドリル・ロールプレイをスムーズに行い、これらの活動の目的を達成するための大切な基礎練習です。学習する文型が与えられたキューからどのように作られるかが例に示されています。例の中の矢印（→）の左側がキューになっており、右側が作られる文で、練習する時に置き換えるところを下線で示してあります。予習・復習などの自習の時には音声テープを聴きながら例にならって文を作る練習をします。教科書には例とキューのみが与えられ、作られる文は示されていません（矢印の右側には何も書いてありません）が、音声テープには作られる文もはいっています。

フォーメーションは置き換え練習の形をとっています。機械的な練習ですが、学習者は積極的に自習をすることが必要です。授業では文型や語彙の定着をはかるとともに発音の正確さを目指します。なお、フォーメーションの番号はSENTENCESの番号と呼応しています。

ドリル： フォーメーションは文単位の練習ですが、ドリルは対話の形とし、教室内でのインターアクションを重視しています。基本的にAとB二人の短いやりとりの形を提示し、置き換え可能な部分を下線で示しています。枠で囲んだ与えられたキューの中から適切なものを選び、下線部分を置き換えて練習するようになっています。これは、実際の場面で、学習者が自分で判断し、適切な言葉や表現を選んで応答できるようにするためです。教室で練習するときは、教科書を見ないで、より現実の場面に近い状況で行うほうが効果があります。ですから授業の前に必ずドリルで使われている表現や言葉を勉強しておくことが必要です。

ロールプレイ： ロールプレイはその課の学習の仕上げと考えてよいでしょう。学習した言葉や文型、表現を総動員して、OBJECTIVESで示されたその課の目標を達成できたかどうか、どの程度できるかを総合的に見ることができます。ロールプレイが上手にできれば、その課の学習を修了したといえます。

コミュニケーションを適切に行えるようにするためには、早い時期から場面や人間関係に適した言葉の使い方に慣れることが大切ですから、インフォーマル（☆★☆のマークで示す）とフォーマルの会話の例をのせました。インフォーマルの場合、男女の言葉の異なるものは女性形／男性形の順で一つの例を示しました。このモデル会話に出てくるEXPRESSIONSはその下に対訳とともにあげられています。これらはあくまでもモデル会話なので巻末にまとめて提示してありますが、それを参考にしてペアになった相手と自発的に適切な会話を作り上げるようにするとよいでしょう。その際まだ学習していない語彙や表現などが必要な場合には先生が提示します。

GRAMMAR NOTES 文法

聴き・話しのセクションで導入された文法項目の説明をしています。
まず、基本的な文型を枠で囲んで示し、その文型の意味とそれがどのような言語機能を果たす目的で使われるのか、また特に注意しなければならない点を説明しています。その後ろに例文を対訳つきで提示しています。時に言語を運用する際に必要な言語的・文化的情報がUSAGE NOTESとして与えられています。学習する前後によく読んで理解し、分からないところは先生に聞いて明確にしておきます。

READING 読み

本文： 各課の聴き・話しセクションの文法項目、語彙と関連づけて、日常生活で実際に目にする読み物の形式（ジャンル）や縦書きと横書き、印刷と手書きといった様々な書き方の読み物が入るよう配慮してあります。また、本文に使われている漢字は各課で新しく導入される漢字に準拠しているので、本文を読み始める前に漢字の学習をしておく必要があります。

「読む前に」： その課のトピックと文章形式を理解します。

「質問」： ここにある項目を使いながら本文の内容の確認をします。

「書きましょう」： その課で扱うトピック、形式、および機能にあわせて、同じような文章を書いたり、または、本文の内容に応じて返事などを書いたりします。

「話しましょう」： 本文で扱っているトピックについてクラス内で話したりインタビューしたりします。

WRITING 書き

「読み方を覚えましょう」「新しい漢字」「書く練習」「読む練習」の4つのパートから成っています。30課まで修了すると、日本語能力試験の3級で扱う245字が書けるようになり、その他155字が読めるようになります。つまり、合計400字の習得を目標としています。
次に、それぞれのパートを解説します。

読み方を覚えましょう： 「新しい漢字」に出てくる漢字を使った語彙を先に紹介したり、「新しい漢字」にない155字の漢字を使った初級語彙を紹介します。その言葉と読み方と意味が書いてあるので、覚えながら新しい漢字語彙を増やします。

新しい漢字： 漢字表を使って、245字と繰り返し符号「々」を紹介し、書く練習ができるようになっています。

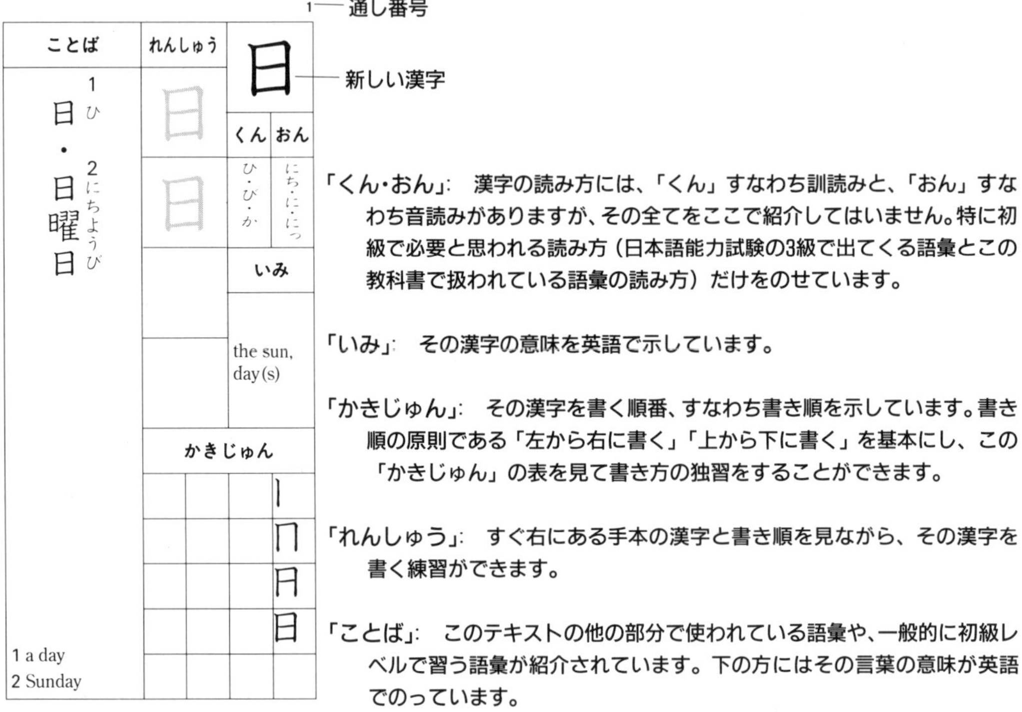

「くん・おん」: 漢字の読み方には、「くん」すなわち訓読みと、「おん」すなわち音読みがありますが、その全てをここで紹介してはいません。特に初級で必要と思われる読み方（日本語能力試験の3級で出てくる語彙とこの教科書で扱われている語彙の読み方）だけをのせています。

「いみ」: その漢字の意味を英語で示しています。

「かきじゅん」: その漢字を書く順番、すなわち書き順を示しています。書き順の原則である「左から右に書く」「上から下に書く」を基本にし、この「かきじゅん」の表を見て書き方の独習をすることができます。

「れんしゅう」: すぐ右にある手本の漢字と書き順を見ながら、その漢字を書く練習ができます。

「ことば」: このテキストの他の部分で使われている語彙や、一般的に初級レベルで習う語彙が紹介されています。下の方にはその言葉の意味が英語でのっています。

書く練習・読む練習： 「書く練習」では「新しい漢字」の漢字を書く練習ができ、「読む練習」では「読み方を覚えましょう」や「新しい漢字」の言葉を読む練習ができます。同じ漢字や語彙が何回か出てきますが、より重ねて練習するためには、このページをコピー（あるいは拡大コピー）などしておくとよいでしょう。

なお、各巻巻末に書きセクションの索引がついていますが、それは第1巻から第3巻までで紹介される漢字の全ての読み方に基づいた音訓索引となっています。この教科書は現行の国語表記の標準に従いました。しかし外国人学習者への教育的な配慮に基づいて慣用的なものも採用しています。

ABOUT KANJI USAGE 漢字表記

聴き・話しセクションの漢字表記は原則としてその課よりあとに紹介される漢字語彙にルビをつけましたが、その漢字語彙にふくまれる漢字がすべて紹介された時点でルビははずされます。未習の漢字をふくむ固有名詞や慣用的に漢字で表記される語彙についてはルビをつけて漢字で表記しました。なお文法は学習者の便宜をはかるため30課までのすべての漢字にルビをつけました。

ROMANIZATION AND ‘WAKACHIGAKI’
ローマ字表記とわかち書きについて

ローマ字表記は原則として修正ヘボン式を採用しています。例えば長音は母音を重ねて［aa］とし、促音は子音を重ねて［itte］、撥音は［n］としました。

この教科書では1課から漢字仮名交じり文で表記していますが、第1巻（1課から10課）は、わかち書きにしてあります。

CASSETTE TAPES オーディオテープについて

前にも述べましたが、この教科書での学習には積極的なテープの利用を勧めます。テープにはGETTING STARTEDと全30課のLISTENING AND SPEAKINGの部分が入っています。

先ず、GETTING STARTEDでは五十音図と日常生活に役に立つ表現を学びながら、日本語の音が練習できるようになっています。第1課に進む前に、ここで十分発音やイントネーション、アクセントなどの練習をしておきます。なお、教科書の本文にはイントネーションやアクセントは表記はされていませんが、巻末の語彙リストにはアクセントが表記されています。

GETTING STARTEDに続く第1課から第30課にはフォーメーションとドリルが入っています。フォーメーションではそれぞれの学習項目が例を使ってキュー（→の左側）と作られるべき表現（→の右側にあり、置き換え部分に下線が付いています）で提示され、続いて置き換え練習ができるようになっています。教科書の練習の箇所には作られるべき表現は書いてありませんが、テープには入っていますから、まずキューを使って自分で言ってみてから、テープの答えを聞き、正確にできたかどうかチェックするといいでしょう。ListeningとSpeakingの能力を高めるためにフォーメーションは教科書を閉じて練習することを勧めます。ドリルの置き換え部分はフォーメーションと同様に下線が付いています。それぞれのドリルのキューの箱から適切なものを選んで下線部分に置き換えます。いくつかの組み合わせが可能で、答えが1つとはかぎりません。ですから、テープにはモデルとして教科書に提示されている短い会話のみが入っています。また、ドリルにはイラストを使ったりしながら練習するものも多く、その場合は教科書を開いて必要な箇所を見ながら練習します。

Some Basic Features of the Japanese Language

Japanese has a number of structural features that it shares with many other languages throughout the world but which are not present in English or the languages of Western Europe. A brief outline of these features is provided here so that students who native tongue does not possess these characteristics can better grasp the grammatical points introduced throughout this course.

1. The headword of a phrase generally comes in the final position. This means that (a) objects, adverbs and adverbial phrases precede the verbs or adjectives they belong to (that is, Japanese is an SOV (subject+object+verb) language rather than an SVO language like English); (b) adjectives and clauses precede the nouns they modify; and (c) noun phrases precede relational particles (that is, Japanese has postpositions rather than prepositions like English).

2. Verbs have complicated conjugations marking tense and aspect. There are two types of adjectives: those that are marked for tense and aspect like verbs, and those that behave rather like nouns. Nouns and noun-like adjectives are accompanied by a copula when used as predicates.

3. In addition to being analyzable as subject and predicate, sentences can typically be broken down into topic and comment. The topic, marked by the particle 'wa', is usually found in the initial position of a sentence or a sequence of sentences.

4. There is no obligatory distinction between singular and plural nouns. Numbers are normally combined with a classifier that categorizes the object being counted.

5. There is an elaborate system for marking speech styles. Utterances may be plain or polite, according to the situation; the style is determined by suffixes being added to the predicate. Honorific forms, which may be markers or distinct words, express respect for those of a higher social status than the speaker.

6. The predicate is the only sentence component that must be present. Other components, including topics, subjects, and objects, can be omitted whenever the speaker considers them to be understood from context. In addition, implied meaning is often given priority over direct statement, making an understanding of context doubly important.

7. Events tend to be described as situations rather than as actions performed by persons: for example. normal Japanese would call for 'Fuji-san ga mieru' ('Mt. Fuji is visible') rather than 'Fuji-san o miru koto ga dekiru' ('I can see Mt. Fuji').

8. The basic unit of rhythm in standard Japanese is the mora, which has a time value equal to a short syllable. Each mora has a pitch accent of either high (H) or low (L), which is determined at the word level.

In contrast to English, in which stressed syllables tend to be elongated, both high and low syllables in Japanese are perceived to have approximately the same length. This is also true of special moras: long vowels (e.g., to-o-kyo-o, of four moras), syllabic nasals (e.g., ni-ho-n-go, of four moras), and doubled consonants (e.g., i-t-ta, of three moras).

For all words, the second accent is low if the first is high, and vice versa. For instance, consider the pitch of nouns when accompanied by the particle 'ga'. Two-mora nouns + 'ga' have the patterns LHH (e.g., あれが), LHL (e.g., やまが), and HLL (e.g., じしょが); three-mora nouns + 'ga' have LHHH (e.g., なまえが), LHHL (e.g., やすみが), LHLL (e.g., あなたが), and HLLL (e.g., なんじが).

In this book, accent is indicated in the appendix "New Vocabulary and Expressions." On the separately available tapes, natural rhythm, pronunciation, accent, and intonation are recorded for repeated listening. Making use of these materials, students should achieve considerable accuracy in the spoken language.

The Writing System

Japanese Script

A number of different scripts are used in the Japanese language: Chinese characters ('kanji'), 'hiragana', 'katakana', the Roman alphabet ('roomaji'), and various types of numbers (Chinese, Roman, and Arabic). Kanji are Chinese in origin and came to be used as Japanese script in the fifth century, and were thereafter augmented by the creation of new kanji by the Japanese.

At the beginning, kanji were the only script available for writing Japanese, but later two phonetic scripts—hiragana and katakana (collectively called 'kana')—were created on the basis of the shapes of selected Chinese characters. Both of these scripts are phonetic, but they differ from phonetic alphabetic scripts in that they represent not individual sounds (phonemes) but syllables. Japanese is commonly written with a combination of kanji and these two kana scripts.

Japanese was first romanized, or written with the Roman alphabet, by Western missionaries in the fifteenth century. Romanized Japanese is called 'roomaji'.

The function of each script in contemporary Japanese may be summarized as follows:

a. Kanji are used for writing nouns and the stems of verbs and adjectives, that is, content words.
b. Hiragana, which were created from cursive forms of kanji, are used to write indigenous adverbs and grammatical function words such as particles and the inflections of verbs and adjectives.
c. Katakana, which were created by extracting a part of a kanji character, are used to write loanwords, foreign names, onomatopoeia, and the scientific names of flora and fauna, thus making these words stand out in the main body of text consisting of hiragana and kanji; in this usage, katakana is similar to italics in English.
d. Roomaji are used for transcribing Japanese sounds (phonemes) as well as those of other languages. The use of roomaji is far from being limited to signboards and literature intended for foreign visitors in Japan. It is often used in the design world for effect.

Next, let us take a brief look at the structure, reading, and meaning of kanji.

Kanji can be categorized structurally into four types and functionally into two. The first structural type is the ideograph. Kanji began as pictorial representations of natural objects, such as mouth (口), tree (木), sun (日), and fish (魚). All scripts throughout the world began in this way, including the Roman alphabet, but at present only kanji remains in use.

To represent abstract concepts such as up, down, and middle, the second structural type was created. In this type, lines in the kanji pointed 'up' (上) or 'down' (下) or passed through the 'middle' of a box (中) to convey the intended meaning; a short line intersecting the trunk of a tree (本) meant 'source'.

A third structural type consisted of combining individual ideographs to form new characters. For example, the character for 'tree' (木) could be doubled (林) to make 'woods' or tripled (森) to make forest, or 'sun' (日) could be overlapped with 'tree' to create the image of the sun rising behind a tree (東), producing the meaning 'east'.

Combining ideographs had clear limitations, however, which led to the invention of the fourth structural type. This type combined a pictorial character with another character that had developed strong associations with a certain sound. The chief characteristic of this structural type is the fact that the pictorial element represents the meaning (this part is called the 'radical' [部首 'bushu']) and the other element the pronunciation. The character 語 is an example of this type. The radical, on the left, represents the meaning 'language', while the part on the right gives the sound, 'go'. Another example of this structure is 悟 ('enlightenment'), with the abbreviated radical for 'heart' on the left suggesting the meaning and the reading 'go' on the right giving the pronunciation. This type of kanji proved so effective that it now accounts for over eighty percent of all kanji.

With the above, the various ways of creating new kanji were exhausted. However, in case of need, there were still ways in which new meanings could be attached to already existing kanji, alluded to earlier as the two functions or uses of kanji. One way was association by meaning. For example, the character 楽 in the compound 音楽 means 'music', and from the association of music with the joy of listening to music, the character 楽 was given the meaning 'enjoyable'.

Another way of attaching new meanings occurred when two spoken words had identical pronunciations but only one of them possessed a kanji with which it could be written. The word having no kanji simply adopted the kanji of its homonymic counterpart, regardless of any differences in meaning. An example of this is 来, the original meaning of which was 'wheat' but whose later, now more common, meaning is 'come'. This method of association by sound rather than meaning was also adopted for transcribing loanwords by means of kanji, an example of which is 亜米利加 'Amerika'.

This is basically the form kanji had assumed when taken up for the transcription of Japanese. Due to differences in the pronunciation and grammar between Chinese and Japanese, however, kanji in Japan underwent some changes.

These changes concern the readings, or pronunciation, applied to the kanji. One type of reading is called the 'on' reading, which is the pronunciation given the kanji when it is read as a Chinese word (or, more accurately, as it is read when a Japanese emulates Chinese pronunciation). Single kanji and kanji compounds which are read in this way are referred to as 'kango', or Chinese words (lit., 'Han words'). An example is 人 ('jin', person). Some kanji have more than one 'on' reading (人 is also read 'nin') because Japanese picked up a variety of readings from different dialectical regions of China and in various historical eras.

The other reading is called the 'kun' reading, which is the meaning of the kanji as translated into native Japanese, or 'wago' (lit., 'Yamato words'). An example is 人 ('hito', person), which uses the same kanji as the kango 'jin' but is read as a native Japanese word.

Turning now to katakana, it was mentioned earlier that katakana is used to write loanwords, of which there are a great many in the Japanese language, as there are in English. During the Meiji period (1868-1912) there was a great influx of loanwords, but most were rendered into Japanese equivalents, often as kanji compounds. Today, however, perhaps because of the speed, volume, and variety of loanwords making their way into the language, there is a strong tendency to render them phonetically into katakana, keeping the pronunciation as close as possible to the original.

Overall, modern Japanese script consists basically of a combination of kanji, hiragana, and katakana. The Ministry of Education has established standards for their use, in particular for official documents, newspapers, and television. The teaching of Japanese script in elementary and middle schools also follows the Ministry's directives. 1,945 kanji have been established by the Ministry to be learned during the years of compulsory education. These are the so-called 'Jooyoo Kanji' (lit., Common Use Kanji) and are considered the minimum number needed to read present-day newspapers, magazines, and contemporary literature. 1,006 of these kanji are learned in elementary school and the remaining 939 in middle school. An additional 284 kanji, along with the Jooyoo Kanji, are available for use in personal names.

Aside from these standards, there are few overriding restrictions at a popular level on how a certain word must be written, whether in kanji or in one of the kana syllabary. There is considerable room for individual choice in a wide variety of writing activities. According to time and place, a person may write the same word in different ways without being rigidly consistent. In this respect, Japanese script stands apart from English and European scripts, where the correct spelling of words is more or less fixed.

In conclusion, a few words might be said about the role that kanji play in the transcription of Japanese, particularly in light of the burden that the complexity of kanji places on the student. For over 1,500 years, kanji have been recognized as a Japanese script, and they continue to be employed today as a matter of course. True, there are some Japanese who feel that kanji should be abandoned in favor of the exclusive use of hiragana and katakana, and there are others who champion the Roman alphabet. Nevertheless, the overwhelming opinion is that kanji are indispensable in expressing through writing the multifaceted aspects of Japanese culture.

Among students of the Japanese language, there are many who find kanji to be a formidable and unwelcome barrier, while there are others who have taken up the study of Japanese precisely because of a fascination with kanji. For these latter students there is a certain satisfaction and even joy in unraveling the meaning and reading of individual kanji as they become familiar with the shapes and structures out of which kanji are formed. Perceiving how one kanji changes in meaning when combined with another is a further source of intellectual satisfaction. All students are encouraged to take this curious-minded, puzzle-solving approach; it makes the study of kanji so much more interesting and rewarding.

It is the hope of the authors of this book that students will familiarize themselves with kanji from the earliest possible stage in their study of the language, so that they can more easily make use of kanji in whatever occupation or walk of life connected with the Japanese language that they choose to undertake. That is the reason kanji have been introduced from the very first lesson of *Japanese for College Students: Basic* and presented so that groups of kanji with associated meanings can be learned and put into practice in the most efficient possible way.

Vertical Versus Horizontal

Japanese is generally written and printed from top to bottom, the lines running from right to left, with the exception of publications and papers that deal with science, mathematics, foreign languages, et cetera. Recently, however, horizontal handwriting has achieved some popularity among young people. In this book, horizontal writing is used in the main text, and vertical writing in the "Reading" and "Writing" sections.

ABBREVIATIONS AND TERMINOLOGY

Adj	= adjective (e.g., 'ookii', 'takai')
Adj'l	= adjectival; a word or phrase that has an adjective-like function (e.g., 'Tanaka-san wa se ga takai desu' "Mr. Tanaka is tall").
Adv	= adverb (e.g., 'yukkuri', 'itsumo')
Adv'l	= adverbial; a word or phrase that has an adverb-like function (e.g., 'dono kurai', 'moo sukoshi')
Agent	= doer of an action
AN	= adjectival noun (e.g., 'genki', 'hima')
Aux	= auxiliary verb; verb used with a preceding verb (e.g., 'tabete iru')
Conj	= conjunction
copula	a verb that identifies the predicate of a sentence with the subject (e.g., 'da', 'desu')
CV	= consonant verb; verb whose stem ends in a consonant (e.g., kak-u, yom-u, hanas-u)
Dem. M	= demonstrative modifier (e.g., 'kono', 'sono', 'ano', 'dono')
Dem. Pro.	= demonstrative pronoun (e.g., 'kore', 'sore', 'are', 'dore', 'koko', 'soko', 'asoko', 'doko')
Exp	= "Expressions" section
GN	= "Grammar Notes" section
Interj	= interjection
IV	= irregular verb (e.g., 'suru', 'kuru', 'benkyoo suru')
N	= noun
nominalizer	a noun which changes a sentence into a noun (e.g., 'no' and 'koto' in the following: 'Supootsu suru no ga suki da', 'Kanji o kaku koto ga dekiru')
P	= particle (e.g., 'wa', 'ga', 'o', 'e', 'de', 'ni', 'kara')
Plain	the plain or dictionary form of copulas, adjectives, and verbs (e.g., 'da', Adj-i, V-(r)u)
Polite	the polite form of copulas, adjectives, and verbs (e.g., 'desu', Adj-i desu, V-(i)masu)
pn	= proper name/noun

Predicate	The four types of predicates are N + da, AN + da, Adj-i, V-(r)u
Pref	= prefix (e.g., 'o' in 'obenkyoo')
Quant	= quantifier
Ques	= question word
S	= sentence
Stem	= Adj-, V- (e.g., ooki- of 'ookii', taka- of 'takai', tabe- of 'taberu', kak- of 'kaku')
Subject	a noun which is normally followed by the particle 'ga'
Suf	= suffix (the inflectional ending of verbs: e.g., tabe-sase-ru, tabe-rare-ru)
Topic	the particle 'wa' indicates that the preceding word/phrase is the topic of the sentence (e.g., Tanaka-san wa hon o yomu)
V_i	= intransitive verb; a verb which does not take a direct object (e.g., 'Tanaka-san ga kuru')
V_t	= transitive verb; a verb which takes a direct object (e.g., 'Tanaka-san ga hon o yomu')
VV	= vowel verb; a verb whose stem ends with a vowel (e.g., tabe-ru, mi-ru)

GETTING STARTED

Objectives

Preparing to study Japanese and live in Japan

Points

- Familiarizing yourself with Japanese pronunciation and the kana scripts
- Exchanging greetings
- Introducing yourself
- Learning some survival expressions

LISTENING AND SPEAKING

1. Exchanging Greetings

A: *Ohayoogozaimasu.* "Good morning."
B: *Ohayoogozaimasu.* "Good morning."

A	B
Konnichiwa. "Hi/Hello/Good afternoon."	*Konnichiwa.*
Konbanwa. "Good evening."	*Konbanwa.*
Sayoonara. "Good-bye."	*Sayoonara.*
Ittekimasu. (said when going out)	*Itterasshai.* (said to someone going out)
Tadaima. (said when returning home, etc.)	*Okaerinasai.* (said to someone returning home, etc.)

2. "Thanks" and Other Standard Formulas

A: *Arigatoogozaimasu.* "Thank you very much."
B: *Dooitashimashite.* "You're welcome."

A	B
Arigatoo. "Thank you."	*Dooitashimashite.* "You are welcome."
Sumimasen. "I'm sorry/Excuse me/ Pardon me."	*Iie.* "Don't mention it."
Doozo. "Please do so." (said when inviting someone to carry out a certain action	*Doomo.* "Thanks/Thank you." (said to someone to acknowledge something)
Doozo. (said before offering food/ refreshment)	*Itadakimasu.* (said when starting a meal)
Gochisoosama. (said when finishing a meal)	*Osomatsusamadeshita* (said in reply to *gochisoosama*)

3. Introducing Oneself

A: *Hajimemashite. (Watashi wa)* *Tanaka* desu. "How do you do. I'm Tanaka."
B: *Hajimemashite. (Watashi wa)* *Suzuki* desu. "How do you do. I'm Suzuki."
A: *Doozo yoroshiku.* "Nice to meet you."
B: *Kochirakoso.* "Nice to meet you, too."

Introduce yourself using the above patterns.

4. Survival Expressions

Nan desu ka.	"What is it?"
Ikura desu ka.	"How much is it?"
Nanji desu ka.	"What time is it?"
Kyooshitsu wa doko desu ka.	"Where is the classroom?"
Kore o kudasai.	"I'll take (buy) this."
Wakarimasen.	"I don't understand/know."
Onegaishimasu.	"(Could you help me), please."
Moo ichido itte kudasai.	"Please say it once more."
Sumimasen.	"Excuse me."
Moshimoshi.	"Hello (on the telephone)."
Chotto matte kudasai.	"Just a minute, please."

5. Japanese Sounds

■ Hiragana

1) The a, i, u, e, o order

	w	r	y	m	h	n	t	s	k		
ん	わ	ら	や	ま	は	な	た	さ	か	あ	a
n	wa	ra[1]	ya	ma	ha	na	ta	sa	ka	a	
		り		み	ひ	に	ち	し	き	い	i
		ri		mi	hi	ni	chi	shi	ki	i	
		る	ゆ	む	ふ	ぬ	つ	す	く	う	u
		ru	yu	mu	fu[2]	nu	tsu	su	ku	u	
		れ		め	へ	ね	て	せ	け	え	e
		re		me	he	ne	te	se	ke	e	
	を[3]	ろ	よ	も	ほ	の	と	そ	こ	お	o
	o	ro	yo	mo	ho	no	to	so	ko	o	

Notes: 1. [r] is a so-called a flap [r], which is made by flicking the tip of the tongue against the area behind the upper teeth.
2. [f] is made by bringing the upper and lower lips close together and blowing air between them.
3. を is used only as a particle and is always pronounced [o].

p/b	d	z	g	
ぱ　ば	だ	ざ	が	a
pa/ba	da	za	ga	
ぴ　び	ぢ[4]	じ	ぎ	i
pi/bi	ji	ji	gi	
ぷ　ぶ	づ[5]	ず	ぐ	u
pu/bu	zu	zu	gu	
ぺ　べ	で	ぜ	げ	e
pe/be	de	ze	ge	
ぽ　ぼ	ど	ぞ	ご	o
po/bo	do	zo	go	

Notes: 4. e.g., はな＋ち［hana＋chi］(nose＋blood) → はなぢ［hanaji］(nosebleed)
5. e.g., つづける［tsuzukeru］(to continue, Lesson 24)

2) Small や, ゆ, よ are combined with [i] row

m	h	b	p	n	t	z	s	g	k	
みゃ	ひゃ	びゃ	ぴゃ	にゃ	ちゃ	じゃ	しゃ	ぎゃ	きゃ	ya
mya	hya	bya	pya	nya	cha	ja	sha	gya	kya	
みゅ	ひゅ	びゅ	ぴゅ	にゅ	ちゅ	じゅ	しゅ	ぎゅ	きゅ	yu
myu	hyu	byu	pyu	nyu	chu	ju	shu	gyu	kyu	
みょ	ひょ	びょ	ぴょ	にょ	ちょ	じょ	しょ	ぎょ	きょ	yo
myo	hyo	byo	pyo	nyo	cho	jo	sho	gyo	kyo	

■ Katakana

	w	r	y	m	h	n	t	s	k		
ン	ワ	ラ	ヤ	マ	ハ	ナ	タ	サ	カ	ア	a
n	wa	ra	ya	ma	ha	na	ta	sa	ka	a	
		リ		ミ	ヒ	ニ	チ	シ	キ	イ	i
		ri		mi	hi	ni	chi	shi	ki	i	
		ル	ユ	ム	フ	ヌ	ツ	ス	ク	ウ	u
		ru	yu	mu	fu	nu	tsu	su	ku	u	
		レ		メ	ヘ	ネ	テ	セ	ケ	エ	e
		re		me	he	ne	te	se	ke	e	
		ロ	ヨ	モ	ホ	ノ	ト	ソ	コ	オ	o
		ro	yo	mo	ho	no	to	so	ko	o	

p/b	d	z	g	
パ／バ	ダ	ザ	ガ	a
pa/ba	da	za	ga	
ピ／ビ	ヂ	ジ	ギ	i
pi/bi	ji	ji	gi	
プ／ブ	ヅ	ズ	グ	u
pu/bu	zu	zu	gu	
ペ／ベ	デ	ゼ	ゲ	e
pe/be	de	ze	ge	
ポ／ボ	ド	ゾ	ゴ	o
po/bo	do	zo	go	

1) Small ヤ, ユ, ヨ are combined with [i] row

m	h	b	p	n	d	t	z	s	g	k	
ミャ	ヒャ	ビャ	ピャ	ニャ		チャ	ジャ	シャ	ギャ	キャ	ya
mya	hya	bya	pya	nya		cha	ja	sha	gya	kya	
ミュ	ヒュ	ビュ	ピュ	ニュ		チュ	ジュ	シュ	ギュ	キュ	yu
myu	hyu	byu	pyu	nyu		chu	ju	shu	gyu	kyu	
ミョ	ヒョ	ビョ	ピョ	ニョ		チョ	ジョ	ショ	ギョ	キョ	yo
myo	hyo	byo	pyo	nyo		cho	jo	sho	gyo	kyo	

2) Small ア, イ, エ, オ combined with ウ、ク、ツ、テ、デ、フ

ファ		ツァ	クァ		a
フィ	ディ	ティ		ウィ	i
	デュ				u
フェ		ツェ		ウェ	e
フォ		ツォ		ウォ	o

READING

Read the following:

1. Exchanging Greetings

おはようございます[6]。
こんにちは[7]。
こんばんは。
さようなら。

いってきます[8]。
いってらっしゃい。
ただいま。
おかえりなさい。

Notes: 6. う after [o] is usually pronounced [o], not [u].
7. は at the end of greeting expressions is pronounced [wa], not [ha].
8. Double consonants are indicated by a small つ preceding the kana syllable beginning with the consonant to be doubled.

2. Thanks and Other Standard Formulas

ありがとうございます。
どういたしまして。
すみません。
いただきます。
ごちそうさま。

3. Introducing Oneself

はじめまして。
わたし　は[9]　たなか　です。
どうぞ　よろしく。

Note: 9. The particle は is always pronounced [wa].

4. Survival Expressions

いくら　です　か。
なんじ　です　か。
これ　を[10]　ください。
もう　いちど　いって　ください。
ちょっと　まって　ください。

Note: 10. The particle を is pronounced [o].

5. Loan Words

オーストラリア[11]、アメリカ、カナダ、フィリピン、タイ、イギリス、インドネシア、シンガポール、スペイン、メキシコ、ロシア、ブラジル、ドイツ、フランス、オランダ

ジョージ、ジョン、リー、スミス、コーヒー、キャンデー、チョコレート、ガム、フォーメーション[12]、ドリル、スケジュール、テスト、フィルム、パーティー[13]、オーディオ・テープ[14]

Notes: 11. A dash in kana indicates that the preceding vowel is given a duration of two moras (syllable-like units).
12. [f] sounds in foreign words are written ファ, フィ, フ, フェ or フォ.
13. [ti] sounds in foreign words are usually written ティ to approximate the original sound more closely.
14. [di] sounds in foreign words are usually written ディ to approximate the original sound more closely.

WRITING

ん	わ	ら	や	ま	は	な	た	さ	か	あ
ん	わ	ら	や	ま	は	な	た	さ	か	あ
ん	わ	ら	や	ま	は	な	た	さ	か	あ
ん	わ	ら	や	ま	は	な	た	さ	か	あ
		り		み	ひ	に	ち	し	き	い
		り		み	ひ	に	ち	し	き	い
		り		み	ひ	に	ち	し	き	い
		り		み	ひ	に	ち	し	き	い
		る	ゆ	む	ふ	ぬ	つ	す	く	う
		る	ゆ	む	ふ	ぬ	つ	す	く	う
		る	ゆ	む	ふ	ぬ	つ	す	く	う
		る	ゆ	む	ふ	ぬ	つ	す	く	う
		れ		め	へ	ね	て	せ	け	え
		れ		め	へ	ね	て	せ	け	え
		れ		め	へ	ね	て	せ	け	え
		れ		め	へ	ね	て	せ	け	え
	を	ろ	よ	も	ほ	の	と	そ	こ	お
	を	ろ	よ	も	ほ	の	と	そ	こ	お
	を	ろ	よ	も	ほ	の	と	そ	こ	お
	を	ろ	よ	も	ほ	の	と	そ	こ	お

ン	ワ	ラ	ヤ	マ	ハ	ナ	タ	サ	カ	ア
ン	ワ	ラ	ヤ	マ	ハ	ナ	タ	サ	カ	ア
ン	ワ	ラ	ヤ	マ	ハ	ナ	タ	サ	カ	ア
		リ		ミ	ヒ	ニ	チ	シ	キ	イ
		リ		ミ	ヒ	ニ	チ	シ	キ	イ
		リ		ミ	ヒ	ニ	チ	シ	キ	イ
		ル	ユ	ム	フ	ヌ	ツ	ス	ク	ウ
		ル	ユ	ム	フ	ヌ	ツ	ス	ク	ウ
		ル	ユ	ム	フ	ヌ	ツ	ス	ク	ウ
		レ		メ	ヘ	ネ	テ	セ	ケ	エ
		レ		メ	ヘ	ネ	テ	セ	ケ	エ
		レ		メ	ヘ	ネ	テ	セ	ケ	エ
	ヲ	ロ	ヨ	モ	ホ	ノ	ト	ソ	コ	オ
	ヲ	ロ	ヨ	モ	ホ	ノ	ト	ソ	コ	オ
	ヲ	ロ	ヨ	モ	ホ	ノ	ト	ソ	コ	オ

ぱ	ば	だ	ざ	が
pa	ba	da	za	ga
ぱ	ば	だ	ざ	が
ぱ	ば	だ	ざ	が
ぱ	ば	だ	ざ	が
ぴ	び	ぢ	じ	ぎ
pi	bi	ji	ji	gi
ぴ	び	ぢ	じ	ぎ
ぴ	び	ぢ	じ	ぎ
ぴ	び	ぢ	じ	ぎ
ぷ	ぶ	づ	ず	ぐ
pu	bu	zu	zu	gu
ぷ	ぶ	づ	ず	ぐ
ぷ	ぶ	づ	ず	ぐ
ぷ	ぶ	づ	ず	ぐ
ぺ	べ	で	ぜ	げ
pe	be	de	ze	ge
ぺ	べ	で	ぜ	げ
ぺ	べ	で	ぜ	げ
ぺ	べ	で	ぜ	げ
ぽ	ぼ	ど	ぞ	ご
po	bo	do	zo	go
ぽ	ぼ	ど	ぞ	ご
ぽ	ぼ	ど	ぞ	ご
ぽ	ぼ	ど	ぞ	ご

パ	バ	ダ	ザ	ガ
pa	ba	da	za	ga
パ	バ	ダ	ザ	ガ
パ	バ	ダ	ザ	ガ
パ	バ	ダ	ザ	ガ
ピ	ビ	ヂ	ジ	ギ
pi	bi	ji	ji	gi
ピ	ビ	ヂ	ジ	ギ
ピ	ビ	ヂ	ジ	ギ
ピ	ビ	ヂ	ジ	ギ
プ	ブ	ヅ	ズ	グ
pu	bu	zu	zu	gu
プ	ブ	ヅ	ズ	グ
プ	ブ	ヅ	ズ	グ
プ	ブ	ヅ	ズ	グ
ペ	ベ	デ	ゼ	ゲ
pe	be	de	ze	ge
ペ	ベ	デ	ゼ	ゲ
ペ	ベ	デ	ゼ	ゲ
ペ	ベ	デ	ゼ	ゲ
ポ	ボ	ド	ゾ	ゴ
po	bo	do	zo	go
ポ	ボ	ド	ゾ	ゴ
ポ	ボ	ド	ゾ	ゴ
ポ	ボ	ド	ゾ	ゴ

みゃ	ひゃ	びゃ	ぴゃ	にゃ	ちゃ	じゃ	しゃ	ぎゃ	きゃ
mya	hya	bya	pya	nya	cha	ja	sha	gya	kya
みゃ	ひゃ	びゃ	ぴゃ	にゃ	ちゃ	じゃ	しゃ	ぎゃ	きゃ
みゃ	ひゃ	びゃ	ぴゃ	にゃ	ちゃ	じゃ	しゃ	ぎゃ	きゃ
みゃ	ひゃ	びゃ	ぴゃ	にゃ	ちゃ	じゃ	しゃ	ぎゃ	きゃ

みゅ	ひゅ	びゅ	ぴゅ	にゅ	ちゅ	じゅ	しゅ	ぎゅ	きゅ
myu	hyu	byu	pyu	nyu	chu	ju	shu	gyu	kyu
みゅ	ひゅ	びゅ	ぴゅ	にゅ	ちゅ	じゅ	しゅ	ぎゅ	きゅ
みゅ	ひゅ	びゅ	ぴゅ	にゅ	ちゅ	じゅ	しゅ	ぎゅ	きゅ
みゅ	ひゅ	びゅ	ぴゅ	にゅ	ちゅ	じゅ	しゅ	ぎゅ	きゅ

みょ	ひょ	びょ	ぴょ	にょ	ちょ	じょ	しょ	ぎょ	きょ
myo	hyo	byo	pyo	nyo	cho	jo	sho	gyo	kyo
みょ	ひょ	びょ	ぴょ	にょ	ちょ	じょ	しょ	ぎょ	きょ
みょ	ひょ	びょ	ぴょ	にょ	ちょ	じょ	しょ	ぎょ	きょ
みょ	ひょ	びょ	ぴょ	にょ	ちょ	じょ	しょ	ぎょ	きょ

ミャ	ヒャ	ビャ	ピャ	ニャ	チャ	ジャ	シャ	ギャ	キャ
mya	hya	bya	pya	nya	cha	ja	sha	gya	kya
ミャ	ヒャ	ビャ	ピャ	ニャ	チャ	ジャ	シャ	ギャ	キャ
ミャ	ヒャ	ビャ	ピャ	ニャ	チャ	ジャ	シャ	ギャ	キャ
ミャ	ヒャ	ビャ	ピャ	ニャ	チャ	ジャ	シャ	ギャ	キャ

ミュ	ヒュ	ビュ	ピュ	ニュ	チュ	ジュ	シュ	ギュ	キュ
myu	hyu	byu	pyu	nyu	chu	ju	shu	gyu	kyu
ミュ	ヒュ	ビュ	ピュ	ニュ	チュ	ジュ	シュ	ギュ	キュ
ミュ	ヒュ	ビュ	ピュ	ニュ	チュ	ジュ	シュ	ギュ	キュ
ミュ	ヒュ	ビュ	ピュ	ニュ	チュ	ジュ	シュ	ギュ	キュ

ミョ	ヒョ	ビョ	ピョ	ニョ	チョ	ジョ	ショ	ギョ	キョ
myo	hyo	byo	pyo	nyo	cho	jo	sho	gyo	kyo
ミョ	ヒョ	ビョ	ピョ	ニョ	チョ	ジョ	ショ	ギョ	キョ
ミョ	ヒョ	ビョ	ピョ	ニョ	チョ	ジョ	ショ	ギョ	キョ
ミョ	ヒョ	ビョ	ピョ	ニョ	チョ	ジョ	ショ	ギョ	キョ

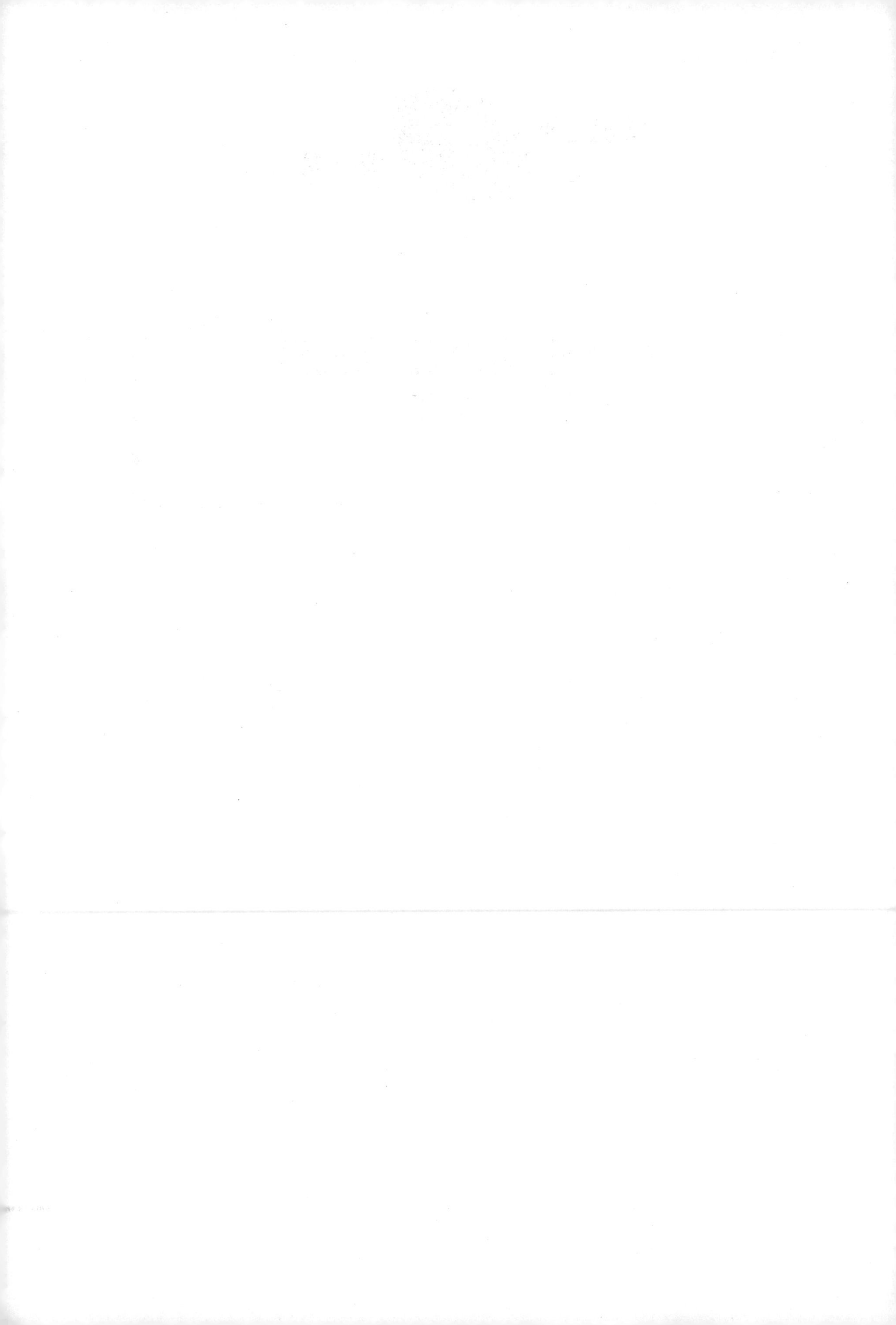

LISTENING AND SPEAKING

Objectives

Simple greetings on meeting someone for the first time
Exchanging personal information

Points

- simple greetings
- conveying basic personal information
- asking/telling the names of everyday objects

Sentences

1 (わたし は) ジョン・スミス です。

2 リーさん の 国(くに) は 中国(ちゅうごく) です。

3 パクさん は 中国(ちゅうごく) の 人 です か。

はい/ええ、 (パクさん は) 中国(ちゅうごく) の 人 です。
そう です。

いいえ、 (パクさん は) 中国(ちゅうごく) の 人 じゃありません。
そう じゃありません。

いいえ。(パクさん は) 韓国(かんこく) の 人 です。

4　あれ　は　何　です　か。

　　（あれ　は）　図書館(としょかん)　です。

5　わたし　の　専攻(せんこう)　は　経済(けいざい)　です。スミスさん　の　専攻(せんこう)　も　経済(けいざい)　です。

Expressions

1　これ　は　日本語(にほんご)　で　何　です　か。What is this in Japanese?　（ドリル　V—2）

フォーメーション

1-1　N　は　N　です

例(れい)）（わたし）、（ジョン・）スミス　→　（わたし　は）（ジョン・）スミス　です。

1)　（わたし）、your full name/family name only　→

2)　（わたし）、学生　→

3)　（わたし）、アメリカ人　→

4)　（わたし）、your nationality　→

2-1　N　の　N

例(れい)）　スミスさん　の　国(くに)

1)__________　の　__________　　3)__________　の　__________

2)__________　の　__________　　4)__________　の　__________

2-2

例(れい)）　リーさん　の　国(くに)、韓国(かんこく)　→　リーさん　の　国(くに)　は　韓国(かんこく)　です。

1)　わたし　の　大学、the name of your university　→

2)　スミスさん、アメリカ　の　人　→

3)　わたし　の　専攻(せんこう)、your major　→

3-1 Affirmative and negative forms of です

例）学生 → 学生 です
→ 学生 じゃありません

1) 辞書 →
2) 図書館 →
3) 本 →
4) 日本 →

3-2

例）リーさん、学生 → リーさん は 学生 です か。
はい／ええ、（リーさん は） 学生 です。／そう です。

1) （あなた）、留学生 →
2) スミスさん、アメリカ人 →
3) 田中さん、先生 →
4) （あなた）、中国 の 人：中国人 →

3-3

例）リーさん、学生 → リーさん は 学生 ですか。
いいえ、（リーさん は）学生 じゃありません。／そう じゃありません。

☆ Use the same cues as in 3-2.

3-4

例）リーさん、先生：学生 → リーさん は 先生 ですか。
いいえ。（リーさん は） 学生 です。

1) リーさん、中国 の 人：韓国 の 人 →
2) 田中さん、学生：先生 →
3) （あなた の） 専攻、日本語：経済 →

4-1 This, that, and that over there

例）あれ、図書館 → あれ は 何 です か。
（あれ は） 図書館 です。

1) あれ、寮 →
2) これ、大学 →

4-2

例)れい 図書館としょかん、これ → 図書館としょかん は どれ ですか。
(図書館としょかん は) これ です。
1) 食堂しょくどう、それ →
2) 寮りょう、これ →
3) 大学、あれ →

4-3 Identifying objects

例)れい これ、田中たなかさん の かばん → これ は 田中たなかさん の かばん です。
1) あれ、スミスさん の 大学 →
2) これ、日本語にほんご の 辞書じしょ →
3) これ、ひらがな の 「あ」 →
4) これ、だれ の かばん →

5 Also

例)れい わたし の 専攻せんこう、経済けいざい：スミスさん の 専攻せんこう
→ わたし の 専攻せんこう は 経済けいざい です。スミスさん の 専攻せんこう も 経済けいざい です。
1) わたし、学生：リーさん →
2) スミスさん、アメリカ の 人：ジョージさん →
3) これ、寮りょう：あれ →

ドリル

I Introducing oneself

A：はじめまして。わたし は 田中たなか です。(わたし は) 日本人 です。どうぞよろしく。

II Asking/Answering

A：わたし は 学生 です。Bさんは？
B：わたし も 学生 です。

A：田中たなかさん は 学生 です か。
B：いいえ、学生 じゃありません。 先生 です。

Ⅲ Asking/Answering about someone's major

A：Bさん　の　専攻(せんこう)　は　文学(ぶんがく)　です　か。

B：ええ、そう　です。

B：いいえ、経済(けいざい)　です。

Ⅳ Asking/Identifying which

A：わたし　の　かさ　は　これ　です。　スミスさん　の　かさ　は　どれ　です　か。

B：それ　です。

* Practice using objects in the classroom, personal belongings, etc. as cues.

Ⅴ Asking for identification of objects

1) A：あれ　は　何　です　か。

B：(あれ　は)　図書館(としょかん)　です。

寮(りょう)　食堂(しょくどう)

2) A：これ　は　日本語(にほんご)　で　何　です　か。

B：かさ　です。

Ⅵ Asking whose

A：これ　は　だれ　の　かぎ　です　か。

B：それ　は　リーさん　の　かぎ　です。

かばん　辞書(じしょ)　かさ

ロールプレイ

CARD A

I First meeting

You meet a person for the first time. Greet him/her, introduce yourself, and have a brief conversation. Find out name, nationality, and what he/she does.

CARD B

I First meeting

You meet a person for the first time. Greet him/her, introduce yourself, and have a brief conversation. Find out name, nationality, and what he/she does.

CARD A

II Asking names of buildings

You are new to the campus. Ask another student to indentify the buildings.

CARD B

II Asking names of buildings

You are asked about the campus. Give answers to the questions.

CARD A

III Asking names of things in Japanese

Ask a person near you what something is called in Japanese.

CARD B

III Asking names of things in Japanese

You are asked what certain things are called in Japanese. Give the answers.

CARD A

IV Self-introduction

Introduce yourself at a small gathering. Tell your name, where you are from, your status (student, graduate student, etc.), and your major.

GRAMMAR NOTES

1. Noun predicate

1) | N_1 は (wa) N_2 です (desu) | As for N_1, it is N_2

The particle は (pronounced 'wa') marks the topic of a sentence. A topic is something that is being talked about. です is called a copula and corresponds to the English 'be'.

ジョン・スミス です。 I am John Smith.
Jon Sumisu desu

スミスさん は アメリカ人(じん) です。 Mr. Smith is an American.
Sumisusan wa amerikajin desu

In the first example above, わたし ('I') is not expressed because it is understood from context. The suffix -さん is a polite marker attached to names but must not be used with the speaker's own name.

2) | N_1 は (wa) N_2 じゃありません (jaarimasen) | As for N_1, it is not N_2

The negative form of です is じゃありません.

スミスさん は アメリカ人(じん) じゃありません。
Sumisusan wa amerikajin jaarimasen
Mr. Smith is not an American.

じゃ is the contracted form of では. In informal speech, the contracted form is usually used.

2. Yes/No questions

N_1 は (wa) N_2 です (desu) か (ka)	As for N_1, is it N_2?

Unlike English, you don't have to change the word order of a sentence to make yes/no question sentences; simply add the question marker か at the end of the sentence.

スミスさん は アメリカ人(じん) です か。
Sumisusan wa amerikajin desu ka
Is Mr. Smith an American?/Are you an American, Mr. Smith?

'You' is expressed by あなた in Japanese, but the use of the word あなた is fairly limited. Names and titles are used instead.

3. Answering questions

N_1 は (wa) N_2 です (desu) か (ka)	Is N_1 N_2?
はい (hai)/ええ (ee)、(N_1 は (wa)) N_2 です (desu)	Yes, N_1 is N_2
そう (soo) です (desu)	Yes, that's right
いいえ (iie)、(N_1 は (wa)) N_2 じゃありません (jaarimasen)	No, N_1 is not N_2
そう (soo) じゃありません (jaarimasen)	No, that's not right

In answering a yes/no question, はい or ええ is 'yes' and いいえ is 'no'. そう means literally 'in that way'.

リーさん は 学生(がくせい) です か。 Riisan wa gakusee desu ka	Is Ms. Lee a student?
はい/ええ、(リーさん は) 学生(がくせい) です。 hai ee Riisan wa gakusee desu	Yes, she is a student.
はい/ええ、そう です。 hai ee soo desu	Yes, that's right.
いいえ、(リーさん は) 学生(がくせい) じゃありません。 iie Riisan wa gakusee jaarimasen	No, she is not.
いいえ、そう じゃありません。 iie soo jaarimasen	No, that's not right.

4. Linking nouns

N_1 の (no) N_2	N_1's N_2/N_2 of N_1

The particle の links nouns. N_1 の is placed before N_2 to modify and explain N_2.

リーさん Riisan	の no	国（くに） kuni	Mr. Lee's country
中国（ちゅうごく） chuugoku	の no	人（ひと） hito	a Chinese
わたし watashi	の no	専攻（せんこう） senkoo	my major

5. Demonstratives (1)

これ kore	this one
それ sore	that one
あれ are	that one over there
どれ dore	which one

Demonstratives are words that are used to indicate the referent in terms of physical distance from the speaker and the hearer. これ is used for things close to the speaker, それ is used for things close to the hearer, and あれ for things away from, but identified by, both the speaker and the hearer. And どれ is the demonstrative question word. These demonstratives are used as pronouns.

あれ は 図書館（としょかん） です。 That over there is the library.
are wa toshokan desu

これ は 田中（たなか）さん の かばん です。 This is Mr. Tanaka's bag.
kore wa Tanakasan no kaban desu

6. Question words

N	は wa	何（なん） nan	です desu	か ka	What is N?
		だれ／どなた dare donata			Who is N?
		どれ dore			Which one is N?

Japanese question words such as 何（なん） 'what', だれ 'who'／どなた 'who' (in polite style), and どれ 'which one' do not have to be placed at the beginning of a sentence, unlike English Wh-words; they are inserted in the place where the answer would appear.

あれ は 何（なん） です か。 What is that over there?
are wa nan desu ka

図書館（としょかん） は どれ です か。 Which one is the library?
toshokan wa dore desu ka

これ は だれ の かばん です か。 Whose bag is this?
kore wa dare no kaban desu ka

7. Also

N も (mo)	N also／N too

The particle も, which corresponds to English 'also' or 'too', focuses attention on the N. N も can be used in both affirmative and negative sentences.

わたし の 専攻(せんこう) は 経済(けいざい) です。スミスさん の 専攻(せんこう) も 経済(けいざい) です。
watashi no senkoo wa keezai desu Sumisusan no senkoo mo keezai desu
My major is economics. Mr. Smith's major is also economics.

わたし は 学生(がくせい) じゃありません。リーさん も 学生(がくせい) じゃありません。
watashi wa gakusee jaarimasen Riisan mo gakusee jaarimasen
I am not a student. Ms. Lee is not a student, either.

READING

Introduction / Identification

田中(たなか)
日本
学生
日本文(ぶん)学

チン
中国(ごく)
留(りゅう)学生
せいじ

パク
韓国(かんこく)
留学生
日本文学

スミス
アメリカ
留学生
けいざい

マイヤー
ドイツ
留学生
せいじ

山田(やまだ)
日本
日本語(ご)の先生

マイヤー	PN	Meiyer
山田（やまだ）	PN	Yamada
せいじ	N	politics

□ Comprehension Check

1. Combine the left and the center columns with the right column by drawing lines.

パク	中国	先生
スミス	韓国	留学生
田中	ドイツ	大学生
山田	アメリカ	
マイヤー	日本	
チン		

2. Who is majoring in the following subjects?

経済(けいざい)	政治(せいじ)	日本文学

□ Writing Activity

1. Draw your own face and that of your friends, and write names, nationalities, student/job status, and major areas of study under the faces.

WRITING
[KANJI]

読み方を覚えましょう

何（なに、なん）: what

新しい漢字

1 日

ことば	れんしゅう	日
1 日（ひ）・2 日曜日（にちようび）	日 日	くん: ひ・び・か / おん: にち・に・にっ
		いみ: the sun, day(s)
1 a day 2 Sunday		かきじゅん: 丨 冂 日 日

2 本

ことば	れんしゅう	本
1 本（ほん）・2 日本（にほん／にっぽん）	本 本	くん: もと / おん: ほん・ぼん・ぽん
		いみ: a book, basis
1 a book 2 Japan		かきじゅん: 一 十 才 木 本

3 人

ことば	れんしゅう	人
1 人（ひと）・2 日本人（にほんじん／にっぽんじん）	人 人	くん: ひと / おん: じん・にん
		いみ: a person
1 a person 2 a Japanese		かきじゅん: ノ 人

4

ことば	れんしゅう	大	
1 大きい（おお）	大	くん	おん
	大	おお・おお（きい）	だい・たい
		いみ	
		big	
	かきじゅん		
	一 ナ 大		
1 big			

5

ことば	れんしゅう	学	
1 大学（だいがく）・2 文学（ぶんがく）	学	くん	おん
	学		がく・がっ
		いみ	
		to learn, study, a school	
	かきじゅん		
	、 ‥ ⺍ 𭕄 ⺍⺍ 学 学 学		
1 a college, a university 2 literature			

6

ことば	れんしゅう	先	
1 先に（さき）	先	くん	おん
	先	さき	せん
		いみ	
		earlier, ahead	
	かきじゅん		
	ノ ⺊ 牛 生 労 先		
1 before			

7

ことば	れんしゅう	生	
1 生まれる（う）・2 生きる（い）・3 学生（がくせい）・4 留学生（りゅうがくせい）・5 先生（せんせい）	生	くん	おん
	生	う（まれる）・い（きる）	せい・しょう・じょう
		いみ	
		to be born, to live, to be alive	
	かきじゅん		
	ノ ⺊ 牛 牛 生		
1 to be born 2 to live 3 a student 4 a foreign student 5 a teacher			

8

ことば	れんしゅう	中	
1 中（なか）・2 中国（ちゅうごく）	中	くん	おん
	中	なか	ちゅう
		いみ	
		middle, inside	
	かきじゅん		
	丨 冂 口 中		
1 the inside 2 China			

書く練習

一、わたしは□□□（にほんじん）です。

二、□国□（ちゅうごくじん）じゃありません。

三、スミスさんは、□□（だいがく）の□□（せんせい）です。

四、□□（がくせい）じゃありません。

五、これは、わたしの□（ほん）です。

六、田□（たなか）さんは、文□（ぶんがく）の□□（せんせい）です。

七、専攻は□□語（にほんご）です。

八、リーさんは、韓国の□（ひと）です。

読む練習

一、わたしは日本人です。

二、チンさんは、中国の人です。

三、留学生は何人ですか。

四、これは何ですか。日本語の本です。

五、田中さんは大学の先生です。
学生じゃありません。

六、これは、日本の大学です。

七、わたしの専攻は文学です。

LESSON 2 第二課(だいにか)

LISTENING AND SPEAKING

Objectives

Inquiring about time and prices
Simple shopping

Points

- responding about time and prices
- responding about beginning/ending and opening/closing times and business hours
- simple shopping

Sentences

1 1, 2, 3, 4, 5, 6, 7, 8, 9, 10,
… 20, … 30, … 40, … 50, … 10000

2 (今(いま)、時間(じかん) は) 午後(ごご) 1時半(じはん) です。
テスト は 火曜日(かようび) です。

3 おかし は 120円 です。

4 この 新聞(しんぶん) は 140円 です。

5 前(まえ)、この 新聞(しんぶん) は 100円 でした。

6 これ と これ を ください。

7 図書館(としょかん) は 午前(ごぜん) 8時半(じはん) から です。
図書館(としょかん) は 午後(ごご) 10時(じ) まで です。
図書館(としょかん) は 午前(ごぜん) 8時半(じはん) から 午後 10時(じ) まで です。

（料金（りょうきん） は） 三鷹（みたか） から 新宿（しんじゅく） まで 210円 です。

8 図書館（としょかん） は 午後（ごご） 10時（じ） まで でしょう。

Expressions

1 210円 です ね。 210 yen, right? （ドリル IV）（ね at the end of a sentence indicates that the speaker is seeking agreement from the hearer.）

2 じゃ、この 新聞（しんぶん） は？ And, this newspaper? （ドリル V）

3 じゃ、これ を ください。 Well then, I'll take this one. （ドリル V）

フォーメーション

1-1 Numbers from 1 to 10000

1	いち	30	さんじゅう	200	にひゃく
2	に	40	よんじゅう	300	さんびゃく
3	さん	50	ごじゅう	400	よんひゃく
4	し／よん	60	ろくじゅう	500	ごひゃく
5	ご	70	ななじゅう	600	ろっぴゃく
6	ろく	80	はちじゅう	700	ななひゃく
7	しち／なな	90	きゅうじゅう	800	はっぴゃく
8	はち	100	ひゃく	900	きゅうひゃく
9	く／きゅう	101	ひゃくいち	1000	せん
10	じゅう	102	ひゃくに	2000	にせん
11	じゅういち	103	ひゃくさん	3000	さんぜん
12	じゅうに	104	ひゃくし／ひゃくよん	4000	よんせん
13	じゅうさん	105	ひゃくご	5000	ごせん
14	じゅうし／じゅうよん	106	ひゃくろく	6000	ろくせん
15	じゅうご	107	ひゃくしち／ひゃくなな	7000	ななせん
16	じゅうろく	108	ひゃくはち	8000	はっせん
17	じゅうしち／じゅうなな	109	ひゃくきゅう	9000	きゅうせん
18	じゅうはち	110	ひゃくじゅう	10000	いちまん
19	じゅうく／じゅうきゅう				
20	にじゅう				

1-2

Read the following numbers.

1, 2, 3, 4, 5, 6, 7, 8, 9, 10, 11, 25, 33, 47, 54, 68, 79, 82, 96, 100

1-3

Read the following numbers.

180, 250, 515, 1030, 2356, 5390, 6821, 7900, 8674, 9172, 10000

2-1 Counters (1): Time

1時	いちじ	8時	はちじ
2時	にじ	9時	くじ
3時	さんじ	10時	じゅうじ
4時	よじ	11時	じゅういちじ
5時	ごじ	12時	じゅうにじ
6時	ろくじ	1時半	いちじはん
7時	しちじ／ななじ		
何時	なんじ		

2-2

Read the following times.

1:00 A.M., 3:00 A.M., 5:30 P.M., 9:30 P.M., 4:00 P.M., 7:00 A.M., 11:00 P.M.

2-3

例) 1:30 P.M. → (今、時間 は) <u>午後 1時半</u> です。

1) 4:00 P.M. →

2) 7:30 A.M. →

3) 9:00 A.M. →

4) 12:30 P.M. →

5) 何時 →

2-4 Days of the week

Sunday 日曜日 (にちようび)	Monday 月曜日 (げつようび)	Tuesday 火曜日 (かようび)	Wednesday 水曜日 (すいようび)	Thursday 木曜日 (もくようび)	Friday 金曜日 (きんようび)	Saturday 土曜日 (どようび)
What day of the week 何曜日 (なんようび)						

Tell the day of the week for the given dates.

9	Sun.	Mon.	Tue.	Wed.	Thu.	Fri.	Sat.
			1	2	3	4	5
	6	7	8	9	10	11	12
	13	14	15	16	17	18	19
	20	21	22	23	24	25	26
	27	28	29	30			

例(れい)) Sept. 1 → 火曜日(かようび)
1) Sept. 13 →
2) Sept. 25 →
3) Sept. 9 →
4) Sept. 3 →
5) Sept. 22 →
6) Sept. 19 →

3-1 Counters (2): Prices

1円 いちえん	10円 じゅうえん
2円 にえん	:
3円 さんえん	100円 ひゃくえん
4円 よえん	:
5円 ごえん	1000円 せんえん
6円 ろくえん	:
7円 ななえん	:
8円 はちえん	:
9円 きゅうえん	10000円 いちまんえん
何円 なんえん いくら	

3-2

例(れい)) ¥120 → ひゃくにじゅう円

例(れい)) おかし、¥120 → おかし は 120円 です。

例(れい) ¥120	1 ¥100	2 ¥250	3 ¥3800	4 ¥680	5 ¥170

LISTENING AND SPEAKING

LESSON 2 第二課

4 Price of something

例(れい)) この、新聞(しんぶん)、¥140 → <u>この 新聞(しんぶん)</u> は <u>140 円</u> です。

1) その、ガム、 ¥100 →

2) あの、ざっし、¥550 →

3) この、かさ、いくら →

4) この、フィルム、¥680 →

5 Price of something in the past

例(れい)) この、新聞(しんぶん)、¥100 → 前(まえ)、<u>この 新聞(しんぶん)</u> は <u>100 円</u> でした。

1) その、ガム、¥50 →

2) あの、ざっし、¥300 →

3) この、かさ、いくら →

4) この、フィルム、¥800 →

6 Asking for something

例(れい)) これ → <u>これ</u> を ください。

1) 新聞(しんぶん) と おかし →

2) ざっし と ガム →

3) この フィルム →

4) その 本 と あの かさ →

7-1 From ~ to ~

例(れい)) 図書館(としょかん)、8:30 A.M.、10:00 P.M. →

①<u>図書館(としょかん)</u> は <u>午前 8時半(じはん)</u> から です。

②<u>図書館(としょかん)</u> は <u>午後 10時(じ)</u> まで です。

③<u>図書館(としょかん)</u> は <u>午前 8時半(じはん)</u> から <u>午後 10時(じ)</u> まで です。

1) コンサート、7:00 P.M.、9:30 P.M. →

2) 郵便局(ゆうびんきょく)、9:00 A.M.、5:00 P.M. →

3) 銀行(ぎんこう)、9:00 A.M.、3:00 P.M. →

4) 図書館(としょかん)、何時(なんじ)、何時(なんじ) →

5) 銀行(ぎんこう)、月曜日(げつようび)、金曜日(きんようび) →

7-2 Fares

例(れい)) 三鷹(みたか)、新宿(しんじゅく)、¥210 → <u>三鷹(みたか)</u> から <u>新宿(しんじゅく)</u> まで (料金(りょうきん) は) <u>210円</u> です。

1) 三鷹(みたか)、吉祥寺(きちじょうじ)、¥120 →

2) 三鷹(みたか)、東京(とうきょう)、¥370 →

3) 武蔵境(むさしさかい)、吉祥寺(きちじょうじ)、¥150 →

4) ICU、三鷹(みたか)、いくら →

8 Estimating

例(れい)) 図書館(としょかん) は 午後 10時(じ) まで です → <u>図書館(としょかん) は 午後 10時(じ) まで</u> でしょう。

1) 三鷹(みたか) から 新宿(しんじゅく) まで 210円 です →
2) その かさ は 田中(たなか)さん の かさ です →
3) あれ は 寮(りょう) です →
4) 郵便局(ゆうびんきょく) は 月曜日(げつようび) から 金曜日(きんようび) まで です →
5) リーさん は イギリス の 人 です →

ドリル

I Asking and telling the time

A：すみません。今(いま) 何時(なんじ) です か。
B：<u>8時(じ)</u> です。
A：<u>8時(じ)</u> です か。どうも。
B：いいえ。

II-1 Asking when it opens

A：<u>図書館(としょかん)</u> は 何時(なんじ) から です か。
B：<u>8時半(じはん)</u> から です。

II-2 Asking when it closes/ends

A：<u>図書館(としょかん)</u> は 何時(なんじ) まで です か。
B：<u>午後 10時(じ)</u> まで です。

II-3 Asking about opening and closing times

A：<u>図書館(としょかん)</u> は 何時(なんじ) から 何時(なんじ) まで です か。
B：<u>8時半(じはん)</u> から <u>午後 10時(じ)</u> まで です。

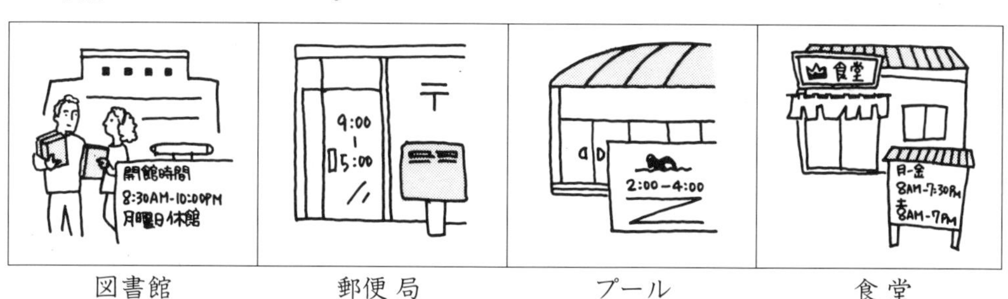

図書館(としょかん)　郵便局(ゆうびんきょく)　プール　食堂(しょくどう)

Ⅲ Asking about the schedule

A：<u>テスト</u>　は　何曜日(なんようび)　です　か。

B：<u>金曜日(きんようび)</u>　です。

スケジュール

月(げつ)	ラボ	フォーメーション
火(か)	ドリル	
水(すい)	会話(かいわ)	読み方(よみかた)
木(もく)	漢字(かんじ)	ビデオ
金(きん)	テスト	作文(さくぶん)
土(ど)	休み(やすみ)	
日(にち)	休み(やすみ)	

Ⅳ Asking the fare

A：<u>新宿(しんじゅく)</u>　まで　いくら　です　か。

B：<u>210円</u>　です。

A：<u>210円</u>　です　ね。

B：ええ。

B

三鷹(みたか)　から			
吉祥寺(きちじょうじ)	¥120	池袋(いけぶくろ)	¥290
新宿(しんじゅく)	¥210	原宿(はらじゅく)	¥290
四谷(よつや)	¥290	渋谷(しぶや)	¥290
東京(とうきょう)	¥370	有楽町(ゆうらくちょう)	¥370

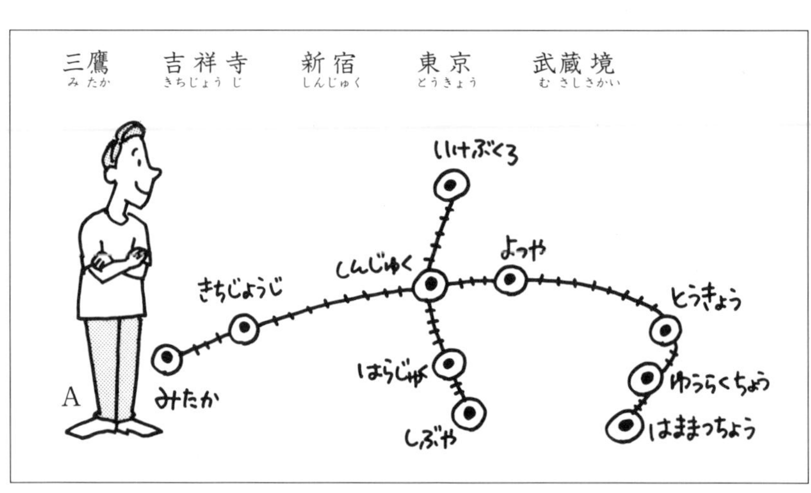

V　This, that, and that over there

A：この　新聞(しんぶん)　は　いくら　です　か。

B：150円　です。

A：じゃ、この　新聞(しんぶん)　は？

B：それ　は　180円　です。

A：じゃ、これ　と　ガム　を　ください。

①新聞(しんぶん)	¥150
②フィルム	¥500
③ガム	¥100
④コーヒー	¥110
⑤かさ	¥700
⑥ざっし	¥450
⑦でんち	¥430
⑧おかし	¥1,500
⑨新聞(しんぶん)	¥180

ロールプレイ

CARD A

I　Asking about opening/closing time

Ask another student the opening and closing time of the library / dining hall / post office.

CARD B

I　Asking about opening/closing time

You are asked the opening and closing time of the library / dining hall / post office. Give the answers to the questions.

CARD A

II　Making a purchase

At a kiosk, ask the price of a few things and make a purchase.

CARD B

II　Making a purchase

You are the salesperson at a kiosk. Respond to the customer's requests.

CARD A

III　Asking the fare

At the station, ask a person nearby the fare to your destination.

CARD B

III　Asking the fare

You are asked the cost of the fare to ________. Give the answer.

CARD A

IV　Purchasing at a fast-food shop

At a fast-food shop, purchase some food and a drink.

CARD B

IV　Purchasing at a fast-food shop

You work at a fast-food shop. Respond to the customer's requests.

GRAMMAR NOTES

1. Numbers

The number 0 is pronounced either ゼロ (zero) or れい (ree). Numbers 1 to 10 and 100, 1000, and 10000 are particularly important since they form the basis of other numbers up to 99999999, which are made by combining these numbers.

11 to 19 are made by combining 10 with 1 through 9:

  11 is じゅういち (juu-ichi), 12 is じゅうに (juu-ni), etc.

20, 30, ..., 90 are made by combining 2 and 10, 3 and 10, ..., 9 and 10:

  20 is にじゅう (ni-juu), 30 is さんじゅう (san-juu), etc.

21, 22, ..., 99 are made by combining 20 and 1, 20 and 2, ..., and 90 and 9:

  21 is にじゅういち (ni-juu-ichi), 22 is にじゅうに (ni-juu-ni), etc.

100 is pronounced ひゃく (hyaku). 200, ..., 900 are made by combining 2 and 100, ..., 9 and 100:

  200 is にひゃく (ni-hyaku), 900 is きゅうひゃく (kyuu-hyaku), etc.

Note that numbers 300, 600, and 800 are pronounced slightly differently:

  300 is さんびゃく (san-byaku), 600 is ろっぴゃく (rop-pyaku), 800 is はっぴゃく (hap-pyaku)

1000 is pronounced せん (sen). 2000, ..., 9000 are made by combining 2 and 1000, ..., 9 and 1000:

  2000 is にせん (ni-sen), 9000 is きゅうせん (kyuu-sen), etc.

Note that numbers 3000 and 8000 are pronounced slightly differently:

  3000 さんぜん (san-zen), 8000 はっせん (has-sen).

10000, ..., 99990000 are made by combining 1, ..., 9999 and まん (man):

  10000 is いちまん (ichi-man), 20000 is にまん (ni-man).

  300000 is さんじゅうまん (san-juu-man), 410000 is よんじゅういちまん (yon-juu-ichi-man).

  99990000 is きゅうせんきゅうひゃくきゅうじゅうきゅうまん (kyuu-sen-kyuu-hyaku-kyuu-juu-kyuu-man).

Note that there is no irregularity in the pronunciation of まん (man).

The Japanese number system is a four-digit system using different names for every four figures, such as 'man', whereas English is a three-digit system using 'thousand', 'million', 'billion', etc. Thus, 99999999 is きゅうせんきゅうひゃくきゅうじ

ゆうきゅうまんきゅうせんきゅうひゃくきゅうじゅうきゅう(kyuu-sen-kyuu-hyaku-kyuu-juu-kyuu-man-kyuu-sen-kyuu-hyaku-kyuu-juu-kyuu).

Japanese numbers

Numbers in bold type need special attention in pronunciation.

1 **いち** (ichi)	20 にじゅう (ni-juu)	200 にひゃく (ni-hyaku)
2 **に** (ni)	30 さんじゅう (san-juu)	300 **さんびゃく** (san-byaku)
3 **さん** (san)	40 よんじゅう (yon-juu)	400 よんひゃく (yon-hyaku)
4 **し** (shi)／**よん** (yon)	50 ごじゅう (go-juu)	500 ごひゃく (go-hyaku)
5 **ご** (go)	60 ろくじゅう (roku-juu)	600 **ろっぴゃく** (rop-pyaku)
6 **ろく** (roku)	70 **ななじゅう** (nana-juu)	700 ななひゃく (nana-hyaku)
7 **しち** (shichi)／**なな** (nana)	80 はちじゅう (hachi-juu)	800 **はっぴゃく** (hap-pyaku)
8 **はち** (hachi)	90 **きゅうじゅう** (kyuu-juu)	900 きゅうひゃく (kyuu-hyaku)
9 **く** (ku)／**きゅう** (kyuu)	100 **ひゃく** (hyaku)	1000 **せん** (sen)
10 **じゅう** (juu)	101 ひゃくいち (hyaku-ichi)	2000 にせん (ni-sen)
11 じゅういち (juu-ichi)	102 ひゃくに (hyaku-ni)	3000 **さんぜん** (san-zen)
12 じゅうに (juu-ni)	103 ひゃくさん (hyaku-san)	4000 よんせん (yon-sen)
13 じゅうさん (juu-san)	104 ひゃくし (hyaku-shi)／ひゃくよん (hyaku-yon)	5000 ごせん (go-sen)
14 じゅうし (juu-shi)／じゅうよん (juu-yon)	105 ひゃくご (hyaku-go)	6000 ろくせん (roku-sen)
15 じゅうご (juu-go)	106 ひゃくろく (hyaku-roku)	7000 ななせん (nana-sen)
16 じゅうろく (juu-roku)	107 ひゃくしち (hyaku-shichi)／ひゃくなな (hyaku-nana)	8000 **はっせん** (has-sen)
17 じゅうしち (juu-shichi)／じゅうなな (juu-nana)	108 ひゃくはち (hyaku-hachi)	9000 きゅうせん (kyuu-sen)
18 じゅうはち (juu-hachi)	109 ひゃくきゅう (hyaku-kyuu)	10000 いちまん (ichi-man)
19 じゅうく (juu-ku)／じゅうきゅう (juu-kyuu)	110 ひゃくじゅう (hyaku-juu)	

For your reference, larger numbers include the following: 100000000 is いちおく (ichi-oku), with the unit おく (oku) being used up to 999900000000; the next higher number is 1000000000000 いっちょう (it-choo), with ちょう (choo) being used up to 9999000000000000. The next higher number unit is けい (kee), which behaves like まん, おく, and ちょう. Few people use numbers larger than けい.

2. Counters (1)

Time expressions (1): o'clock

NUMBER 時 (じ ji)	＿＿ o'clock

The word for 'o'clock' is 時 (じ, ji), and it follows the number.

1時 (いちじ, ichi-ji) 1 o'clock

Note that 4時 is pronounced よじ (yo-ji), and 9時 is くじ (ku-ji).

The word 半 (はん, han) is used to show 'half past'.

12時半 (じゅうにじはん, juuni-ji-han) half past 12

Expressions for 'minutes' will be introduced in the next lesson.

'A.M.' and 'P.M.' are indicated by ごぜん (gozen) and ごご (gogo), respectively. Note, however, that these words precede the time words.

ごぜん7時 (gozen shichi-ji) 7 A.M.

ごご1時半 (gogo ichi-ji-han) 1:30 P.M.

The question word for time is 何時 (なんじ, nanji), which literally means 'what o'clock?'

1時	いちじ (ichi-ji)	8時	はちじ (hachi-ji)
2時	にじ (ni-ji)	9時	くじ (ku-ji)
3時	さんじ (san-ji)	10時	じゅうじ (juu-ji)
4時	よじ (yo-ji)	11時	じゅういちじ (juuichi-ji)
5時	ごじ (go-ji)	12時	じゅうにじ (juuni-ji)
6時	ろくじ (roku-ji)	1時半	いちじはん (ichi-ji-han)
7時	しちじ (shichi-ji)/ななじ (nana-ji)		
何時	なんじ (nanji)		

Telling time.

(＿＿は) TIMEです wa desu	(As for ＿＿), it's ＿＿

今、時間 は 午後 1時半 です。 It's now 1:30 P.M.
いま じかん ご ご じ はん
ima, jikan wa gogo ichi-ji -han desu

今 何時 です か。 What time is it now?
いま なんじ
ima nanji desu ka

3. Days of the week

The word ようび (yoobi) means the day of the week. It follows words indicating Sun, Moon, Fire, Water, Tree, Gold/Metal, and Earth: thus, にちようび (nichi-yoobi) 'Sunday', げつようび (getsu-yoobi) 'Monday', かようび (ka-yoobi) 'Tuesday', すいようび (sui-yoobi) 'Wednesday', もくようび (moku-yoobi) 'Thursday', きんようび (kin-yoobi) 'Friday', and どようび (do-yoobi) 'Saturday'.

テスト は 火曜日 です。 The test is (on) Tuesday.
かようび
tesuto wa kayoobi desu

4. Counters (2): Price (¥)

NUMBER 円 えん en	¥＿＿

円 (えん, en) is the Japanese currency unit. It follows the numbers. Note that it is pronounced 'en', not 'yen'.

5000円 (ごせんえん, go-sen-en), 10000円 (いちまんえん, ichi-man-en)

おかし は 120円 です。 The candy is ¥120.
えん
okashi wa hyakunijuu-en desu

5. Demonstratives (2)

この N kono	this N
その N sono	that N
あの N ano	that N over there

どの dono	N

which N

The word for 'this' is この (kono), as in このほん (kono hon, 'this book'). この, その, あの, and どの must precede a noun. Compare these with これ, それ, あれ, and どれ (Lesson 1), which are used as pronouns.

The relationship between the use of この, その, あの, and どの and the referent's proximity to the speaker and the hearer is the same as in the case of これ, それ, あれ, and どれ, as explained in Lesson 1.

この kono 新聞 (しんぶん) shinbun は wa 140円 hyakuyonjuu-en です。 desu — This newspaper is ¥140.

cf. これ kore は wa 140円 hyakuyonjuu-en です。 desu — This is ¥140.

6. Connectives (1) : と

N_1	と to	N_2

N_1 and N_2

The conjunctive particle と (to) is used to join two or more nouns. Note that と can be used with nouns only. The forms that join verbs, adjectives, sentences, etc. will be introduced later.

新聞 (しんぶん) shinbun と to おかし okashi — newspaper and snacks

これ kore と to これ kore — this and this

7. Buying things

N	を o	ください kudasai

Please give me N

The particle を (o) indicates that the noun it follows is the object of the verb. More details will be given in Lesson 3. The word ください (kudasai) means 'please give me'.

この kono フィルム firumu を o ください。 kudasai
Please give me this film. (I will buy this film.)

ざっし zasshi と to ガム gamu を o ください。 kudasai
Please give me a magazine and some chewing gum.

8. From ~ to ~

X から kara	Y まで made

from X to/until Y

Various nouns, such as time words, place names, numbers, prices, etc. may be used for X and Y in the above pattern.

月曜日(げつようび) から 金曜日(きんようび) まで　from Monday to Friday
getsu-yoobi kara kin-yoobi made

三鷹(みたか) から 新宿(しんじゅく) まで　from Mitaka to Shinjuku
Mitaka kara Shinjuku made

1 から 10 まで　from 1 to 10
ichi kara juu made

Either から (kara) or まで (made) may be omitted when it is obvious or unnecessary.

図書館(としょかん) は 午前(ごぜん) 8時半(じはん) から 午後(ごご) 10時(じ) まで です。
toshokan wa gozen hachi-ji-han kara gogo juu-ji made desu
The library is (open) from 8:30 A.M. to 10:00 P.M.

銀行(ぎんこう) は 午前(ごぜん) 9時(じ) から です。
ginkoo wa gozen ku-ji kara desu
Banks are (open) from 9:00 A.M.

郵便局(ゆうびんきょく) は 午後(ごご) 5時(じ) まで です。
yuubinkyoku wa gogo go-ji made desu
The post office is (open) till 5:00 P.M.

9. Conjecture (1)

________ でしょう deshoo

Probably ________
I think that ________

The form でしょう (deshoo) used in place of です (desu) indicates the speaker's uncertainty. In this sense, it can also be used to make a statement sound less direct or straightforward in order to express the speaker's modesty or politeness.

図書館(としょかん) は 午後(ごご) 10時(じ) まで でしょう。
toshokan wa gogo juu-ji made deshoo
I think the library is (open) till 10 P.M.

10. Past forms

Affirmative

________ でした deshita

was ________

The past form of the copula です (desu) is でした (deshita), with た (ta) indicating the past tense.

> この　かさ　は　1000円(えん)　でした。
> kono　kasa　wa　sen-en　deshita
> This umbrella was ¥1000.

> 今(いま)、1ドル　は　100円(えん)　です。　前(まえ)　は　250円(えん)　でした。　（まえ 'before'）
> ima　ichi-doru　wa　hyaku-en　desu　mae　wa　nihyakugojuu-en　deshita
> Now $1 is ¥100. Before it was ¥250.

> わたし　の　専攻(せんこう)　は　文学(ぶんがく)　です。　前(まえ)　は　経済(けいざい)　でした。
> watashi　no　senkoo　wa　bungaku　desu　mae　wa　keezai　deshita
> My major is literature. Before it was economics.

Negative

________ じゃありません でした
jaarimasen deshita

was not ______

The past negative form of the copula is じゃありません　でした (jaarimasen deshita).

> わたし　の　専攻(せんこう)　は　経済(けいざい)　じゃありません　でした。
> watashi　no　senkoo　wa　keezai　jaarimasen　deshita
> My major was not economics.

Summary of copula forms

	Non-past	Past
Affirmative	～です desu	～でした deshita
Negative	～じゃありません jaarimasen	～じゃありません でした jaarimasen deshita

GRAMMAR NOTES

LESSON 2

第二課

READING

Library Hours / Swimming Pool Hours / Menus

大学プール	1:00-4:00	(月一金)	
みたかプール	10:00-5:00	(月一金)	¥200
しんじゅくプール	1:00-9:30	(月やすみ)	¥150
東京プール	12:00-8:00	(月一土)	¥250

みたか図書館

水、金、土、日	九時半から五時まで
火、木	九時半から七時まで
月	やすみ

ICU　図書館

月曜日一金曜日	8:30-20:00
土曜日と日曜日	9:00-17:00

月曜日　(げつようび)
火曜日　(かようび)
水曜日　(すいようび)
木曜日　(もくようび)
金曜日　(きんようび)
土曜日　(どようび)
日曜日　(にちようび)
時　(じ)
半　(はん)
東京　(とうきょう)

しぶや　はなぶさ

すし	一五〇〇円
そば	八〇〇円
うどん	七五〇円
てんぷら	二〇〇〇円
しゃぶしゃぶ	二五〇〇円
すきやき	三〇〇〇円
ビール	五〇〇円
おさけ	四〇〇円

すし	N	sushi
そば	N	buckwheat noodles
うどん	N	wheat noodles
てんぷら	N	tempura (deep-fried fish and vegetables)
しゃぶしゃぶ	N	shabushabu (slices of meat dipped into pot of boiling broth and other ingredients)
すきやき	N	sukiyaki (meat, vegetables, etc. cooked in pot)
ビール	N	beer
おさけ	N	sake (Japanese wine made from fermented rice)

□ **Comprehension Check**

1. Where do you go to swim in the morning?
2. Which pools are open on weekends?
3. Which pool is the most expensive?
4. Which library is open longer?

□ **Speaking Activity**

1. Suppose you have ¥4,000 to spend at はなぶさ Restaurant. Choose food and drinks within your budget.

WRITING
[KANJI]

読み方を覚えましょう

午前（ごぜん）: morning, A.M.
午後（ごご）: afternoon, P.M.
～円（～えん）: yen
郵便局（ゆうびんきょく）: post office

新しい漢字

9 一

ことば	
1 一（いち）・2 一つ（ひとつ）	
くん	ひと・ひと(つ)
おん	いち・いっ
いみ	one
かきじゅん	一

1 one
2 one item

10 二

ことば	
1 二（に）・2 二つ（ふたつ）	
くん	ふた・ふた(つ)・ふっ
おん	に
いみ	two
かきじゅん	一 二

1 two
2 two items

11 三

ことば	
1 三（さん）・2 三つ（みっつ）	
くん	み・みっ(つ)
おん	さん
いみ	three
かきじゅん	一 二 三

1 three
2 three items

12

ことば	れんしゅう	四
1 四（し／よん）・2 四つ（よっつ）		くん: よ・よっ(つ)・よん　おん: し
		いみ: four
1 four 2 four items		かきじゅん

13

ことば	れんしゅう	五
1 五（ご）・2 五つ（いつつ）・3 五人（ごにん）		くん: いつ・いつ(つ)　おん: ご
		いみ: five
1 five 2 five items 3 five persons		かきじゅん

14

ことば	れんしゅう	六
1 六（ろく）・2 六つ（むっつ）		くん: む・むっ(つ)・むい　おん: ろく・ろっ
		いみ: six
1 six 2 six items		かきじゅん

15

ことば	れんしゅう	七
1 七（しち／なな）・2 七つ（ななつ）・3 七本（ななほん）		くん: なな・なな(つ)・なの　おん: しち
		いみ: seven
1 seven 2 seven items 3 seven long items		かきじゅん

16

ことば	れんしゅう	八
1 八（はち）・2 八つ（やっつ）		くん: や・やっ(つ)・よう　おん: はち・はっ
		いみ: eight
1 eight 2 eight items		かきじゅん

17

ことば	れんしゅう	九
1 九（きゅう）・2 九つ（ここのつ）・3 九円（きゅうえん）		くん: ここの・ここの(つ)　おん: きゅう・く
		いみ: nine
1 nine 2 nine items 3 nine yen		かきじゅん

18

ことば	れんしゅう	十	
十・十五日 1 とお／じゅう 2 じゅうごにち 1 ten 2 fifteen days	十 十	くん	おん
		とお・と	じゅう・じっ・じゅっ
		いみ	
		ten	
	かきじゅん		
	一 十		

WRITING LESSON 2 第二課

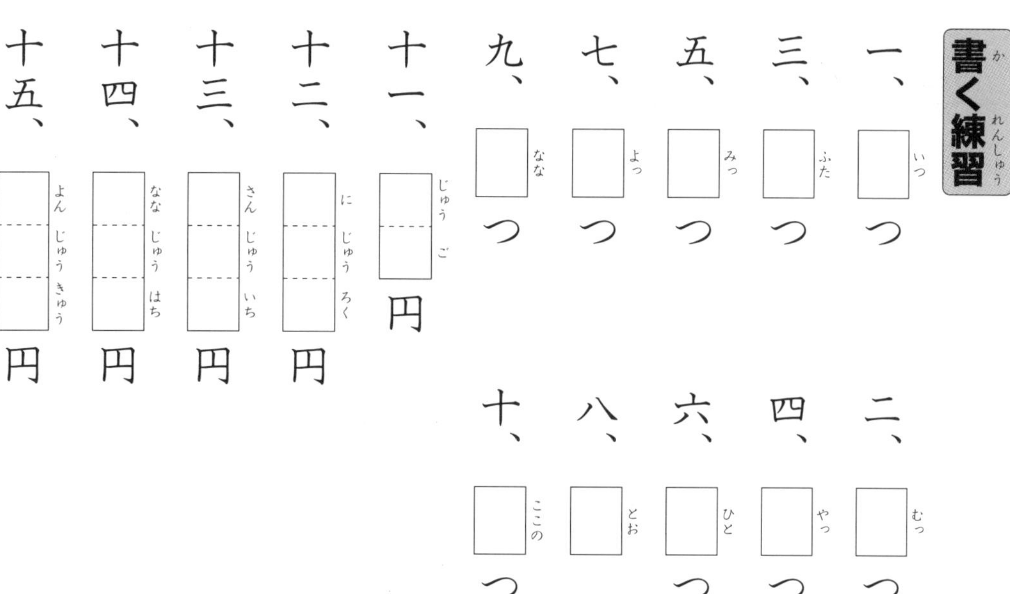

書く練習（かくれんしゅう）

一、□つ（いつ）
三、□つ（ふた）
五、□つ（みっ）
七、□つ（よっ）
九、□つ（なな）
十一、□□円（じゅう ご）
十二、□□□円（に じゅう ろく）
十三、□□□円（さん じゅう いち）
十四、□□□円（なな じゅう はち）
十五、□□□円（よん じゅう きゅう）

二、□つ（むっ）
四、□つ（やっ）
六、□つ（ひと）
八、□（とお）
十、□つ（ここの）

読む練習（よむれんしゅう）

一、六つ
三、一つ
五、二つ
七、九つ
九、七つ
十一、四十五円
十二、九十八円
十三、午前十一時（じ）
十四、午後六時（じ）
十五、これは郵（ゆう）便局です。

二、十
四、五つ
六、三つ
八、四つ
十、八つ

LISTENING AND SPEAKING

Objectives

Conversing sociably about daily life
Relating past experiences and activities

Points

- responding about customary activities and plans for future activities
- inquiring about time needed

Sentences

1 1分、2分、3分、・・・10分、・・・60分、

2 (わたし は) いつも 6時 45分 に 起(お)きます。

3 (あなた は) あした 大学 へ 行きます か。

はい/ええ、(わたし は あした 大学 へ) 行きます。

いいえ、(わたし は あした 大学 へ) 行きません。

4 (わたし は) きのう 映画(えいが) を 見ました。

(わたし は) きのう 映画(えいが) を 見ません でした。

5 (わたし は) 夜(よる) 新宿(しんじゅく) で 映画(えいが) を 見ます。

6 学生 は バス で 大学 に 来ます。

7 (わたし は) 朝 コーヒー や お茶(ちゃ) を 飲(の)みます。

フォーメーション

1-1 Counters (3): Time: minutes

1分 いっぷん	11分 じゅういっぷん	30分 さんじゅっぷん／さんじっぷん
2分 にふん	12分 じゅうにふん	40分 よんじゅっぷん／よんじっぷん
3分 さんぷん	13分 じゅうさんぷん	50分 ごじゅっぷん／ごじっぷん
4分 よんぷん	14分 じゅうよんぷん	60分 ろくじゅっぷん／ろくじっぷん
5分 ごふん	15分 じゅうごふん	
6分 ろっぷん	16分 じゅうろっぷん	
7分 ななふん	17分 じゅうななふん	
8分 はっぷん／はちふん	18分 じゅうはっぷん／じゅうはちふん	
9分 きゅうふん	19分 じゅうきゅうふん	
10分 じゅっぷん／じっぷん	20分 にじゅっぷん／にじっぷん	何分 なんぷん

1-2

Read the following times.

例(れい)) 6:45 → ろくじ　よんじゅうごふん

1) 8:03 →
2) 4:37 →
3) 9:24 →
4) 5:19 →
5) 11:46 →

2-1 Verb practice

例(れい)) 見る → 見ます
見ません

1) 書(か)く →
2) 泳(およ)ぐ →
3) 話(はな)す →
4) 待(ま)つ →
5) 死(し)ぬ →
6) よぶ →
7) 飲(の)む →
8) 帰(かえ)る →
9) 買(か)う →
10) 食べる →
11) 起(お)きる →
12) 来る →
13) する →

2-2 When you get up/go to bed

例)(わたし)、いつも、6:45、起きる
→ (わたし は) いつも 6時 45分 に 起きます。

1) (わたし)、きょう、12:30、寝る →
2) (わたし)、あした、6:20、起きる →
3) (わたし)、いつも、何時、寝る →

3 Coming and going

例)(わたし)、あした、大学、行く → (わたし は) あした 大学 へ 行きます。

1) (わたし)、今晩、友だち の うち、行く →
2) ～さん、きょう、どこ、行く →
3) ～さん、いつ、(わたし の) うち、来る →

4 Verb practice

例)見る → 見ます → 見ました
→ 見ません → 見ません でした

1) 行く →
→
2) 書く →
→
3) 読む →
→
4) 帰る →
→
5) 買う →
→
6) 起きる →
→
7) 寝る →
→
8) 食べる →
→
9) 始まる →
→
10) 来る →
→
11) する →
→

5 What you did

例)(わたし)、きのう、新宿、映画、見る
→ (わたし は) きのう 新宿 で 映画 を 見ました。

1) (わたし)、朝、うち、新聞、読む →
2) ～さん、昼、大学 の 食堂、昼ご飯、食べる →

3) （わたし）、けさ、うち、ラジオ　の　ニュース、聞(き)く　→

4) ～さん、夜(よる)、レストラン、晩(ばん)ご飯(はん)、食べる　→

6-1 What you use

例(れい)) （わたし）、はし、食べる　→　（わたし　は）はし　で　食べます。

1) （わたし）、フォーク　→

2) （わたし）、手(て)　→

3) （わたし）、ナイフ　と　フォーク　→

6-2 How you get somewhere

例(れい)) 学生、バス、大学、来る

→　学生　は　バス　で　大学　に　来ます。

1) ～さん、飛行機(ひこうき)、イギリス、行く　→

2) ～さん、自転車(じてんしゃ)、大学、行く　→

3) （わたし）、歩(ある)いて、うち、帰(かえ)る　→

7 Mentioning examples

例(れい)) 学生、バス　や　自転車(じてんしゃ)、大学、来る

→　学生　は　バス　や　自転車(じてんしゃ)　で　大学　に　来ます。

1) （わたし）、午後、図書館(としょかん)　や　プール、行く　→

2) ～さん、きのう、おかし　や　パン、買(か)う　→

3) ～さん、いつも、新宿(しんじゅく)　や　吉祥寺(きちじょうじ)、映画(えいが)、見る　→

ドリル

Ⅰ-1 Talking about daily schedules

6:00	起(お)きる	7:00	勉強(べんきょう)
7:00	朝(あさ)ご飯(はん)	10:00	テレビ
9:00	クラス	11:00	寝(ね)る
12:00	昼(ひる)ご飯(はん)		
1:00	クラス		
4:00	図書館(としょかん)		
6:00	晩(ばん)ご飯(はん)		

A：Bさん　は　何時　に　起(お)きます　か。

B：6時　に　起(お)きます。

A：それから　何　を　します　か。

Ⅰ-2

A：Bさん　は　8時　に　起(お)きます　か。

B：ええ、8時　に　起(お)きます。　　B：いいえ。6時　に　起(お)きます。

Ⅱ-1　Talking about everyday life

A：Bさん　は　コーヒー　を　飲(の)みます　か。

B：ええ、飲(の)みます。

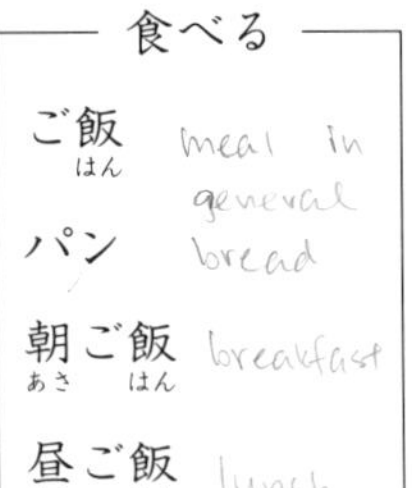

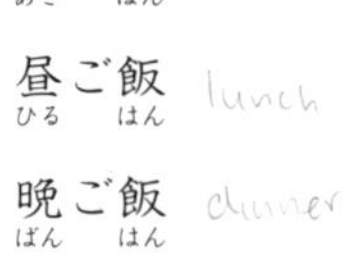

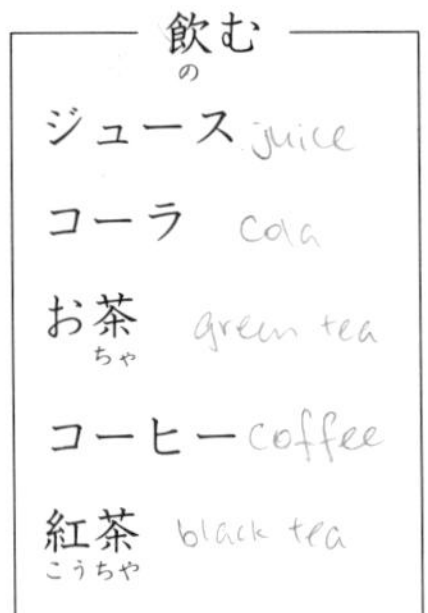

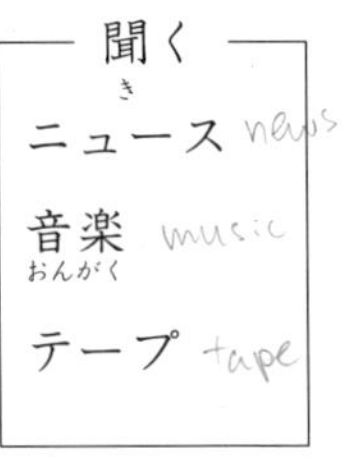

Ⅱ-2

A：Bさん　は　パン　を　食べます　か。

B：いいえ、食べません。

ご飯(はん)　を　食べます。

Ⅲ　Talking about where you're going and what you're going to do

A：どこ　へ　行きます　か。

B：喫茶店(きっさてん)　へ　行きます。そして、喫茶店(きっさてん)　で　コーヒー　を　飲(の)みます。

どこ	何
喫茶店(きっさてん)	コーヒー　を　飲(の)む
レストラン	昼(ひる)ご飯(はん)　を　食べる
デパート	映画(えいが)　を　見る
本屋(ほんや)	買(か)い物(もの)　を　する
花屋(はなや)	テニス　を　する
	花(はな)　を　買(か)う
	友(とも)だち　に　会(あ)う

Ⅳ Doing this and that

A：きのうは 図書館(としょかん) に 行きました か。

B：ええ。図書館(としょかん) で 新聞(しんぶん) や ざっし を 読(よ)みました。

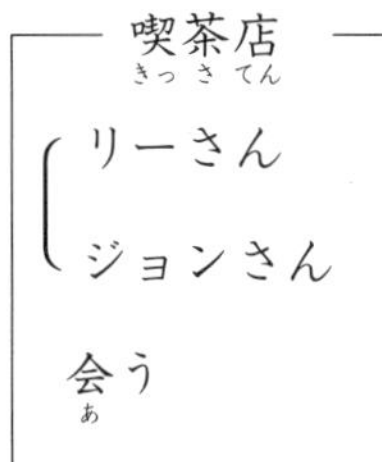

喫茶店(きっさてん)	本屋(ほんや)	大学	デパート
リーさん / ジョンさん	本 / 辞書(じしょ)	勉強(べんきょう) / テニス	コーヒー / パン
会(あ)う	見る	する	買(か)う

ロールプレイ

CARD A

I Talking about daily life

You want to find out more about 1) new people in your class, 2) close friends.

Ask the following:

① what time they get up
② if they eat breakfast and what they eat
③ what time they arrive at school
④ how they get to school

CARD B

I Talking about daily life

You are asked about your daily schedule by 1) a new person, 2) a close friend. Answer the questions.

CARD A

II Talking about weekends

You want to find out how your new classmates spent last Sunday.

Ask the following:

① what time they got up
② what they did afterwards
③ where they went
④ what time they returned home

CARD B

II Talking about weekends

You are asked about what you did last Sunday by a new friend in your class. Answer the questions.

GRAMMAR NOTES

1. Verb predicates

1) Verb-ます form: Affirmative

N は (wa) V-ます (masu)	As for N, it V

The above sentence pattern has a verb predicate, the second type among three kinds of predicates in Japanese. The topic of the sentence, which is marked by は (wa) in this pattern, also functions as the subject (or the doer in the case of action) of the verb.

Verbs in Japanese are basically categorized into three groups: ① vowel verbs, ② consonant verbs, and ③ irregular verbs. This categorization is important for understanding how conjugation suffixes vary from one verb to another.

① Vowel verbs: As illustrated below, the stems of vowel verbs end in either -[i]- or -[e]-, and the plain non-past form ends in -[ru](-る).

m**i**-**ru**	(見る)	see, look
ok**i**-**ru**	(起きる)	get up
n**e**-**ru**	(寝る)	go to bed
tab**e**-**ru**	(食べる)	eat

② Consonant verbs: The stems of consonant verbs end in one of nine sounds [k, g, s, ts, n, b, m, r, or (w)], and the plain non-past form ends in -[u].

ka**k**-**u**	(書く)	write
oyo**g**-**u**	(泳ぐ)	swim
ka**s**-**u**	(貸す)	lend
ma**ts**-**u**	(待つ)	wait
shi**n**-**u**	(死ぬ)	die

ka**(w)**-**u**	(買う)	buy
yo**b**-**u**	(よぶ)	call
yo**m**-**u**	(読む)	read
u**r**-**u**	(売る)	sell

Note that -(w)-u stands for [u] on the [w]-column of the Japanese syllabary table (see "Getting Started").

There are a few exceptions to this categorization. Some verbs in the non-past plain affirmative form, such as 入る (hairu) and 帰る (kaeru), end in -[ru] and appear to have a stem ending in -[i] or -[e]. However, they do not belong to the vowel verbs as they would appear to, but rather to the consonant verbs. A few more examples of this type of verb are 切る (kiru) 'cut', いる (iru) 'need', しゃべる (shaberu) 'chat', and へる (heru) 'decrease'.

③ Irregular verbs: Only two verbs, 来る (ku-ru, 'to come') and する (su-ru, 'to do'), belong to this group. Their conjugation is irregular.

ku-ru	(来る)	to come
su-ru	(する)	to do

The plain non-past affirmative form of verbs is the form in which verbs appear in most dictionaries. For this reason this form is often referred to as the dictionary form.

The conjugation introduced in this lesson is the -ます conjugation. Attached to the stem of a verb, the suffix -ます conveys politeness to the hearer. The -ます form of verbs is often used in talking with acquaintances, those who have higher social status, and strangers.

The -ます form is derived from the dictionary form in the following way: attach -[(i)masu] to the dictionary form stem. For vowel verbs, the suffix -[masu] is attached to the stem, and for consonant verbs -[imasu] is attached. For the verbs 来る and する, the -ます forms are conjugated irregularly.

The variants -[imasu] and -[masu] result from the fact that the Japanese sounds have a fixed order of CVCV... (C stands for consonants and V for vowels.) When this order is violated by a grammatical phenomenon such as suffixing, there is a return to the CVCV order by the insertion or omission of a vowel or consonant. In the case of the -ます suffix, it is necessary to rectify the order of the -ます form of a consonant verb by inserting the vowel [i] before -[masu]; otherwise the sequence of CVCCV... (e.g., kak-masu) would be produced, violating the regularly repeated order of consonant/vowel.

① Vowel verbs:

Dictionary form		-ます form		
mi- **ru**	(見る)	mi- **masu**	(見ます)	see, look
oki- **ru**	(起きる)	oki- **masu**	(起きます)	get up
ne- **ru**	(寝る)	ne- **masu**	(寝ます)	go to bed
tabe- **ru**	(食べる)	tabe- **masu**	(食べます)	eat

② Consonant verbs:

Dictionary form		-ます form		
kak- **u**	(書く)	kak- **imasu**	(書きます)	write
oyog- **u**	(泳ぐ)	oyog- **imasu**	(泳ぎます)	swim
kas- **u**	(貸す)	kash- **imasu**	(貸します)	lend
mats- **u**	(待つ)	mach- **imasu**	(待ちます)	wait
shin- **u**	(死ぬ)	shin- **imasu**	(死にます)	die
yob- **u**	(よぶ)	yob- **imasu**	(よびます)	call
yom- **u**	(読む)	yom- **imasu**	(読みます)	read
ur- **u**	(売る)	ur- **imasu**	(売ります)	sell

③ Irregular verbs:

Dictionary form		-ます form		
kuru	(来る)	ki- **masu**	(来ます)	come
suru	(する)	shi- **masu**	(します)	do

Using the Japanese syllabary table below, the way to attach the -[masu] suffix to the ます form stem of a consonant verb can be explained from a different perspective as follows: the endings of consonant verbs, -く, -ぐ, -す, -つ, -ぬ, -ぶ, -む, -る, -う, which are the last syllables of the dictionary form, all belong to the -[u] row. Replace each of the last syllables with its corresponding sound in the -[i] row, -き, -ぎ, -し, -ち, -に, -び, -み, -り, or -い, respectively. And then add -[masu] to it.

[n]	[w-]	[r-]	[y-]	[m-]	[b-]	[h-]	[n-]	[t-]	[s-]	[g-]	[k-]		
ん	わ	ら	や	ま	ば	は	な	た	さ	が	か	あ	-[a]

ます Form Stem Ending

(い)	り	(い)	み	び	ひ	に	ち	し	ぎ	き	い	-[i] +ます

GRAMMAR NOTES

LESSON

第三課

Dictionary Form Stem Ending

(う)	る	ゆ	む	ぶ	ふ	ぬ	つ	す	ぐ	く	う	-[u]
(え)	れ	(え)	め	べ	へ	ね	て	せ	げ	け	え	-[e]
を	ろ	よ	も	ぼ	ほ	の	と	そ	ご	こ	お	-[o]

V-ます indicates the non-past tense (something is going to happen, will happen, or is done habitually) or the speaker's volition.

(わたし　は) 寝(ね)ます。　(I) go to bed/(I) am going to go to bed/(I) will go to bed.
watashi　wa　nemasu

2) V-ます form: Negative

N　は　V-ません wa　masen	As for N, it does not V

The negative form of V-ます is V-ません.

A yes/no question with a verb predicate and the answer to it are formed in the same way as a yes/no question with a noun predicate (L1 GN3). It should be noted, however, that unlike answering a noun predicate question, the set phrases そうです 'That's right' and そうじゃありません 'That's not right' cannot be used in answering a question with a verb predicate.

わたし　は　帰(かえ)りません。　I am not going to return.
watashi　wa　kaerimasen

リーさん　は　寝(ね)ますか。　Are you going to go to bed, Mr. Lee?/Is Mr. Lee going to go to bed?
Riisan　wa　nemasu　ka

はい／ええ、(わたし／リーさん　は) 寝(ね)ます。　Yes, I am/he is.
hai/ee　(watashi/　Riisan　wa)　nemasu

いいえ、(わたし／リーさん　は) 寝(ね)ません。　No, I'm not/he isn't.
iie　(watashi/　Riisan　wa)　nemasen

2. Time expressions (2): Minutes

NUMBER-ふん／ぷん fun　pun	____ minutes

The word for 'minutes' is ふん／ぷん, and it follows the number. The corresponding question word is 何分(なんぷん). The choice of ふん or ぷん depends on the immediately preceding number: ふん immediately follows the numbers 2, 5, 7, 8, 9; andぷん, the numbers

1, 3, 4, 6, 8, 10, with 8 taking either. Sound change occurs in the numbers 1, 6, 8, and 10, in combination with the counter ぷん.

2分 (にふん ni-fun) two minutes
6分 (ろっぷん rop-pun) six minutes
何分 (なんぷん nan-pun) how many minutes
4時35分 (よじ さんじゅうごふん yo-ji sanjuugo-fun) four thirty-five

1分 いっぷん	11分 じゅういっぷん	30分 さんじゅっぷん／さんじっぷん
2分 にふん	12分 じゅうにふん	40分 よんじゅっぷん／よんじっぷん
3分 さんぷん	13分 じゅうさんぷん	50分 ごじゅっぷん／ごじっぷん
4分 よんぷん	14分 じゅうよんぷん	60分 ろくじゅっぷん／ろくじっぷん
5分 ごふん	15分 じゅうごふん	
6分 ろっぷん	16分 じゅうろっぷん	
7分 ななふん	17分 じゅうななふん	
8分 はっぷん／はちふん	18分 じゅうはっぷん／じゅうはちふん	
9分 きゅうふん	19分 じゅうきゅうふん	
10分 じゅっぷん／じっぷん	20分 にじゅっぷん／にじっぷん	何分 なんぷん

3. Time marker に

TIME に (ni)	＿＿＿

The particle に marks a point of time at which a denoted action takes place.

It can follow time expressions like ～時(じ)～分(ふん) which were introduced above in GN2, Time Expressions (2). Time words followed by the time marker に can occur with verbs in any tense.

(わたし は) 6時(じ) 45分(ふん) に 起(お)きます。(I) get up at 6:45.
(watashi wa rokuji yonjuugofun ni okimasu)

リーさん は 何時(なんじ) に 寝(ね)ます か。 What time do you go to bed, Mr. Lee? / What time does Mr. Lee go to bed?
(Riisan wa nanji ni nemasu ka)

4. Verbs with an object

N_1 は (wa) N_2 (OBJECT) を V-ます (masu)	As for N_1, it V N_2

The particle を marks the object of a verb. Verbs that require an object are generally

GRAMMAR NOTES
LESSON

第三課

called transitive verbs, as opposed to intransitive verbs, which essentially do not require an object. Note that verbs introduced in section 1 are intransitive.

Transitive verbs in English do not necessarily correspond to Japanese transitive verbs. For example, the verb 'meet', as in 'I meet my friend,' is expressed in Japanese as follows:

わたし は 友(とも)だち に 会(あ)います。
watashi wa tomodachi ni aimasu

As seen here, the verb 会(あ)う (au, 'to meet') is accompanied by the particle に, instead of the object marker を, to indicate the person one meets.

ラジオ の ニュース を 聞(き)きます。 (I) listen to the radio news.
rajio no nyuusu o kikimasu

スミスさん は 昼(ひる)ご飯(はん) を 食(た)べます。 Mr. Smith eats lunch.
Sumisusan wa hirugohan o tabemasu

田中(たなか)さん は 何(なに) を します か。
Tanakasan wa nani o shimasu ka
What does Mr. Tanaka do? / What do you do, Mr. Tanaka?

5. At/In ～

N で PLACE de	at/in ______

The particle で marks the location where the action takes place.

わたし は 新宿(しんじゅく) で 映画(えいが) を 見(み)ます。 I'll see a movie in Shinjuku.
watashi wa shinjuku de eega o mimasu

うち で 新聞(しんぶん) を 読(よ)み ます。 (I) read a newspaper at home.
uchi de shinbun o yomimasu

リーさん は どこ で 晩(ばん)ご飯(はん) を 食(た)べます か。
Riisan wa doko de bangohan o tabemasu ka
Where does Mr. Lee eat dinner? / Where do you eat dinner, Mr. Lee?

6. Motion verbs with direction

N_1 は N_2 へ／に V-ます PLACE e ni masu	As for N_1, it V to N_2

Verbs used in this pattern denote motion. 行(い)く (iku, 'to go'), 来(く)る (kuru, 'to come'), 帰(かえ)る (kaeru, 'to return') are three representatives of this group. Motion verbs by nature require an element expressing direction, which is marked by the particle へ (pronounced 'e') or に.

大学(だいがく) へ 行(い)きます。 (I) go to the university.
daigaku e ikimasu

パクさん は (わたし の) うち に 来(き)ます。 Mr. Park comes to my house.
Pakusan wa watashi no uchi ni kimasu

田中(たなか)さん は どこ へ 行(い)きます か。 Where does Mr. Tanaka go? / Where do you go, Mr. Tanaka?
Tanakasan wa doko e ikimasu ka

7. Instrumental marker

N (INSTRUMENT) で (de)	by means of/with N

The particle で marks the means of an action.

はし で 食(た)べます。 (I) eat with chopsticks.
hashi de tabemasu

学生(がくせい) は バス で 大学(だいがく) に 来(き)ます。 Students come to the university by bus.
gakusee wa basu de daigaku ni kimasu

リーさん は 何(なん) で 食(た)べますか。 What does Mr. Lee eat with? / What do you eat with, Mr. Lee?
Riisan wa nan de tabemasu ka

8. Time expressions (3)

きのう kinoo	yesterday	昼(ひる) hiru	lunch time, daytime
きょう kyoo	today	夜(よる) yoru	evening, night
あした ashita	tomorrow	けさ kesa	this morning
いつ itsu	when	今晩(こんばん) konban	this evening/tonight
朝(あさ) asa	morning		

The words listed above denote time in relation to the time of speech and must be used without the time marker に. They are normally placed immediately after the topic of a sentence (or as the first word in the sentence when the topic is not explicitly mentioned). They can occur with other time expressions.

きょう 12時(じ) 30分(ぷん) に 寝(ね)ます。
kyoo juuniji sanjuppun ni nemasu
(I) will go to bed at 12:30 today.

わたし は 朝(あさ) うち で 新聞(しんぶん) を 読(よ)みます。
watashi wa asa uchi de shinbun o yomimasu
I read a newspaper at home in the morning.

スミスさん は いつ 大学(だいがく) へ 行(い)きます か。
Sumisusan wa itsu daigaku e ikimasu ka
When does Mr. Smith go to the university? /
When do you go to the university, Mr. Smith?

9. Past tense

N は V-ました wa mashita	As for N, it did V
N は V-ませんでした wa masendeshita	As for N, it did not V

The past form of V-ます is V-ました, and that of V-ません, V-ませんでした。

きのう 新宿(しんじゅく) で 映画(えいが) を 見(み)ました。(I) saw a movie in Shinjuku yesterday.
kinoo shinjuku de eega o mimashita

けさ 新聞(しんぶん) を 読(よ)みませんでした。 (I) didn't read a newspaper this morning.
kesa shinbun o yomimasen deshita

The following table shows all the forms of V-ます for non-past/past and affirmative/negative.

	Non-past	Past
Affirmative	V-ます masu	V-ました mashita
Negative	V-ません masen	V-ませんでした masendeshita

READING

Letter to a Japanese Friend

たなかさん、おげんきですか。

わたしは、九月に東京に来ました。今、ＩＣＵの学生です。月よう日から金よう日までまいにち大学へ行きます。

きのうは、日よう日でした。大学に行きませんでした。ともだちと新宿に行きました。デパートとほんやでかいものしました。それからえいがも見ました。ばんごはんは、レストランで食べました。よる十時ごろうちにかえりました。

たなかさんは、何をしましたか。

では、また。

ヤノス・マイヤー

東京（とうきょう）
新宿（しんじゅく）

□ Comprehension Check

1. Where is the writer of the letter now?
2. What did he do last Sunday?

□ Writing Activity

1. Describe your daily routine in Japanese.
2. Describe what you did last weekend.

WRITING
[KANJI]

読(よ)み方(かた)を覚(おぼ)えましょう

行く（いく）: to go　　食べる（たべる）: to eat
来る（くる）: to come　　朝（あさ）: morning
見る（みる）: to look at　　今晩（こんばん）: tonight

新(あたら)しい漢字(かんじ)

19 今

ことば	くん	おん	いみ
1 今(いま)・2 今月(こんげつ)	いま	こん	now, present

かきじゅん: ノ 𠆢 今

1 now
2 this month

20 時

ことば	くん	おん	いみ
1 時(とき)・2 三時(さんじ)・3 時間(じかん)・4 一時間(いちじかん)	とき・と	じ	time

かきじゅん: 丨 冂 日 日 日一 日十 旪 旹 時 時

1 time
2 three o'clock
3 time, hour(s)
4 one hour

21 分

ことば	くん	おん	いみ
1 分かる(わかる)・2 二分(にふん)・3 六分(ろっぷん)	わ(かる)	ぶん・ふん・ぷん	minute(s), to divide

かきじゅん: ノ 八 分 分

1 to understand
2 two minutes
3 six minutes

22

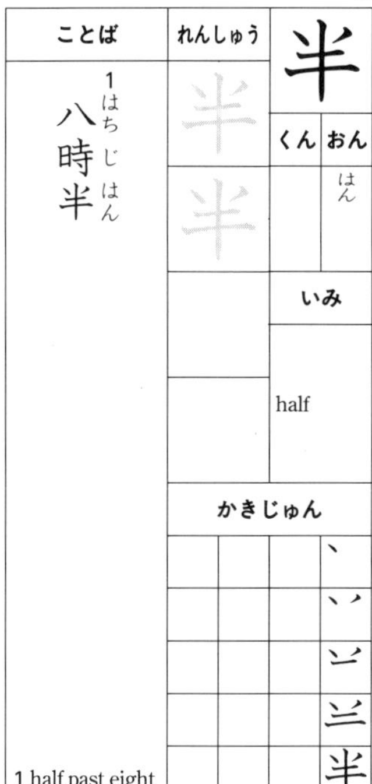

ことば	れんしゅう	半
八時半 (1 はちじはん)		くん: — / おん: はん
		いみ: half
1 half past eight		かきじゅん

23

ことば	れんしゅう	前
前 (1 まえ)		くん: まえ / おん: ぜん
		いみ: before, front
1 the front		かきじゅん

24

ことば	れんしゅう	後
後ろ (1 うし)・後 (2 あと)		くん: うし(ろ)・あと / おん: ご
		いみ: after, later, behind
1 the back 2 later		かきじゅん

25

ことば	れんしゅう	午
午前 (1 ごぜん)・午後 (2 ごご)		くん: — / おん: ご
		いみ: noon
1 A.M. 2 P.M.		かきじゅん

26

ことば	れんしゅう	何
何 (1 なに)・何ですか (2 なん)・何時 (3 なんじ)		くん: なに・なん / おん: —
		いみ: what, how many
1 what 2 What is it? 3 what time		かきじゅん

書く練習

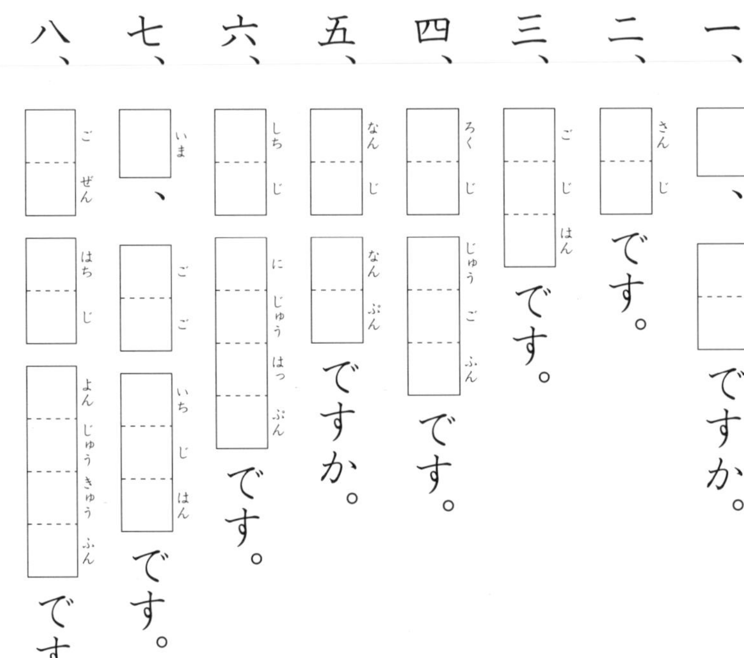

読む練習

一、今、四時二十三分です。

二、九時半です。

三、六時十八分です。

四、朝、何時に朝ご飯を食べますか。

五、午前八時四十五分に大学へ行きます。

六、午後七時半にテレビを見ます。

七、今晩、何時に来ますか。

八、朝、何を食べますか。

LISTENING AND SPEAKING

Objectives

Making invitations
Arranging date and time when invited

Points

- asking questions using WH-question words
- making proposals/inviting
- expressing pleasure and sympathy

Sentences

1 1時間、2時間、3時間、・・・、24時間

2 1日、2日、3日、・・・、31日

3 (わたし は) 友だち に 家族 の 写真 を 見せました。

4 いっしょ に テニス を しません か。

5 来週 どこ か へ 旅行 しましょう。

6 (わたし は) 週末 (に) は 何 も 勉強 しません。

7 (わたし は) 毎日 3時間 図書館 で 勉強 します。

8 (わたし は) 11月 20日 に 飛行機 で 北海道 へ 行きます。

Expressions

1　いい　です　ね。　That would be nice.　（ドリル　II-1）

フォーメーション

1-1　Counters (4): Time spans

1時間	いちじかん
2時間	にじかん
3時間	さんじかん
4時間	よじかん
5時間	ごじかん
6時間	ろくじかん
7時間	ななじかん／しちじかん
8時間	はちじかん
9時間	くじかん
10時間	じゅうじかん
11時間	じゅういちじかん
12時間	じゅうにじかん
何時間	なんじかん
どのくらい	

1-2

例）8：30－9：35

→　いち時間　ご分

1）　9：00－11：30　→

2）12：21－15：05　→

3）13：10－13：58　→

4）　4：30－22：30　→

5）14：40－18：15　→

2-1 Months and dates

1月	いちがつ
2月	にがつ
3月	さんがつ
4月	しがつ
5月	ごがつ
6月	ろくがつ
7月	しちがつ
8月	はちがつ
9月	くがつ
10月	じゅうがつ
11月	じゅういちがつ
12月	じゅうにがつ
何月	なんがつ

1日	ついたち	16日	じゅうろくにち
2日	ふつか	17日	じゅうしちにち
3日	みっか	18日	じゅうはちにち
4日	よっか	19日	じゅうくにち
5日	いつか	20日	はつか
6日	むいか	21日	にじゅういちにち
7日	なのか	22日	にじゅうににち
8日	ようか	23日	にじゅうさんにち
9日	ここのか	24日	にじゅうよっか
10日	とおか	25日	にじゅうごにち
11日	じゅういちにち	26日	にじゅうろくにち
12日	じゅうににち	27日	にじゅうしちにち
13日	じゅうさんにち	28日	にじゅうはちにち
14日	じゅうよっか	29日	にじゅうくにち
15日	じゅうごにち	30日	さんじゅうにち
		31日	さんじゅういちにち
何日	なんにち		

2-2

例(れい)) 1月1日 → いちがつ ついたち

1) 2月 4日 →
2) 4月10日 →
3) 6月20日 →
4) 8月 2日 →
5) 10月17日 →
6) 12月14日 →
7) 3月 8日 →
8) 5月 5日 →
9) 7月13日 →
10) 9月26日 →
11) 11月30日 →
12) 1月29日 →

3 To someone

例(れい)) (わたし)、友(とも)だち、(わたし の) 家族(かぞく) の 写真(しゃしん)、見せる

→ (わたし は) 友(とも)だち に (わたし の) 家族(かぞく) の 写真(しゃしん) を 見せました。

1) (わたし)、(わたし の) 家族(かぞく)、手紙(てがみ)、書く →
2) ～さん、友(とも)だち、自転車(じてんしゃ)、貸(か)す →
3) (わたし)、子(こ)ども、英語(えいご)、教(おし)える →
4) (わたし)、(わたし の) 家族(かぞく)、えはがき、送(おく)る →

4 Inviting

例)ジョギング、する → いっしょ に ジョギング を しません か。
れい

1) お茶、飲む →
ちゃ
2) テニス、する →
3) 図書館、勉強 する →
としょかん べんきょう
4) 食堂、昼ご飯、食べる →
しょくどう ひる はん

5 Suggesting

例)来週、どこ か、旅行 → 来週 どこ か へ 旅行 しましょう。
れい らいしゅう りょこう らいしゅう りょこう

1) 今週 の 週末、どこ か、買い物 する →
こんしゅう しゅうまつ か もの
2) わたし の アパート、何 か、作る →
つく
3) だれ か、道、聞く →
みち き
4) あの 喫茶店、何 か、飲む →
きっさてん

6-1 Nothing, nobody, nowhere

例)(わたし)、週末、何 も、勉強 する
れい しゅうまつ べんきょう

→ (わたし は) 週末 (に) は 何 も 勉強 しません。
しゅうまつ べんきょう

1) (わたし)、けさ、何 も、食べる →
2) (わたし)、先週、だれ に も、会う →
せんしゅう
3) (わたし)、きのう、どこ へ も、行く →
4) (わたし)、きのう、デパート、何 も、買う →

6-2 Something, somebody, somewhere; nothing, nobody, nowhere

例)(あなた)、先週、どこ か、行く
れい せんしゅう

→ (あなた は) 先週 どこ か へ 行きました か。
せんしゅう

はい/ええ、行きました。

いいえ、(わたし は) どこ へ も 行きません でした。

1) (あなた)、けさ、何 か、食べる →
2) (あなた)、図書館、だれ か、会う →
としょかん
3) だれ か、わたし の 部屋、来る →
へや
4) きのう の 夜、(あなた)、何 か、する →
よる

7 Duration

例) (わたし)、毎日、3時間、図書館、勉強　する

→　(わたし　は)　毎日　3時間　図書館　で　勉強　します。

1) リーさん、火曜日　と　木曜日、1時間　30分、子ども、英語、教える　→

2) ～さん、毎日、45分、テープ、日本語　の　勉強、する　→

3) (わたし)、毎日　2時間　15分、電車、乗る　→

4) チェンさん、毎日、25分、ニュース、見る　→

8 Dates

例) (わたし)、20日、飛行機、北海道、行く

→　(わたし　は)　20日　に　飛行機　で　北海道　へ　行きます。

1) リーさん、4日、秋葉原、ワープロ、買う　→

2) (わたし)、8日、九州　の　友だち、会う　→

3) チェンさん、31日、友だち、テープレコーダー、貸す　→

4) パメラさん、29日、飛行機、日本、来る　→

ドリル

I Asking/Telling to whom

A：ジョンさん　は　だれ　に　えはがき　を　送ります　か。

B：日本人　の　友だち　に　送ります。

友だち	写真	送る
家族	本	貸す
子ども	ビデオ	見せる
	自転車	

II-1 Inviting someone to do something

A：いっしょ　に　テニス　を　しませんか。

B：いい　です　ね。

映画　を　見る	本屋　に　行く
昼ご飯　を　食べる	帰る

II-2 Inviting someone to do something

A：Bさん　は　テニス　を　します　か。

B：ええ、します。

A：週末(しゅうまつ)　に　いっしょ　に
　テニス　を　しません　か。

B：いい　です　ね。　そう　しましょう。

B：いいえ、テニス　は　しません。

A：そう　です　か。

III Did you (do) something

A：きのう　は　何か　しました　か。

B：ええ、買い物(かいもの)　を　しました。

B：いいえ、何も　しません　でした。
　Aさん　は　どこか　へ　行きました　か。

A：いいえ、どこ　へ　も　行きません　でした。

Give your own response.

IV Asking about the duration of activities

A：Bさん　は、朝、何時間　勉強(べんきょう)　を　しました　か。

B：3時間半　勉強(べんきょう)　を　しました。

Bさんの土曜日(どようび)

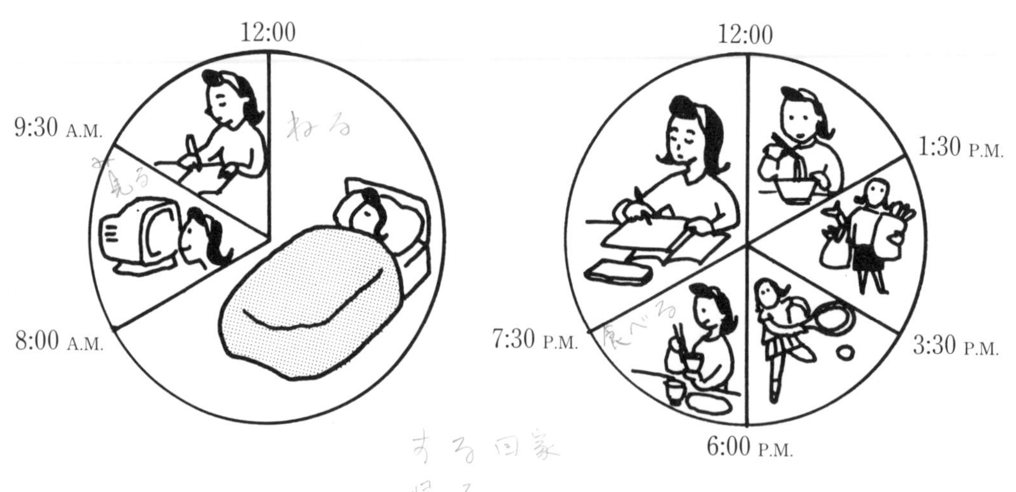

ロールプレイ

CARD A

I　Inviting someone to do something

Ask your classmate to play tennis this Saturday. Arrange the meeting time and place.

CARD B

I　Inviting someone to do something

You are asked to play tennis this Saturday. You accept the invitation. Arrange the meeting time and place.

CARD A

II　Being served tea/cold drinks

At someone's house, you are offered something to drink. State your preference and thank them.

CARD B

II　Being served tea/cold drinks

You offer a guest something to drink.

CARD A

III　Inviting someone to do something

Ask your friend to go to the movies with you this weekend. Arrange the meeting time and place.

CARD B

III　Inviting someone to do something

You are invited to go to see a movie. Arrange the meeting time and place.

GRAMMAR NOTES

1. Time spans

TIME-間 (かん kan)

In order to express duration of time, the suffix -かん is attached to the time, as in いちじかん ('one hour') and じゅっぷんかん ('ten minutes'). In the case of -ふん／-ぷん, however, the suffix -かん is optional. なんじかん corresponds to the English 'how many hours' and なんぷんかん, or なんぷん, to 'how many minutes'.

よじかん yo-ji-kan	four hours
さんじゅうごふん（かん） sanjuugo-fun (kan)	thirty-five minutes

2. Dates

NUMBER-月 (がつ gatsu)

The names of the months of the year are expressed with the numbers 1 to 12 followed by -がつ, as shown in the chart below. Note that 4-がつ ('April'), 7-がつ ('July'), and 9-がつ ('September') are pronounced しがつ, しちがつ, and くがつ, respectively. なんがつ corresponds to 'what month' in English.

1月	いちがつ ichigatsu	January	5月	ごがつ gogatsu	May
2月	にがつ nigatsu	February	6月	ろくがつ rokugatsu	June
3月	さんがつ sangatsu	March	7月	しちがつ shichigatsu	July
4月	しがつ shigatsu	April	8月	はちがつ hachigatsu	August

9 月	くがつ kugatsu	September	11 月	じゅういちがつ juuichigatsu	November
10 月	じゅうがつ juugatsu	October	12 月	じゅうにがつ juunigatsu	December

NUMBER-日 (nichi)

The days of the month are indicated with the numbers 1 to 31 followed by -にち, with the exception of the 1st to the 10th, the 14th, 20th, and 24th (which are shown in bold type).

1 日	**ついたち** tsuitachi	16 日	じゅうろくにち juurokunichi
2 日	**ふつか** futsuka	17 日	じゅうしちにち juushichinichi
3 日	**みっか** mikka	18 日	じゅうはちにち juuhachinichi
4 日	**よっか** yokka	19 日	じゅうくにち juukunichi
5 日	**いつか** itsuka	20 日	**はつか** hatsuka
6 日	**むいか** muika	21 日	にじゅういちにち nijuuichinichi
7 日	**なのか** nanoka	22 日	にじゅうににち nijuuninichi
8 日	**ようか** yooka	23 日	にじゅうさんにち nijuusannichi
9 日	**ここのか** kokonoka	24 日	**にじゅうよっか** nijuuyokka
10 日	**とおか** tooka	25 日	にじゅうごにち nijuugonichi
11 日	じゅういちにち juuichinichi	26 日	にじゅうろくにち nijuurokunichi
12 日	じゅうににち juuninichi	27 日	にじゅうしちにち nijuushichinichi
13 日	じゅうさんにち juusannichi	28 日	にじゅうはちにち nijuuhachinichi
14 日	**じゅうよっか** juuyokka	29 日	にじゅうくにち nijuukunichi
15 日	じゅうごにち juugonichi	30 日	さんじゅうにち sanjuunichi
		31 日	さんじゅういちにち sanjuuichinichi
何日	なんにち nannichi		

なんにち correponds to 'what day of the month' in English.

3. Indirect object

N_1 は (wa) N_2 に (ni) N_3 を (o) V-ます (masu)	N_1 V N_3 to N_2

The particle に corresponds to the English 'to' and indicates the indirect object of a verb. The phrase [N_2 に] explains to or for whom someone does something.

スミスさん は 友だち(とも) に 手紙(てがみ) を 書(か)きました。
Sumisusan wa tomodachi ni tegami o kakimashita
Mr. Smith wrote a letter to a friend.

子(こ)ども に 英語(えいご) を 教(おし)えます。
kodomo ni eego o oshiemasu
I teach English to children.

4. Inviting someone to do something

いっしょに (isshoni) V-ません (masen) か (ka)	Would you like to V together? Why don't we V together?

This expression is used for inviting the hearer(s) to do something together. いっしょに means 'together' with someone else. When you are invited to do something with someone and you want to accept the invitation, you should say いい です ね ('That's a good idea') or ええ、そう しましょう ('Yes, let's'). Expressions for declining an invitation will be introduced later.

いっしょに ジョギング を しません か。 — Why don't we jog together?
isshoni jogingu o shimasen ka

いい です ね。 — That's a good idea.
ii desu ne

5. Suggesting

Let's V

The form V-ましょう is called the volitional form of V-ます. Its most common use is in suggestions, and it corresponds to the English 'let's'. As in GN4 above, when someone suggests something to you and you want to accept the suggestion, the expression そう しましょう can be used.

お茶(ちゃ) を 飲(の)みましょう。 — Let's have tea.
ocha o nomimashoo

ええ、そう しましょう。 — Yes, let's.
ee soo shimashoo

6. Something, somebody, somewhere

QUESTION WORD-か	
なにか nanika	something
だれか dareka	someone
どこか dokoka	somewhere
いつか itsuka	sometime

When か is attached to question words like なに ('what'), だれ ('who'), どこ ('where') and いつ ('when'), they correspond to English indefinite pronouns such as 'something, somebody, somewhere, and sometime' when used in statements, or to indefinite pronouns such as 'anything, anyone, anywhere, and anytime' when used in questions.

(あなた は) 先週 どこか へ 行きました か。
anata wa senshuu dokoka e ikimashita ka
Did you go anywhere last week?

わたし の アパート で 何か 作りましょう。
watashi no apaato de nanika tsukurimashoo
Let's cook something at my apartment.

だれか に 道 を 聞きましょう。
dareka ni michi o kikimashoo
Let's ask someone for directions.

A：だれか 来ました か。
dareka kimashita ka
Did someone come?

B：田中さん が 来ました。
Tanakasan ga kimashita
Mr. Tanaka came.

A：いっしょに 何か 食べません か。
isshoni nanika tabemasen ka
Shall we eat something together?

B：ええ、昼ご飯 を 食べましょう。
ee hirugohan o tabemashoo
Yes: Let's eat lunch.

Note that the particles が and を are dropped after だれか and なにか.

7. Nothing, nobody, nowhere

QUESTION WORD-も	V-NEGATIVE	
なにも nanimo	ません masen	nothing
だれも daremo	ません masen	no one
どこへも dokoemo	ません masen	nowhere

Followed by も and used in negative sentences, question words like なに, だれ, and どこ correspond to English negative pronouns, such as 'nothing, no one, and nowhere', or to indefinite pronouns such as 'anything, anyone, and anywhere'.

(わたし　は) けさ　何(なに)も　食(た)べません　でした。
watashi wa kesa nanimo tabemasen deshita
I didn't eat anything this morning.

cf. (わたし　は) けさ　朝(あさ)ご飯(はん)　を　食(た)べません　でした。
watashi wa kesa asagohan o tabemasen deshita
I didn't eat breakfast this morning.

だれも　来(き)ません　でした。
daremo kimasen deshita
Nobody came.

cf. 田中(たなか)さん　が　来(き)ません　でした。
Tanakasan ga kimasen deshita
Mr. Tanaka didn't come.

(わたし　は) きのう　どこ　へ　も　行(い)きません　でした。
watashi wa kinoo doko e mo ikimasen deshita
I didn't go anywhere yesterday.

cf. きのう　新宿(しんじゅく)　へ　行(い)きません　でした。
kinoo Shinjuku e ikimasen deshita
I didn't go to Shinjuku yesterday.

Here, again, the particles が and を are dropped after だれも and なにも.

READING

Memo

リーさんへ
わたしとスミスさんは、
あしたしんじゅくでえいがを
見ます。フランスのえいがです。
それから、買い物をします。
リーさんもいっしょに行きま
せんか。
それから、今度の土曜日に
大学でテニスをします。
リーさんも来ませんか。
九月十五日（木）7:30
すずき

買い物　（かいもの）
今度　　（こんど）

□ Comprehension Check

1. What does the memo writer intend to do?

    a.

    b.

□ Writing Activity

1. Suppose you received the memo. Write a reply to the writer.

WRITING
[KANJI]

読み方を覚えましょう
(よ かた おぼ)

～時間 (～じかん): hour(s)
書く (かく): to write
飲む (のむ): to drink
買う (かう): to buy
会う (あう): to meet, see
乗る (のる): to get on, ride

新しい漢字
(あたら かんじ)

27 月

ことば: 1 月(つき)・2 月曜日(げつようび)・3 四月(しがつ)・4 今月(こんげつ)・5 先月(せんげつ)

1 the moon
2 Monday
3 April
4 this month
5 last month

くん	おん
つき	げつ・がつ

いみ: the moon, month(s)

かきじゅん: 丿 冂 月 月

28 火

ことば: 1 火(ひ)・2 火曜日(かようび)

1 (a) fire
2 Tuesday

くん	おん
ひ	か

いみ: fire

かきじゅん: 丶 丷 少 火

29 水

ことば: 1 水(みず)・2 水曜日(すいようび)

1 water
2 Wednesday

くん	おん
みず	すい

いみ: water

かきじゅん: 亅 刀 水 水

30

ことば	れんしゅう	木
1 木（き）・2 木曜日（もくようび）	木 木	くん: き / おん: もく
		いみ: a tree, wood
1 a tree, wood 2 Thursday	かきじゅん	一 十 才 木

31

ことば	れんしゅう	金
1 金（きん）・2 お金（かね）・3 金曜日（きんようび）	金 金	くん: かね / おん: きん
		いみ: gold, money
1 gold 2 money 3 Friday	かきじゅん	ノ 入 亼 今 全 余 金 金

32

ことば	れんしゅう	土
1 土（つち）・2 土曜日（どようび）	土 土	くん: つち / おん: ど
		いみ: soil
1 earth, soil 2 Saturday	かきじゅん	一 十 土

33

ことば	れんしゅう	行
1 行く（い）・2 銀行（ぎんこう）	行 行	くん: い（く） / おん: こう
		いみ: to go
1 to go 2 a bank	かきじゅん	ノ ク 彳 行 行 行

34

ことば	れんしゅう	来
1 来る（く）・2 来月（らいげつ）	来 来	くん: く（る）・き（ます）・こ（ない） / おん: らい
		いみ: to come
1 to come 2 next month	かきじゅん	一 厂 冖 立 平 来 来

WRITING LESSON 4 第四課

書く練習（れんしゅう）

一、□曜□（にちようび）

二、□曜□（すいようび）

三、□曜□（もくようび）

四、□曜□（げつようび）

五、□曜□（きんようび）

六、□曜□（かようび）

七、□曜□（どようび）に、□国（ちゅうごく）へ□（い）きます。

八、□曜□（なんようび）に□□（だいがく）へ□（き）ますか。

九、□曜□（すいようび）の□□（ごご）□□（よじ）に□（き）ます。

十、□曜□（きんようび）の□□（ごぜん）□□（くじ）に銀□（ぎんこう）へ□（い）きます。

読む練習（よむれんしゅう）

一、木曜日

二、火曜日

三、土曜日

四、日曜日に来ます。

五、月曜日に行きます。

六、水曜日に、本を買います。

七、金曜日に、一時間バスに乗ります。

八、水曜日の午後、友だちに会います。

九、三十分、日本語を書きます。

十、朝六時にコーヒーを飲みます。

LISTENING AND SPEAKING

Objectives

Responding when asked for impressions of life in Japan

Points

- stating opinions and impressions with regard to weather, lodgings, daily life, and products

Sentences

1 寮(りょう) の 部屋 は 広(ひろ)い です か。

  はい／ええ、(寮(りょう) の 部屋 は) 広(ひろ)い です。

  いいえ、(寮(りょう) の 部屋 は (広(ひろ)く ありません。 / 広(ひろ)く ない です。)

寮(りょう) の 部屋 は 静(しず)か です か。

  はい／ええ、(寮(りょう) の 部屋 は) 静(しず)か です。

  いいえ、(寮(りょう) の 部屋 は) 静(しず)か じゃありません。

寮(りょう) の 部屋 は どう です か。

  静(しず)か です。

2 リーさん の 部屋 は どんな 部屋 です か。

（わたし の 部屋 は） 広い(ひろ) 部屋 です。

（わたし の 部屋 は） 静か(しず) な 部屋 です。

3 わたし の かさ は その 赤い(あか) の です。

4 新しい アパート は きれい です。 それに、（新しい アパート は） 便利 です。

新しい アパート は きれい です。 でも、（新しい アパート は） 高い です。

5 東京 は 交通(こうつう) が 便利 です。

Expressions

1 そう です か。　Really? / Is that right? （ドリル Ⅲ）

2 そう です ね。　It sure is. / That's right. （ドリル Ⅲ）

フォーメーション

1-1 Non-past conjugation of adjectival nouns and adjectives

例(れい)） 静か(しず)：静か(しず) です → 静か(しず) じゃありません

広い(ひろ)：広い(ひろ) です → 広く(ひろ) ありません / 広く(ひろ) ない です

1) おもしろい →
2) 高い →
3) 大きい →
4) 新しい →
5) 明るい →
6) 少ない →
7) 便利 →
8) かんたん →
9) きれい →
10) いや →
11) 親切(しんせつ) →
12) 安全(あんぜん) →

1-2

例(れい)） 寮(りょう) の 部屋、広い(ひろ)

→ 寮(りょう) の 部屋 は 広い(ひろ) です か。

はい／ええ、（寮(りょう) の 部屋 は） 広い(ひろ) です。

いいえ、(寮(りょう) の 部屋 は) 〔広(ひろ)く ありません。／広(ひろ)く ない です。〕

1) その 仕事、かんたん →
2) 東京、安全(あんぜん) →
3) きょう、暑(あつ)い →
4) タイ語(ご)、むずかしい →
5) この アパート、静(しず)か →
6) この 本、安(やす)い →

2-1 Adjectival nouns and adjectives modifying nouns

例(れい)) 部屋：静(しず)か → 静(しず)か な 部屋
部屋：広(ひろ)い → 広(ひろ)い 部屋

1) 家賃(やちん)：高い →
2) 本：つまらない →
3) 空気(くうき)：きれい →
4) 自転車(じてんしゃ)：赤(あか)い →
5) 日本語(にほんご)：やさしい →
6) 道(みち)：安全(あんぜん) →

2-2

例(れい)) わたし の 部屋、静(しず)か な 部屋 → わたし の 部屋 は 静(しず)か な 部屋 です。

1) 日本 の 車、小さい 車 →
2) ハンバーガー、おいしい 食(た)べ物(もの) →
3) きょう、いい 天気(てんき) →
4) 新幹線(しんかんせん)、便利 な 乗(の)り物(もの) →

3-1 Replacing a noun understood from context with の

例(れい)) わたし の かさ は その 赤(あか)い かさ です
→ わたし の かさ は その 赤(あか)い の です。

1) 日本語(にほんご) の 辞書(じしょ) は あの 小さい 辞書(じしょ) です →
2) わたし の アパート は あの きれい な アパート です →

3-2 Omitting a noun understood from context

例(れい)) この電話番号(でんわばんごう) は 大学 の 電話番号(でんわばんごう) です
→ この 電話番号(でんわばんごう) は 大学 の です。

1) その 新しい 自転車(じてんしゃ) は 佐藤(さとう)さん の 自転車(じてんしゃ) です →
2) その 本 は わたし の 本 です →

4-1 Expanding a description

例(れい)) 新しい アパート、きれい：便利
→ 新しい アパート は きれい です。それに、(新しい アパート は)便利 です。

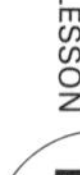

1) 古い 寮、せまい：暗い →
2) バス、便利：安い →
3) この 本、高い：つまらない →

4-2

例) 新しい アパート、きれい：高い
→ 新しい アパート は きれい です。でも、(新しい アパート は) 高い です。
1) 古い 寮、せまい：安い →
2) バス、便利：高い →
3) この 本、高い：おもしろい →

5 ～は～が～

例) 東京、交通、便利 → 東京 は 交通 が 便利 です。
1) 日本語、漢字、むずかしい →
2) 新しい アパート、家賃、高い →
3) きょう、天気、いい →
4) 東京、道、せまい →
5) あの建物、まど、少ない →

ドリル

I Questions and answers

A：この 本 は 高い です か。

B：はい、高い です。　　B：いいえ、高く ありません。

本	安い cheap
ざっし	おもしろい interesting, fun
	むずかしい difficult
	新しい new あたら

II Game: What kind of car is it?

A：～さん の 車 (くるま) は 大きい です か。
B：ええ、大きい です。
A：赤い です か。

B：いいえ、赤く(あか) ありません。白い です。

① 赤い(あか)

② 白い

③ 白い

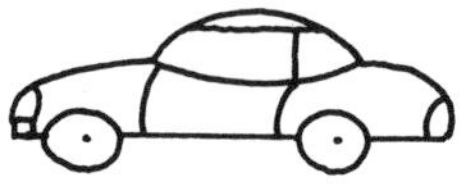

④ 赤い(あか)

① 黒い(くろ)

② 赤い(あか)

③ 赤い(あか)

Ⅲ Asking for and stating impressions

A：日本 の 食べ物(たもの) は どう です か。

B：とても おいしい です。

それに 新しいです。 A：そう です か。

でも、高い です。 A：そう です ね。

テレビ 人 学生 生活(せいかつ) 大学 乗り物(のもの)	Give your own response.

Ⅳ Asking for and stating impressions

(Comparing Tokyo to other cities in the world)

A：東京 は どう です か。

B：東京 は 人 が 多い です。

でも、人 が 親切(しんせつ) です。 A：そう です か。

それに 物(もの) が 高い です。 A：そう です ね。

食べ物(たもの) が おいしい
乗り物(のもの) が きれい
交通(こうつう) が 便利
うち が 小さい
車 が 多い
道(みち) が せまい

V-1 Describing a person

A：～先生　は　どんな　先生　です　か。

B：～先生　は　きれい　な　先生　です。

親切（しんせつ）
せ　が　高い
せ　が　低い（ひく）
やさしい

V-2 Describing a place

A：Bさん　の　アパート　は　どんな　アパート　です　か。

B：静か（しず）　な　アパート　です。

広い（ひろ）／せまい
便利／不便
新しい／古い
きれい／きたない

ロールプレイ

CARD A

I Asking for and stating impressions

You meet a foreign student at a party. Ask the student some questions about his/her impressions of Tokyo/ICU.

CARD B

I Asking for and stating impressions

You are a foreign student who arrived a month ago. You meet a Japanese student and respond to questions about your impressions of Tokyo/ICU.

CARD A

II Asking/telling about someone's country or hometown

You meet a foreign student at a party. Ask about his/her country.

CARD B

II Asking/telling about someone's country or hometown

You are a foreign student who arrived a month ago. You meet a Japanese student and respond to questions about your country.

CARD A

III Making a purchase

You are a shop assistant. Greet a customer, find out what they want, and make some suggestions.

CARD B

III Making a purchase

You go to a store to buy ____. You have a price limit. Ask the sales person a few questions to find out what you need to know. You can leave the shop without buying anything.

GRAMMAR NOTES

1. Adjectives and adjectival nouns

There are two kinds of adjectivals in Japanese : adjectives and adjectival nouns.

1) Adjectives
Adjectives in Japanese resemble verbs by taking a variety of forms, depending on their meaning or the grammatical context in which they are used. This differs from English, in which adjectives as predicates are always used with the verb 'be'.

Japanese adjectives consist of the stem plus a suffix. The stem of adjectives always ends in a vowel (either a, i, u, or o). The plain non-past form consists of the stem plus the suffix -い. This is the form in which adjectives appear in the vocabulary lists in this book and in most dictionaries. Hence it is often referred to as the dictionary form.

Plain non-past form (dictionary form, -い form)

Stem -i		
taka-i	(高い)	is high, is expensive
ooki-i	(大きい)	is big
akaru-i	(明るい)	is bright
omoshiro-i	(おもしろい)	is interesting, is funny

The suffix -い indicates the non-past tense.

The adjective いい (i-i), which corresponds to the English 'good', is irregular. The irregularity consists of a change of the stem from よ to い in the non-past form; all other forms have よ. (See the negative form of adjectives in GN3 below.) Although いい is more common as a non-past from, よい (yo-i) is still used as a variant, especially in formal writing.

i-i	(いい)	is good
(yo-i → i-i)		

2) Adjectival nouns
Not all Japanese words that correspond in meaning to English adjectives are

functionally adjectives in Japanese; some are verbs, and many are nouns. Japanese nouns that have adjectival meanings and are primarily used in adjective constructions are called adjectival nouns (abbreviated AN). Examples:

kiree	(きれい)	clean, pretty
shizuka	(静か)	quiet

Adjectival nouns are listed in the uninflected forms given above in vocabulary lists and dictionaries.

2. Adjectives and adjectival nouns as predicates

Like verbs, adjectives and adjectival nouns can take polite forms when used as predicates.

A subject can be specified in sentences with adjective and adjectival noun predicates just as with ordinary noun predicate sentences.

1) Adjectives

(N は) Adj-い です	(As for N,) it's Adj

The polite form of adjectives consists of the -い form plus です.

おもしろい です。	It's interesting/funny.
新しい です。	It's new.
この 本 は 安い です。	This book is inexpensive.

2) Adjectival nouns

(N は) AN です	(As for N,) it's Adj

The polite form of adjectival nouns used as predicates consists of its use with です, as with other nouns.

静か です。	It's quiet.
便利 です。	It's convenient.
部屋 は きれい です。	The room is clean.

It may appear from these polite forms that adjectives and adjectival nouns are the same, but です plays a different role in the two forms. With adjectives, です merely indicates politeness; it is not required in order for adjectives to function as predicates (adjectives can do that independently). With adjectival nouns, however, です not only indicates politeness but is also required for an adjectival noun (or any noun) to function as a predicate.

3. Negative forms of adjectives and adjectival nouns as predicates

The non-past negative predicate forms of adjectives and adjectival nouns are distinct.

1) Adjectives

(N　は)　Adj-く　ありません 　　　　　　　　ない　です	(As for N,) it is not Adj

The negative forms of adjectives consist of the stem plus suffix -く (the -く form) followed by negative predicates.

-く Form of Adjectives

Stem + -ku		
taka-ku	(高(たか)く)	high, expensive
ooki-ku	(大(おお)きく)	big
akaru-ku	(明(あか)るく)	bright
omoshiro-ku	(おもしろく)	interesting, funny
yo-ku	(よく)	good　(See GN1.1 above.)

There are two polite forms of adjectives used as negative predicates. One consists of the -く form plus ありません, and the other of the -く form plus ない　です. The former sounds slightly more polite than the latter.

暑(あつ)く　ありません。　It's not hot.
暑(あつ)く　ない　です。　It's not hot.
広(ひろ)く　ありません。　It's not wide.
広(ひろ)く　ない　です。　It's not wide.
きょうは　暑(あつ)く　ありません。　It's not hot today.
きょうは　暑(あつ)く　ない　です。　It's not hot today.

2) Adjectival nouns

(N　は)　AN　じゃありません	(As for N,) it is not Adj

To make negative predicates of adjectival nouns add じゃありません in place of です. では replaces じゃ in formal speech, as shown in the third example sentence below.

きれい　じゃありません。　It's not clean.
この　部屋(へや)　は　便利(べんり)　じゃありません。　This room is not convenient.
すし　は　好(す)き　では　ありません。　I don't like sushi.

Note also that きれい is an adjectival noun and not an adjective, even though it happens to end in い.

4. Adjectives and adjectival nouns as noun modifiers

Adjectives and adjectival nouns may be used to modify nouns. They are placed before the noun they modify.

1) Adjectives

Adj-い N	Adj N

An adjective appears in its -い form.

広(ひろ)い 部屋(へや)	a spacious room
高(たか)い 家賃(やちん)	high rent

2) Adjectival nouns

AN な N	Adj N

An adjectival noun is followed by な, a form of the copula used for modification.

きれい な 本(ほん)	a beautiful book
静(しず)か な 部屋(へや)	a quiet room

Remember that when one noun modifies another noun, the initial noun is followed by の rather than な (L1 GN4).

アパート の 部屋(へや)	a room in an apartment house

Two or more adjectives or adjectival nouns can modify a noun. A slight pause (indicated by a comma) occurs between adjectives or adjectival nouns.

安(やす)い、おいしい 食(た)べ物(もの)	cheap, tasty food
広(ひろ)い、静(しず)か な 部屋(へや)	a big, quiet room
きれい な、便利(べんり) な 部屋(へや)	a clean, convenient room

5. Question words: どう and どんな

Adjectives or adjectival nouns may be used to answer questions employing the words どう or どんな. The former immediately precedes です, and the latter modifies a noun.

1) N は どう です か　　How is N?

部屋(へや) は どう です か。

How is the room?

静(しず)か です。

It's quiet.

2) (N_1 は) どんな N_1 です か　　(As for N_1,) what kind of N_1 is it?

どんな 部屋(へや) です か。　What kind of a room is it?

静(しず)か な 部屋(へや) です。 It's a quiet room.

These are to be compared with なん の and どの. なん の modifies a noun and is answered by a function or use; どの also modifies nouns and is answered by a demonstrative or some other specific reference.

何(なん) の 部屋(へや) です か。	What is the room for?
教室(きょうしつ) です。	It's a classroom.
どの 部屋(へや) です か。	Which room is it?
あの 部屋(へや) です。	It's that room.

6. の as the pronoun 'one'

Adj-い / AN な N	⇨	Adj-い / AN な の

A noun modified by an adjective or another noun may be replaced by の if it is understood in context. This の corresponds to the English 'one'.

白(しろ)い かさ は 大(おお)きい です。	The white umbrella is big.
赤(あか)い の は 小さい です。	The red one is small.

きれい な 部屋(へや)は 大(おお)きい です。	The pretty room is large.
静(しず)か な の は 小(ちい)さい です。	The quiet one is small.

わたし の かさ は その 赤(あか)い の です。 My umbrella is that red one.

7. Omitting a noun understood in context

N_1 の N_2 ⇨ N_1 の

A noun modified by another noun may be omitted if it is understood in context.

リーさん の 車(くるま) は 赤(あか)い です。	Lee's car is red.
わたし の は 白(しろ)い です。	Mine is white.
その 本(ほん) は わたし の です。	That book is mine.

8. Topic-Subject construction with adjective or adjectival noun predicates

N_1 は N_2 が Adj-い です AN です	As for N_1, its N_2 is Adj

Adjectives or adjectival nouns are often used in a topic-subject construction in which the topic (N_1) is marked by は and the subject (N_2) is marked by が. The latter usually belongs to the former in some sense.

この　アパート　は　家賃(やちん)　が　高(たか)い　です。
As for this apartment, the rent is high.

きょう　は　天気(てんき)　が　いい　です。
Today, the weather is fine.

東京(とうきょう)　は　交通(こうつう)　が　便利(べんり)　です。
As for Tokyo, its transportation system is convenient.

9. Sentence connectives (1): それに and でも

1) | S_1。　それに、　S_2 | S_1. And in addition, S_2 |
|---|---|

The conjunctive それに, which means 'in addition to', is used to connect two sentences. It is placed at the beginning of the second sentence to join it to the first.

新(あたら)しい　アパート　は　きれい　です。それに、便利(べんり)　です。
The new apartment is clean. And in addition, it is convenient.

2) | S_1。　でも、　S_2 | S_1. But, S_2 |
|---|---|

The conjunctive でも, meaning 'but, however', is also used to connect two sentences. It is placed at the beginning of the second sentence.

新(あたら)しい　アパート　は　きれい　です。でも、家賃(やちん)　が　高(たか)い　です。
The new apartment is clean. But the rent is high.

わたし　は　いつも　6時半(じはん)　に　起(お)きます。でも、きょう　は　8時(じ)　に　起(お)きました。
I always get up at 6:30. But today I got up at 8:00.

READING

Student Housing

リーさんの寮(りょう)は古いです。部屋は広(ひろ)くありません。それに、静(しず)かではありません。でも、リーさんは寮(りょう)に友(とも)だちが多いです。寮(りょう)の友だちは親切(しんせつ)です。いつも日本語(ご)で話(はな)します。寮(りょう)の生活(せいかつ)は、おもしろいです。

スミスさんのアパートは新しいです。部屋はきれいです。そのアパートは、大学から10分ぐらいです。とても便利です。スミスさんは、いつも歩(ある)いて大学に行きます。でも、そのアパートのやちんは高いです。7万(まん)円です。

□ Comprehension Check

1. Where does Mr./Ms. Lee live?
2. What are Mr./Ms. Lee's living accommodations like?
3. Where does Mr./Ms. Smith live?
4. What are Mr./Ms. Smith's living accommodations like?

□ Writing Activity

1. Describe in Japanese where you live.

WRITING
[KANJI]

読み方を覚えましょう
よ　かた　おぼ

部屋 (へや): a room
便利 (べんり): convenient
不便 (ふべん): inconvenient
仕事 (しごと): work
東京 (とうきょう): Tokyo
車 (くるま): car

新しい漢字
かんじ

35

ことば	れんしゅう	白
白(1 しろ)・白(2 しろ)い	白 白	くん: しろ・しろ(い) / おん:
		いみ: white
		かきじゅん: ノ ｲ 冂 白 白
1 white 2 white		

36

ことば	れんしゅう	古
古(1 ふる)い	古 古	くん: ふる(い) / おん:
		いみ: old
		かきじゅん: 一 十 十 古 古
1 old		

37

ことば	れんしゅう	明
明(1 あか)るい	明 明	くん: あか(るい) / おん: めい
		いみ: bright
		かきじゅん: 丨 冂 日 日 日) 明 明 明
1 bright		

38

ことば	れんしゅう	小	
1 小さい（ちいさい）		くん	おん
		ちい（さい）	しょう
		いみ	
		small	
	かきじゅん		
	亅 亅丨 小		
1 small, little			

39

ことば	れんしゅう	少	
1 少ない（すくない）・2 少し（すこし）		くん	おん
		すく（ない）・すこ（し）	
		いみ	
		a few, a little	
	かきじゅん		
	亅 小 小 少		
1 a few, a little 2 a little			

40

ことば	れんしゅう	多	
1 多い（おおい）		くん	おん
		おお（い）	
		いみ	
		many, much	
	かきじゅん		
	ノ ク タ 多 多 多		
1 many, much			

41

ことば	れんしゅう	高	
1 高い（たかい）		くん	おん
		たか（い）	こう
		いみ	
		high, expensive	
	かきじゅん		
	丶 亠 亣 亨 古 吉 高 高 高 高		
1 high, expensive			

42

ことば	れんしゅう	新	
1 新しい（あたらしい）・2 新聞（しんぶん）		くん	おん
		あたら（しい）	しん
		いみ	
		new	
	かきじゅん		
	丶 亠 亣 立 立 立 辛 辛 亲 亲 新 新 新		
1 new 2 a newspaper			

WRITING

LESSON 5

第五課

書く練習（れんしゅう）

一、□（しろ）いです。

二、この部屋は□（あか）るいです。

三、□（あたら）しい□（ほん）を買います。

四、□（ふる）いです。

五、□（おお）きい部屋と□（ちい）さい部屋です。

六、ここは車が□（おお）いです。

七、□（ひと）が□（すく）ないです。

八、この車は□（たか）いですか。

九、この□□（だいがく）は、□□（がくせい）が□（すく）ないです。

十、□□（せんせい）が□（おお）いです。

読（よ）む練習（れんしゅう）

一、東京は便利です。

二、不便じゃありません。

三、仕事が多いです。

四、この白い車は高いです。

五、この新しい部屋は、明るいです。

六、その部屋は、小さいです。

七、この新しい大学は、学生が少ないです。

八、古い車を買いました。

九、東京は人が多いです。

十、大きい車に乗ります。

LISTENING AND SPEAKING

Objectives

Asking for information in order to obtain basic necessities
Purchasing groceries at a store

Points

- purchasing the required quantity of items
- inquiring about possessions
- asking about the existence/nonexistence or location of people and objects
- exchanging information about the immediate neighborhood

Sentences

1 ～枚、～台(だい)、～人、～さつ、～こ、～本、～ひき、～つ

2 ここ に 美術館(びじゅつかん) が あります。

3 この クラス に 学生 が 10人 います。

4 前 は ここ に 映画館 が ありました。

5 (この 店(みせ) に) 切手(きって) は あります か。

6 (この 店(みせ) に) はがき か えはがき は あります か。

はい／ええ、(この 店(みせ) に) はがき も えはがき も あります。

いいえ、(この 店(みせ) に) はがき も えはがき も ありません。

(この 店(みせ) に) はがき は あります が、(この 店(みせ) に) えはがき は ありません。

(この 店(みせ) に) はがき しか ありません。

Expressions

1 すみません。 Excuse me. (ドリル I)

2 ありますよ。 Yes, we do. (ドリル IV) (よ at the end of a sentence indicates that the speaker is making an emphatic statement.)

フォーメーション

1-1 Counters (5)

	～枚	～台(だい)	～人	～さつ	～こ	～本	～ひき	～つ
1	いちまい	いちだい	ひとり	いっさつ	いっこ	いっぽん	いっぴき	ひとつ
2	にまい	にだい	ふたり	にさつ	にこ	にほん	にひき	ふたつ
3	さんまい	さんだい	さんにん	さんさつ	さんこ	さんぼん	さんびき	みっつ
4	よんまい	よんだい	よにん	よんさつ	よんこ	よんほん	よんひき	よっつ
5	ごまい	ごだい	ごにん	ごさつ	ごこ	ごほん	ごひき	いつつ
6	ろくまい	ろくだい	ろくにん	ろくさつ	ろっこ	ろっぽん	ろっぴき	むっつ
7	ななまい	ななだい	ななにん	ななさつ	ななこ	ななほん	ななひき	ななつ
8	はちまい	はちだい	はちにん	はっさつ	はっこ	はっぽん	はっぴき	やっつ
9	きゅうまい	きゅうだい	きゅうにん くにん	きゅうさつ	きゅうこ	きゅうほん	きゅうひき	ここのつ
10	じゅうまい	じゅうだい	じゅうにん	じゅっさつ じっさつ	じゅっこ じっこ	じゅっぽん じっぽん	じゅっぴき じっぴき	とお
?	なんまい	なんだい	なんにん	なんさつ	なんこ	なんぼん	なんびき	いくつ

1-2 Counting various things

例(れい)) 切手(きって) (～枚) → いちまい、にまい、さんまい、・・・じゅうまい

1) 紙(かみ)（〜枚） →
2) コンピュータ（〜台(だい)） →
3) かさ（〜本：ほん／ぽん／ぼん） →
4) 消(け)しゴム（〜つ） →
5) ねこ、犬(いぬ)（〜ひき／ぴき／びき） →
6) 車（〜台(だい)） →
7) えんぴつ（〜本：ほん／ぽん／ぼん） →
8) 学生（〜人） →
9) りんご（〜こ） →
10) 本（〜さつ） →

1-3

例(れい)）（わたし）、切手(きって)、4、買う → （わたし は） 切手(きって) を 4枚 買いました。

1) （わたし）、りんご、1、食べる →
2) （わたし）、本、9、読む →
3) （わたし）、公園、犬(いぬ)、3、見る →
4) （わたし）、えんぴつ、6、買う →

2 There is/there isn't (inanimate)

例(れい)）あなた の 町(まち)、 図書館(としょかん)

→ あなた の 町(まち) に 図書館(としょかん) が ありますか。

はい／ええ、（わたし の 町(まち) に 図書館(としょかん) が） あります。

いいえ、（わたし の 町(まち) に 図書館(としょかん) は） ありません。

1) あなた の 町(まち)、映画館 →
2) この 町(まち)、銀行 →
3) その 町(まち)、空港(くうこう) →
4) あなた の 町(まち)、公園 →

3-1 There is/are (animate)

例(れい)）この クラス、学生、10人 → この クラス に 学生 が 10人 います。

1) この 大学、外国人(がいこくじん) の 先生、35人 →
2) わたし の 寮(りょう)、中国人(ちゅうごくじん)、2人 →
3) わたし の クラブ、留学生(りゅうがくせい)、1人 →

3-2

例(れい)）わたし の 町(まち)、大学、3 → わたし の 町(まち) には 大学 が 3つ あります。

1) この 町(まち)、外国(がいこく) の 人、300 →
2) わたし の 大学、コンピュータ、150 →
3) （わたし の） うち、ねこ、3 →
4) （わたし の） うち の 近所、公園、2 →

4 There was/there wasn't

例(れい)) ここ、映画館

→ 前 は ここ に 映画館 が ありました か。

はい／ええ、(前 は ここ に 映画館 が) ありました。

いいえ、(前 は ここ に 映画館 は) ありません でした。

例(れい)) あなたのうち、犬(いぬ)

→ 前 は あなた の うち に 犬(いぬ) が いました か。

はい／ええ、(前 は わたし の うち に 犬(いぬ) が) いました。

いいえ、(前 は わたし の うち に 犬(いぬ) は) いません でした。

1) そこ、銀行 →

2) あそこ、交番(こうばん) →

3) ここ、郵便局(ゆうびんきょく) →

4) 先生 の うち、ねこ →

5 Do you have or not

例(れい)) 切手(きって) → (この 店(みせ) に) 切手(きって) は あります か。

1) 新聞(しんぶん) →

2) 消(け)しゴム →

3) フィルム →

4) でんち →

6 Is there A or B

例(れい)) (この 店(みせ))、はがき、えはがき

→ (この 店(みせ) に) はがき か えはがき は あります か。

はい／ええ、(この 店(みせ) に) はがき も えはがき も あります。

いいえ、(この 店(みせ) に) はがき も えはがき も ありません。

(この 店(みせ) に) はがき は あります が、(この 店(みせ) に) えはがき は ありません。

(この 店(みせ) に) はがき しか ありません。

1) (そこ)、リーさん、チェンさん →

2) (あなた の 町(まち))、郵便局(ゆうびんきょく)、銀行 →

3) (そこ)、ワープロ、コンピュータ →

4) (そこ)、中国人(ちゅうごくじん) の 学生、韓国人(かんこくじん) の 学生 →

ドリル

I Asking for things at a store

A：すみません。この フィルム を 1本 ください。

B：はい、どうぞ。

フィルム(1)	切手(4)	ハンカチ(9)
ボールペン(3)	りんご(5)	消しゴム(2)

II Asking and responding about where you will be

A：あした の 2時 ごろ どこ に います か。

B：大学 に います。

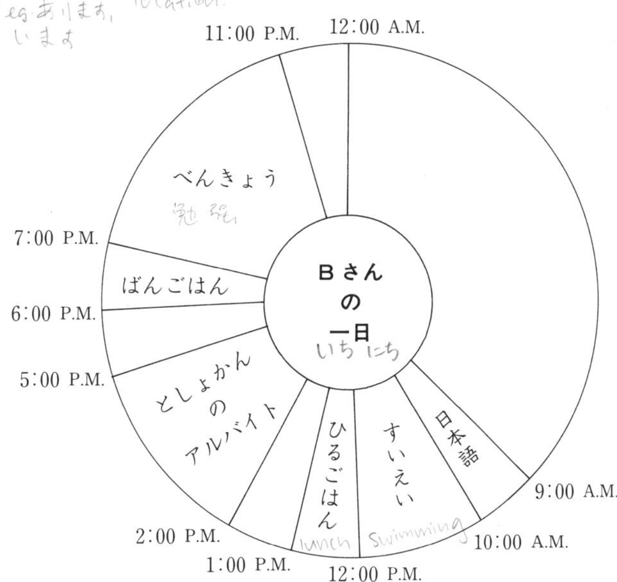

III-1 Describing what is in the town/in the room

A：Bさん の 町 に デパート か スーパー が あります か。

B：デパート は あります が、スーパー は ありません。

あります	ありません	あります	ありません
銀行	動物園	つくえ	テーブル
デパート	プール	いす	電話
公園	映画館	テレビ	ベッド
駅	図書館	コンピュータ	いす
		テープレコーダー	れいぞうこ

Ⅲ-2

A：Bさん　の　町（まち）　に　デパート　か　スーパー　が　あります　か。

B：ええ、デパート　も　スーパー　も　あります。

☆　Use the cues in Ⅲ-1.

Ⅲ-3

A：Bさん　の　部屋　には　テーブル　が　あります　か。

B：いいえ、つくえ　しか　ありません。

☆　Use the cues in Ⅲ-1.

Ⅳ　Asking for things at a store

A：すみません。　切手（きって）　は　あります　か。

B：あります　よ。

A：じゃ、50円の　を　5枚　ください。

フィルム	切手（きって）	かんコーヒー	ボールペン
カラー	120円	あたたかい	赤い（あか）
白黒（しろくろ）	80円	冷たい（つめ）	青い（あお）
			黒い（くろ）

☆　You decide how many you want.

ロールプレイ

CARD A

I Making a purchase

You go to a store to buy ___. You are not sure if the store sells ___. Ask the salesperson a few questions to find out what you need to know to buy ___ (e.g., film, audiotapes, videotapes, batteries).

CARD B

I Making a purchase

You work at a store. Serve the customer.

CARD A

II Asking the way

You are walking around the town and looking for a post office. Ask someone if there is a post office in the area.

CARD B

II Asking the way

You are asked if there is a post office in the area. Give the answer.

CARD A

III Making a purchase at a post office

Do the following things:

① purchase some stamps

② ask for postcards

CARD B

III Making a purchase at a post office

You work at a post office. Serve the customer.

GRAMMAR NOTES

1. Existence of objects, persons, and animals

1) Affirmative

N_1 PLACE	に	N_2 THING	が　あります
N_1 PLACE	に	N_2 PERSON/ANIMAL	が　います

There is/are N_2 in/at N_1

There are two different verbs for expressing the existence of animate and inanimate objects. When the subject of the sentence is animate, います is used. Otherwise, あります is used. (Here, animate means a human being, an animal, or occasionally something that is or appears to be capable of self-locomotion, e.g., a bus, a taxi, etc.)

The particle に marks the location where the thing, person, or animal exists. Demonstratives indicating spatial location can be placed in the location slot.

ここ	here, this place
そこ	there, that place
あそこ	over there, that place over there
どこ	where

The particle が marks the subject of the predicate. In this pattern the subject is what/who exists.

その　町(まち)　に　空港(くうこう)　が　あります。	There is an airport in that city.
ここ　に　ねこ　が　います。	There is a cat here.
この　クラス　に　イタリア人(じん)　が　います。	There is an Italian in this class.

In some cases, this pattern denotes a situation expressed by the English verb 'have'.

この　部屋(へや)　に　トイレ　が　あります。	This room has a toilet.

わたし　の　うち　に　車(くるま)　が　あります。 We have a car at home.

2) Negative

N_1 (PLACE) に　N_2 (THING)　は　ありません N_1 (PLACE) に　N_2 (PERSON/ANIMAL)　は　いません	There isn't/aren't N_2 in/at N_1

The negative form of V-ます is V-ません. Therefore, ありません and いません are the negative forms of あります and います, respectively.

The particle は also functions as a contrast marker as well as a topic marker. In this pattern, it denotes that the referent of the preceding noun phrase (thing, person, or animal) is contrasted with other things, persons, or animals that are implied through the context. Although the contrastive は is frequently observed in sentences in the negative, it may occur in sentences in the affirmative as well.

その　町(まち)　に　銀行(ぎんこう)　は　ありません。
There isn't a bank in that city (although there is a post office).

わたし　は　コーヒー　は　飲(の)みません。
I don't drink coffee (although I drink tea).

この　クラス　には　中国(ちゅうごく)　の　人(ひと)　が　います。
There is a Chinese in this class (but not in other classes).

To indicate the location of something/someone that has already been introduced into the context either explicitly or implicitly, the pattern N_2 は　N_1 に　あります／います is used. (You will practice this pattern in Lesson 9.)

新聞(しんぶん)　は　ここ　に　あります。

Thus, the above sentence literally means something like 'As for the newspaper (that we have been talking about, or that you are looking for now, etc.), it is here'.

This pattern is derived from the pattern N_1 (location) に N_2 (thing/person/animal) が　あります／います by topicalizing the thing/person/animal which is the subject of the verb あります or います, and by moving the topicalized element to the initial position of the sentence. When the subject is transformed into a topic, the subject marker が is replaced by the topic marker は.

N_1 (LOCATION) に N_2 (THING/PERSON/ANIMAL) が　あります／います。
|
[topicalization of the subject of the verb: は replaces が]
↓
N_1 (LOCATION) に　N_2 (THING/PERSON/ANIMAL) は　あります／います。
|

[moving the topic to the initial position in the sentence]

↓

N_2 (THING/PERSON/ANIMAL) は　N_1 (LOCATION) に　あります／います。

3) Summary of the functions of the particle は

First, the particle は marks the topic of discourse. The topic has to be something both the speaker and the hearer can identify. Therefore what has been already referred to implicitly or explicitly in discourse can be the topic, and that may be marked by は.

チェン：大学　の　そば　に　公園　が　あります。

Chen　：There is a park in the vicinity of the university.

キム：その　公園　は　静か　です　か。

Kim　：As for that park, is it quiet?

チェン：キムさん、この　え　は　おもしろい　です。（この　え　を）　だれ　が　かきました　か。

Chen　：Mr. Kim, this picture is interesting. Who painted (this picture)?

キム：その　え　は　友だち　が　かきました。

Kim　：As for the picture, my friend painted it.

There are two other cases in which the topic marker は is used. Besides what has already been referred to, these two cases can be readily identified by both the speaker and the hearer, and are thus candidates for the topic of a sentence, even without a preceding context.

① Nouns used in a generic sense: e.g., 人 'human beings', くじら 'whales'

人　は　足　で　歩きます。

As for human beings, they walk with their legs.

くじら　は　ほにゅうるい　です。

As for whales, they are mammals.

② Something/somebody is physically present at the place of discourse:, e.g., わたし 'I-the-speaker', あなた 'you-the-hearer'

わたし　は　田中　です。どうぞ　よろしく。

As for me, I am Mr. Tanaka. Nice to meet you.

チェンさん　は　学生　です　か。

As for you, Mr. Chen, are you a student?

あの　建物　は　何　です　か。

As for that building, what is it?

この　におい　は　何（なん）　です　か。
As for this smell, what is it?

Remember that a topicalized element is generally placed at the beginning of a sentence.

Secondly, apart from what is known from context and what is known generically or from actual physical presence, the particle は marks what is contrasted implicitly or explicitly in a given context.

ここ　に　映画館（えいがかん）　が　ありました　か。
Was there a movie theater here?
いいえ、　ここ　には　映画館（えいがかん）　は　ありませんでした。
No, there wasn't a movie theater here (though there was something else).
リーさん　は　コーヒー　や　紅茶（こうちゃ）　を　飲（の）みます　か。
As for you, Mr. Lee, do you drink coffee, tea, and the like?
（わたし　は）コーヒー　は　飲（の）みます。でも、　紅茶（こうちゃ）　は　飲（の）みません。
I drink coffee, but I don't drink tea.
ジョージさん　は　去年（きょねん）　北海道（ほっかいどう）　へ　行（い）きました　か。
Speaking of you, George, did you go to Hokkaido last year?
いいえ、（わたし　は）北海道（ほっかいどう）　へは　行（い）きません　でした。でも、九州（きゅうしゅう）　へは　行きました。
No, I didn't go to Hokkaido. But I went to Kyushu.

As the above examples show, a contrasted element, which is followed by は, is not moved to the initial position of a sentence. It also should be noted that the subject marker が and the object marker を are replaced by は when they are topicalized. However, other particles, such as the direction markers へ/に and the location-of-action marker で, remain in the sentence and are followed by は when they are topicalized.

2. Locative expressions (1)

N_1 の N_2 (LOCATIVE NOUN)	LOCATIVE NOUN of N_1

The locative nouns to be introduced in this lesson are そば ('nearby, next to') and まえ ('front'). N のそば and N のまえ mean 'in the vicinity of N' and 'in front of N', respectively. The phrases can be placed in the location slot in the patterns given in GN1.1 and 1.2, above).

大学（だいがく）　の　そば　に　公園（こうえん）　が　あります。
There is a park near the university.

わたし の うち の 前(まえ) に バスてい が あります。

There is a bus stop in front of my house.

3. Past tense

1)

N_1 (PLACE) に N_2 (THING) が ありました N_1 (PLACE) に N_2 (PERSON/ANIMAL) が いました	There was/were N_2 in/at N_1

The past form of あります is ありました, and that of います is いました. The table below shows the conjugation of the verbs あります and います.

	'to exist'-animate		'to exist'-inanimate	
	Non-past	Past	Non-Past	Past
Affirmative	います	いました	あります	ありました
Negative	いません	いませんでした	ありません	ありませんでした

前(まえ) は ここ に 映画館(えいがかん) が ありました。

There was a movie theater here before.

うち には ねこ が いませんでした。

We didn't have cats at home.

大学(だいがく) の そば には 銀行(ぎんこう) は ありませんでした。

There wasn't a bank near the university.

4. At a shop: Do you sell/have ~?

(この 店(みせ) に) N (THING) は あります か	As for N, do you sell/have it (in this/your shop)?

The sentence literally means 'Does N exist (at this shop)?' and is used when one would like to find out whether a certain item (N) is sold or not. The topic/contrastive marker は that follows N is often omitted in conversation.

切手(きって) は あります か。	Do you sell/have stamps?
あの 店(みせ) に でんち は あります か。	Do they sell batteries in that shop?
フィルム、あります か。	Do you sell/have film?

5. Noun connectives: particle か

N_1 か N_2	N_1 or N_2

The particle か connects two or more nouns that are alternatives, and the noun phrase corresponds to the English N_1 or N_2. This noun phrase can be used in the noun slot of a sentence.

わたし は 食堂(しょくどう) で そば か カレー を 食(た)べます。
I will eat soba ('buckwheat noodles') or curry with rice in the cafeteria.

ジョンさん は 11時(じ) か 12時(じ) に 寝(ね)ます。
John goes to bed at 11:00 or 12:00.

喫茶店(きっさてん) か レストラン へ 行(い)きましょう。
Let's go to a coffee shop or a restaurant.

この 店(みせ) に はがき か えはがき は あります か。
Do you sell/have postcards or picture postcards in this shop?

6. Both ~ and ~/neither ~ nor ~

N_1 も N_2 も	both N_1 and N_2/neither N_1 nor N_2

The particle も basically means 'also' or 'too' (L1 GN7). N_1も N_2も can be used in a noun slot. It corresponds to English 'both ~ and ~' or 'neither ~ nor ~', depending on whether the predicate of the sentence is affirmative or negative.

きのう は スミスさん も パクさん も 大学(だいがく) に 来(き)ませんでした。
As for yesterday, neither Mr. Smith nor Mr. Park came to the university.

わたし は コーヒー も 紅茶(こうちゃ) も 飲(の)みます。
I drink both coffee and tea.

この 店(みせ) には はがき も えはがき も あります。
They sell/have both postcards and picture postcards at this shop.

わたし の うち には ねこ も 犬(いぬ) も いません。
We have neither a cat nor a dog at home.

7. Sentence connectives (2): ～ が、～

S_1 が、S_2	S_1, but S_2

The particle が is used to connect two sentences. It means 'but, however'. It has the same meaning and function as the conjunctive でも (L5 GN8), but it is syntactically different: while でも is placed at the beginning of S_2 as an independent word, が is attached to the end of S_1 as a dependent element.

きのう パクさん は 大学(だいがく) に 来(き)ました が、スミスさん は 来(き)ませんでした。
Yesterday Mr. Park came to the university, but Mr. Smith didn't.

紅茶(こうちゃ) は 飲(の)みます が、 コーヒー は 飲(の)みません。
I drink tea, but I don't drink coffee.

この 店(みせ) には はがき は あります が、 えはがき は ありません。
In this shop they sell/have postcards, but they don't have picture postcards.

わたし の うち には ねこ は います が、 犬(いぬ) は いません。
At my home we have a cat, but we don't have a dog.

8. Counters (5)

The counters are roughly classified according to what is counted.

Counters	What is counted
-本(ほん):	long, narrow objects, such as pencils or umbrellas
-枚(まい):	flat objects such as sheets of paper or handkerchiefs
-台(だい):	large machines, such as cars or computers
-人(にん):	people
-匹(ひき):	relatively small animals (e.g., dogs, cats)
-個(こ) :	small objects (e.g., buttons, candies, batteries)
-冊(さつ):	bound objects (e.g., books, albums)
-つ :	a relative neutral counter for a wide variety of objects

Like the counters for time spans, dates, and so on, these counters also exhibit sound changes when combined with certain numbers. Study the table below, where the corresponding question word for each counter is also listed.

	～まい	～だい	～人(にん)	～つ	～さつ	～こ
1	いちまい	いちだい	ひとり	ひとつ	いっさつ	いっこ
2	にまい	にだい	ふたり	ふたつ	にさつ	にこ
3	さんまい	さんだい	さんにん	みっつ	さんさつ	さんこ
4	よんまい	よんだい	よにん	よっつ	よんさつ	よんこ
5	ごまい	ごだい	ごにん	いつつ	ごさつ	ごこ
6	ろくまい	ろくだい	ろくにん	むっつ	ろくさつ	ろっこ
7	ななまい	ななだい	ななにん	ななつ	ななさつ	ななこ
8	はちまい	はちだい	はちにん	やっつ	はっさつ	はっこ
9	きゅうまい	きゅうだい	きゅうにん	ここのつ	きゅうさつ	きゅうこ
10	じゅうまい	じゅうだい	じゅうにん	とお	じゅっさつ/ じっさつ	じゅっこ/ じっこ
?	なんまい	なんだい	なんにん	いくつ	なんさつ	なんこ

	～本(ほん/ぽん/ぼん)	～ひき
1	いっぽん	いっぴき
2	にほん	にひき
3	さんぼん	さんびき
4	よんほん	よんひき
5	ごほん	ごひき
6	ろっぽん	ろっぴき
7	ななほん	ななひき
8	はっぽん	はっぴき
9	きゅうほん	きゅうひき
10	じゅっぽん/ じっぽん	じゅっぴき/ じっぴき
?	なんぼん	なんびき

切手(きって) を 4枚(まい) 買(か)いました。
I bought four stamps.

この クラス に 学生(がくせい) が 10人(にん) います。
There are ten students in this class.

その 町(まち) に 大学(だいがく) が いくつ あります か。
How many universities do they have in that city?

パクさん は りんご を 何(なん)こ 食(た)べました か。
Mr. Park, how many apples did you eat?

うち には 犬(いぬ) が 3びき います。
We have three dogs at home.

9. Only/No more than

N しか (NEGATIVE PREDICATE)	only/no more than N

The dependent word しか always follows a noun or noun phrase. It has to occur with a negative predicate and corresponds to the English ‘only/no more than’. By using しか, the speaker emphasizes that there is not as much N as there should be.

きのう　は　パクさん　しか　大学(だいがく)　に　来(き)ませんでした。
As for yesterday, only Mr. Park came to the university.

わたし　は　紅茶(こうちゃ)　しか　飲(の)みません。
I drink only tea.

この　店(みせ)　には　はがき　しか　ありません。
In this shop they sell/have only postcards.

わたし　の　うち　には　ねこ　しか　いません。
At home we have only a cat.

READING

Tanaka's Town

田(た)中さんの町(まち)は、きちじょうじです。きちじょうじには、公園や映画館があります。それから、銀行やデパートもあります。それに、大学もあります。きちじょうじには、いつも人がたくさんいます。とてもにぎやかな町です。

きちじょうじ駅は、大きい駅です。電車(でんしゃ)がたくさん来ます。きちじょうじ駅には店(みせ)がたくさんあります。田中さんはそこでよく買い物(もの)をします。レストランもあります。時々(ときどき)、友(とも)だちと食事(しょくじ)をします。

たくさん	Adv	many
にぎやか	AN	lively
食事(しょくじ)	N	meal

□ Comprehension Check

1. Where is Tanaka-san's town?
2. What does the town have?
3. Describe the place Tanaka-san often goes to in town.

□ Writing Activity

1. あなたの町(まち)はどんな町(まち)ですか。何がありますか。

WRITING
[KANJI]

読み方を覚えましょう
(かた　おぼ)

～枚（～まい）: (counter for flat objects like paper)

公園（こうえん）: park

映画館（えいがかん）: movie theater

駅（えき）: railroad station

近所（きんじょ）: neighborhood

銀行（ぎんこう）: bank

新しい漢字
(かんじ)

43 見

くん	おん
み(る)・み(える)・み(せる)・み(つかる)・み(つける)	けん

いみ: to see, to look at

ことば: 1 見る（み）・2 見える（み）・3 見せる（み）・4 見つかる（み）・5 見つける（み）

1 to look at
2 to be seen, to be visible
3 to show
4 to be found
5 to find

れんしゅう: 見 見

かきじゅん: 丨 冂 月 月 目 貝 見

44 買

くん	おん
か(う)	

いみ: to buy

ことば: 1 買う（か）

1 to buy

れんしゅう: 買 買

かきじゅん: 丶 冖 冖 罒 罒 罒 罒 罒 罒 罒 買 買

45 言

くん	おん
い(う)・こと	

いみ: to say

ことば: 1 言う（い）

1 to say

れんしゅう: 言 言

かきじゅん: 丶 亠 亠 亖 言 言 言

46

ことば	れんしゅう	話	
1 話す（はな）・2 話（はなし）		くん	おん
		はな（す）・はなし	わ
		いみ	
		to speak, to talk	
1 to talk 2 a story	かきじゅん: 、 ⺀ 亖 亖 言 言 言 訁 訁 許 許 話 話		

47

ことば	れんしゅう	読	
1 読む（よ）		くん	おん
		よ（む）	どく
		いみ	
		to read	
1 to read	かきじゅん: 、 ⺀ 亖 亖 言 言 言 言 言 計 計 計 訪 詩 詩 読		

48

ことば	れんしゅう	書	
1 書く（か）・2 読書（どくしょ）		くん	おん
		か（く）	しょ
		いみ	
		to write, a book	
1 to write 2 reading	かきじゅん: フ ⺕ ⺕ ⺕ 圭 聿 聿 書 書 書		

49

ことば	れんしゅう	食	
1 食べる（た）		くん	おん
		た（べる）	しょく・しょっ
		いみ	
		to eat	
1 to eat	かきじゅん: ノ 人 𠆢 今 今 今 食 食 食		

50

ことば	れんしゅう	飲	
1 飲む（の）		くん	おん
		の（む）	
		いみ	
		to drink	
1 to drink	かきじゅん: ノ 人 𠆢 今 今 今 食 食 食 飠 飲 飲		

書く練習（れんしゅう）

一、映画を□（み）ます。

二、□（ほん）を□（か）います。

三、朝ご飯（はん）を□（た）べます。

四、コーヒーを□（の）みます。

五、□（なん）と□（い）いますか。

六、□□語（にほんご）を□（はな）します。

七、□（ほん）を□（よ）みます。

八、手紙（てがみ）を□（か）きます。

九、□（たか）い車を□（か）います。

十、□晩（こん）□□（なんじ）にテレビを□（み）ますか。

読む練習（れんしゅう）

一、手紙（てがみ）を三枚書きます。

二、公園の前に映画館があります。

三、近所に銀行があります。

四、東京駅で新聞（ぶん）を買います。

五、公園で友（とも）だちと話します。

六、日本語（ご）の本を読みます。

七、午後六時にご飯（はん）を食べます。

八、水を飲みます。

九、何と言いますか。

十、銀行の前の映画館で映画を見ます。

LISTENING AND SPEAKING

Objectives

Engaging in conversation about interests/hobbies
Saying the appropriate courtesies at meal time

Points

- talking about preferences
- making suggestions

Sentences

1 ～日、～週間、～か月、～年、～回

2 （わたし は） 旅行 が 好き です。

（わたし は） 音楽 を 聞く の が 好き です。

3 （わたし は） 時々 ドライブ を します。

4 （あなた は） 1週間 に 何回 テニス を します か。

（わたし は） 1週間 に 3回 （テニス を） します。

Expressions

1 はい、いただきます。 Thanks, I will (have some more). （ドリル IV）

2 もう けっこう です。 No more, thanks. （ドリル IV）

3 たくさん 食べました から。(Since) I've had enough. （ドリル IV）

フォーメーション

1-1 Counters (6)

	days 〜日	weeks 〜週間(しゅうかん)	months 〜か月	years 〜年	how often 〜回
1	いちにち	**いっしゅうかん**	**いっかげつ**	いちねん	**いっかい**
2	ふつか	にしゅうかん	にかげつ	にねん	にかい
3	みっか	さんしゅうかん	さんかげつ	さんねん	さんかい
4	よっか	よんしゅうかん	よんかげつ	**よねん**	よんかい
5	いつか	ごしゅうかん	ごかげつ	ごねん	ごかい
6	むいか	ろくしゅうかん	**ろっかげつ**	ろくねん	**ろっかい**
7	なのか	ななしゅうかん	ななかげつ	(しち / なな) ねん	ななかい
8	ようか	**はっしゅうかん**	**はっかげつ**	はちねん	**はっかい**
9	ここのか	きゅうしゅうかん	きゅうかげつ	(きゅう / く) ねん	きゅうかい
10	とおか	**(じゅっ / じっ) しゅうかん**	**(じゅっ / じっ) かげつ**	じゅうねん	**(じゅっ / じっ) かい**
?	なんにち	なんしゅうかん	なんかげつ	なんねん	なんかい

Bold type indicates that a phonetic change occurs in the number immediately preceding the counter.

1-2

Read the following

1) 1 day →	8 days →	14 days →	20 days →	31 days →
2) 1 week →	4 weeks →	7 weeks →	8 weeks →	10 weeks →
3) 1 month →	5 months →	6 months →	8 months →	12 months →
4) 1 year →	4 years →	17 years →	49 years →	100 years →
5) 1 time →	6 times →	9 times →	13 times →	20 times →

2-1 Likes and dislikes and skills

例(れい)) (わたし)、旅行、好き → (わたし は) 旅行 が 好き です。

1) (わたし)、野菜(やさい)、きらい →

2) あの 先生、スキー、じょうず →

3) (わたし)、料理、へた →

4) キムさん、水泳(すいえい)、とくい →

2-2

例(れい)) (わたし)、音楽 を 聞(き)く、好き

→ (わたし は) 音楽 を 聞(き)く の が 好き です。

1) (わたし)、歌(うた) を 歌(うた)う、きらい →

2) 鈴木(すずき)さん、山のぼり を する、にがて →

3) スミスさん、ピアノ を ひく、じょうず →

4) リーさん、読書 を する、好き →

3 Frequency

例(れい)) (わたし)、時々、ドライブ → (わたし は) 時々 ドライブ を します。

1) (わたし)、いつも、テニス →

2) 学生、たいてい、週末、買(か)い物(もの) →

3) 佐藤(さとう)さん、あまり、料理 →

4) (わたし)、ぜんぜん、読書 →

4-1 How often

例(れい)) 3 days/week → 1 週間(しゅうかん) に 3 日

1) 5 days/week →

2) 4 times/month →

3) 2 times/year →

4) 1 time/3 months →

4-2

例(れい)) (あなた)、1 週間(しゅうかん)、何回、テニス を する：3 回

→ (あなた は) 1 週間(しゅうかん) に 何回 テニス を します か。

1 週間(しゅうかん) に 3 回 します。

1) (あなた)、1 日、何時間、日本語(にほんご) の テープ を 聞(き)く：2 時間 →

2) (あなた)、1年、何回、旅行　を　する：1回　→

3) (あなた)、1か月、何回、映画　を　見る：5回　ぐらい　→

4) (あなた)、1日、どの　くらい、新聞(しんぶん)　を　読む：1時間30分　→

ドリル

I　Talking about daily activities

A：日曜日(にちようび)　は　何　を　します　か。

B：たいてい　テニス　を　します。

いつも
よく
時々

映画	読書
スキー	手紙(てがみ)
水泳(すいえい)	ドライブ
山のぼり	料理
音楽	買い物(かもの)

II-1　Talking about likes and dislikes

A：Bさん　は　スポーツ　が　好き　です　か。

B：ええ、好き　です　よ。

B：いいえ、あまり　好き　じゃありません。

A：どんな　スポーツ　が　好き　です　か。

B：テニス　が　好き　です。

A：そう　です　か。

わたし　も　好き　です。

II-2

A：テニス　は　好き　です　か。

B：見る　の　は　好き　です　が、する　の　は　にがて　です。

	好き	きらい／にがて／へた
すし	(すし　を)　食べます	(すし　を)　作(つく)ります
日本語(にほんご)　の　勉強(べんきょう)	(日本語(にほんご)　を)　話します	(日本語(にほんご)　で)　書きます
歌(うた)	(歌(うた)　を)　聞(き)きます	(歌(うた)　を)　歌(うた)います

Ⅲ Talking about daily activities in more detail

A：Bさん　は、毎日（まいにち）　テレビ　を　見ます　か。

B：ええ。１日　に　１時間　ぐらい　見ます。

テレビニュース	１時間／日	テニス	３回／週（しゅう）
山のぼり	１回／月	ビール	１本／日
本	１さつ／週（しゅう）	音楽	３時間／日
水泳（すいえい）	２回／週（しゅう）	ディスコ	１回／週（しゅう）

Ⅳ At the table: Accepting and refusing

A：もう　少し　いかが　です　か。

B：はい、いただきます。

B：もう　けっこう　です。
たくさん　食べました　から。

おなか　が　いっぱい　です
たくさん　飲みました
車　で　帰（かえ）ります

ロールプレイ

CARD A

I Talking about hobbies

At an informal gathering, you ask a person you have met about the following:

① their hobbies

② how often they do them

You may be asked the same things.

CARD B

I Talking about hobbies

At an informal gathering, a new acquaintance asks you about your hobbies. Find out about their hobbies, too.

CARD A

II A blind date

You meet your date for the first time. Try to find out what you have in common so you can plan some activity together for the next date.

CARD B

II A blind date

You meet your date for the first time. You like the person and want to see him／her again.

GRAMMAR NOTES

1. Counters (6)

Expressions for the duration of time in minutes and hours were introduced in Lesson 4. In this lesson other time-span expressions are introduced.

1) NUMBER-日(か/にち) (間(かん))　　NUMBER days

The number of days is expressed basically the same as the days of the month (see L4 GN2). The only exception is いちにち which means 'for one day' (cf., the first day of the month, ついたち).

Note that both いちにち and ついたち are written in kanji as 一日, and therefore the correct reading or pronunciation must be determined from context. The suffix -間(かん) may or may not be attached to the words for the number of days.

2) NUMBER-週(しゅう)間(かん)　　NUMBER weeks

In counting weeks, the suffix -週(しゅう), which means 'week', is followed by 間(かん), as in 1週間(いっしゅうかん) (for one week) and 4週間(よんしゅうかん) (for four weeks).

1週間(いっしゅうかん)	for one week
2週間(にしゅうかん)	for two weeks
3週間(さんしゅうかん)	for three weeks
4週間(よんしゅうかん)	for four weeks
5週間(ごしゅうかん)	for five weeks
6週間(ろくしゅうかん)	for six weeks
7週間(ななしゅうかん)	for seven weeks
8週間(はっしゅうかん)	for eight weeks

9週間（きゅうしゅうかん）	for nine weeks
10週間（じゅっしゅうかん／じっしゅうかん）	for ten weeks
何週間（なんしゅうかん）	for how many weeks

3) NUMBER-か月（かげつ）(間（かん）) _____ months

The duration of months is expressed with -か月（かげつ）, which means 'months', attached to a number, as in 1か月（いっかげつ） (for one month), 6か月（ろっかげつ） (for six months), and 8か月（はっかげつ） (for eight months). The suffix 間（かん） may or may not be attached.

1か月（いっかげつ） (間（かん）)	for one month
2か月（にかげつ） (間（かん）)	for two months
3か月（さんかげつ） (間（かん）)	for three months
4か月（よんかげつ） (間（かん）)	for four months
5か月（ごかげつ） (間（かん）)	for five months
6か月（ろっかげつ） (間（かん）)	for six months
7か月（ななかげつ） (間（かん）)	for seven months
8か月（はっかげつ） (間（かん）)	for eight months
9か月（きゅうかげつ） (間（かん）)	for nine months
10か月（じゅっかげつ／じっかげつかん） (間（かん）)	for ten months
何か月（なんかげつ） (間（かん）)	for how many months

4) NUMBER-年（ねん） (間（かん）) _____ years

The duration of years is indicated with -年（ねん）, which means 'years', attached to a number. The suffix -間（かん） may or may not follow. Note that the expression 'for 4 years' is pronounced 4年（よねん）(間（かん）) and that 'for 9 years' is 9年（きゅうねん）(間（かん）) or 9年（くねん）(間（かん）).

1年（いちねん） (間（かん）)	for one year
2年（にねん） (間（かん）)	for two years
3年（さんねん） (間（かん）)	for three years
4年（よねん） (間（かん）)	for four years
5年（ごねん） (間（かん）)	for five years
6年（ろくねん） (間（かん）)	for six years
7年（しちねん） (間（かん）) ／ななねんかん	for seven years

8年(間) はちねん かん	for eight years
9年(間) きゅうねん かん /くねん	for nine years
10年(間) じゅうねん かん	for ten years
何年(間) なんねん かん	for how many years

5) NUMBER-回 (かい) ______ times

This expression is used to indicate how often you do something, as in 1回 (いっかい) (once, one time) and 6回 (ろっかい) (six times). The suffix -回 (かい) literally means 'times'.

1回 いっかい	once
2回 にかい	twice
3回 さんかい	three times
4回 よんかい	four times
5回 ごかい	five times
6回 ろっかい	six times
7回 ななかい	seven times
8回 はっかい	eight times
9回 きゅうかい	nine times
10回 じゅっかい/じっかい	ten times
何回 なんかい	how many times / how often

2. Frequency

In addition to GN1.5 above, there is another way to express frequency or how often something is done; namely, the use of adverbs such as いつも (always), たいてい (usually), よく (often), 時々 (ときどき) (sometimes), あまり (seldom), and ぜんぜん (never). Note that あまり and ぜんぜん require a negative predicate.

わたし は いつも テニス を します。	I always play tennis.
学生(がくせい) は たいてい 週末(しゅうまつ) 買い物(かいもの) を します。	Students usually go shopping on weekends.
わたし は よく テニス を します。	I often play tennis.
わたし は 時々(ときどき) ドライブ を します。	Sometimes I go for a drive.
佐藤(さとう)さん は あまり 料理(りょうり) を しません。	Mr. Sato seldom cooks.
わたし は ぜんぜん 読書(どくしょ) を しません。	I never read books.

3. Amount or frequency per time unit

LENGTH OF TIME に AMOUNTS/FREQUENCY

This pattern is used to express amounts or frequency per time unit. The phrase following the に indicates amounts or frequency, and the phrase preceding the に indicates 'per time unit'. The corresponding question word is どのくらい.

1年(いちねん) に 2回(にかい)	twice a year
1か月(いっかげつ) に 4回(よんかい)	4 times a month
8週間(はっしゅうかん) に 6回(ろっかい)	6 times in 8 weeks
1週間(いっしゅうかん) に 5日(いつか)	5 days a week
1日(いちにち) に 2時間(にじかん)	2 hours a day
1日(いちにち) に 何時間(なんじかん)	how many hours a day
1日(いちにち) に どの くらい	how long/how often in a day

4. Likes/Dislikes etc.

<table><tr><td>PERSON は N
Verb plain の</td><td>が AN です</td></tr></table>

A person's likes/dislikes and skills are expressed in the form of adjectival nouns, such as 好(す)き (like), きらい (dislike), じょうず and とくい (good at), and へた (poor at).

The phrase N が indicates what a person likes/dislikes, is good at/poor at, using the topic-subject construction (L5 GN8).

(わたし は) 旅行(りょこう) が 好(す)き です。	I like to travel.
キムさん は 水泳(すいえい) が とくい です。	Mr. Kim is good at swimming.

N in the above construction can be a sentence. When N is expressed as a sentence, the construction is changed as follows: the verb appears in its plain non-past form (L3 GN1) followed by の. In other words, this の makes the immediately preceding sentence a noun phrase, and for that reason is called a nominalizer.

(わたし は) 音楽(おんがく) を 聞(き)く の が 好(す)き です。

I like to listen to music.

スミスさん は ピアノ を ひく の が じょうず です。

Mr. Smith is good at playing the piano.

READING

Introducing People in a Photo Album

山川さんは、音楽が好きです。ピアノをよくひきます。とくに、モーツアルトをひくのがじょうずです。今、大学の音楽クラブにいます。一年に一回コンサートをします。

パクさんはテニスが大好きです。するのも見るのも好きです。週末はいつも友だちとテニスをします。パクさんは、今、町(まち)のテニスクラブにいます。

大田(おおた)さんは旅行が好きです。一年に三回ぐらい外国(がいこく)を旅行します。ことしは、スペインとメキシコに行きました。12月にはオーストラリアにも行きます。大田(おおた)さんは英語(えいご)とスペイン語を話します。

チンさんは料理がじょうずです。日本料理と中国(ちゅうごく)料理がとくいです。毎週(まいしゅう)金曜(よう)日は友(とも)だちといっしょに料理をします。チンさんは料理をするのも好きですが、食べるのも好きです。

山川	PN	Yamakawa	大田(おおた)	PN	Oota
モーツァルト	N	pn: Mozart	スペイン	N	Spain
クラブ	N	club	メキシコ	N	Mexico
コンサート	N	concert	チン	PN	Ching

□ Before Reading

1. あなたは何をするのが好きですか。

□ Comprehension Check

1. List related items under each person.

チン	パク	山川	大田
______	______	______	______
______	______	______	______
______	______	______	______
______	______	______	______

スペイン　中国　テニス　音楽　一週間(しゅうかん)に一回　料理

旅行　クラブ　メキシコ　英語(えいご)　ピアノ

□ Writing Activity

1. Describe your friends in terms of things they like to do, things they are good/bad at, and how often they do those activities.

WRITING
[KANJI]

読み方を覚えましょう

週末（しゅうまつ）: weekend
好き（すき）: to like
〜回（〜かい）: counter for times
旅行する（りょこうする）: to travel
音楽（おんがく）: music
料理する（りょうりする）: to cook

新しい漢字

51

百	
くん	おん
	ひゃく・びゃく・ぴゃく
いみ	hundred

ことば: 1 百（ひゃく）・2 百人（ひゃくにん）・3 百本（ひゃっぽん）・4 三百（さんびゃく）・5 六百人（ろっぴゃくにん）・6 八百（はっぴゃく）

1 one hundred
2 one hundred persons
3 one hundred (long items)
4 three hundred
5 six hundred persons
6 eight hundred

かきじゅん: 一 丆 丆 丙 百 百

52

千	
くん	おん
	せん・ぜん
いみ	thousand

ことば: 1 千（せん）・2 千人（せんにん）・3 四千人（よんせんにん）

1 one thousand
2 one thousand persons
3 four thousand persons

かきじゅん: ノ 二 千

53

万	
くん	おん
	まん
いみ	ten thousand

ことば: 1 一万（いちまん）・2 一万人（いちまんにん）・3 五百万人（ごひゃくまんにん）・4 七千万（ななせんまん）

1 ten thousand
2 ten thousand persons
3 five million persons
4 seventy million

かきじゅん: 一 丁 万

54

ことば	れんしゅう	円
1 十円(じゅうえん)・2 百円(ひゃくえん)・3 千円(せんえん)・4 一万円(いちまんえん)・5 二万九千八百円(にまんきゅうせんはっぴゃくえん)		くん: — / おん: えん
		いみ: yen, a circle, round
1 ten yen 2 one hundred yen 3 one thousand yen 4 ten thousand yen 5 twenty-nine thousand and eight hundred yen	かきじゅん	丨 冂 円 円

55

ことば	れんしゅう	山
1 山(やま)		くん: やま / おん: —
		いみ: mountain
1 a mountain	かきじゅん	丨 山 山

56

ことば	れんしゅう	川
1 川(かわ)		くん: かわ / おん: —
		いみ: river
1 a river	かきじゅん	丿 川 川

57

ことば	れんしゅう	年
1 年(とし)・2 十年(じゅうねん)・3 百年(ひゃくねん)・4 千年(せんねん)・5 一万年(いちまんねん)		くん: とし / おん: ねん
		いみ: year(s)
1 a year 2 ten years 3 one hundred years 4 one thousand years 5 ten thousand years	かきじゅん	ノ 𠂉 𠂇 午 左 年

Repetition symbol

ことば	れんしゅう	々
1 人々(ひとびと)・2 時々(ときどき)・3 年々(ねんねん)		くん: — / おん: —
		いみ: a repetition symbol
1 people 2 sometimes 3 year by year	かきじゅん	ノ ク 々

書く練習(れんしゅう)

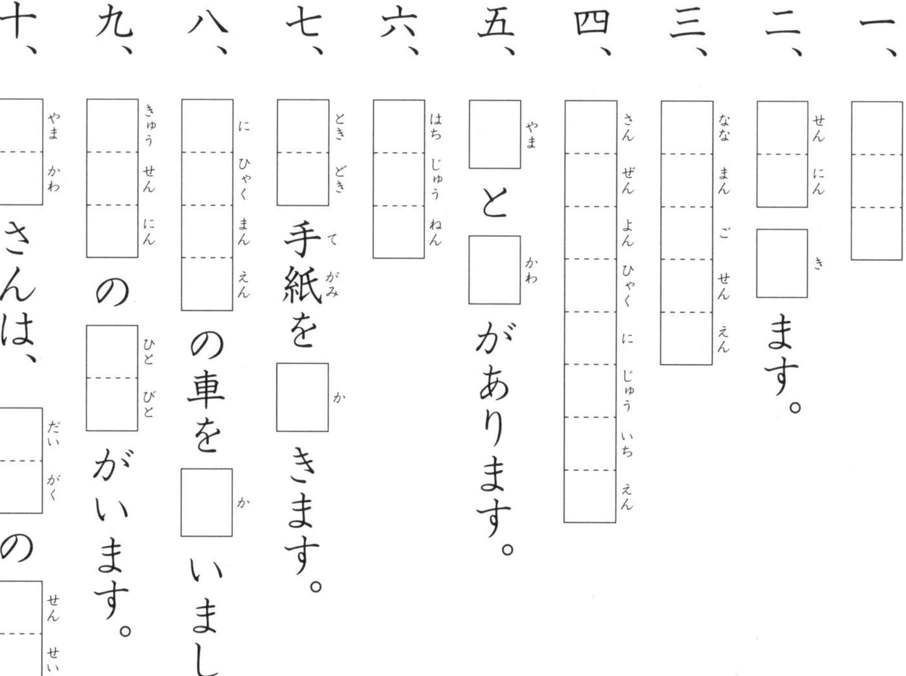

読む練習(れんしゅう)

一、週末は何をしますか。
二、時々、音楽を聞(き)きます。
三、料理するのが好きです。
四、一年に一回旅行します。
五、この本は、三千八百円です。
六、四万二千円のカメラを買います。
七、山川さんは、映画を見るのが好きです。
八、わたしは、公園で本を読むのが好きです。
九、大学に学生が二千人います。
十、時々、週末も仕事します。

LESSON 8 第八課(だいはっか)

LISTENING AND SPEAKING

Objectives

Expressing desires
Discussing choices
Explaining or giving reasons

Points

- conveying wishes and desires
- ordering at a restaurant
- extending invitations
- stating reasons for declining invitations

Sentences

1 (わたし は) 先生 に なります。

2 (わたし は) いい 辞書(じしょ) が ほしい です。でも、(わたし は) 小さい の は {ほしく ありません。/ほしく ないです。}

3 (わたし は) 将来(しょうらい) 医者(いしゃ) に なりたいです。
(わたし は) 先生 に {なりたく ありません。/なりたく ないです。}

（わたし　は）　やきとり　〔が／を〕　食べたい　です。

4　きっぷ　が　出ない　〔の／ん〕　です。

Expressions

1　どうしたんですか。　What happened?/What's the matter?　（ドリル　Ⅲ）

2　今度　の　日曜日　に　友だち　と　海　に　行く　ん　です　が、
Bさん　も　いっしょ　に　行きません　か。（ドリル　Ⅴ）
I'm going to the beach with some friends next Sunday....Why don't you come with us?

3　ざんねん　です。　That's too bad.（ドリルⅤ）

4　食事　でも　しません　か。　Why don't we eat or something?　（ドリル　Ⅵ）

5　Aさん　は　何　に　します　か。　What would you like, Mr. A?　（ドリル　Ⅵ）

フォーメーション

1-1　To become ～/come to ～

例）先生　→　（わたし　は）　先生　に　なります。

1) 医者　→
2) べんごし　→
3) 英語　の　先生　→

1-2

例）子ども、元気　→　子ども　が　元気　に　なりました。
家賃、高い　→　家賃　が　高く　なりました。

1) 円、安い　→
2) 子ども、大きい　→
3) コーヒー、冷たい　→
4) 交通、便利　→
5) 町、きれい　→

2 I want (something)

例) いい 辞書：小さい 辞書→(わたし は) いい 辞書 が ほしい です。
でも、(わたし は) 小さい の は
(ほしく ありません。/ほしく ないです。)

1) コンパクト な ワープロ：高い ワープロ →
2) 外国 の 車：大きい 車 →
3) 新しい テレビ：高い テレビ →

3-1 I want to (do ~)

例) 食べる → 食べたい です → (食べたく ありません/食べたく ない です)

食べたい → 食べたく ない

1) 行く →
2) 話す →
3) 待つ →
4) 死ぬ →
5) 読む →
6) 休む →
7) 帰る →
8) 買う →
9) 泳ぐ →
10) 遊ぶ →
11) 見る →
12) 起きる →
13) 来る →
14) する →

3-2

例) やきとり、食べる → (わたし は) やきとり (が/を) 食べたい です。

1) あつい 物、飲む →
2) (わたし の) 部屋、音楽、聞く →
3) いっしょ に、レストラン、行く →
4) 車、帰る →
5) 週末、友だち、会う →

4-1 Non-past plain forms of predicates

例) 医者 です → 医者 だ
医者 じゃありません → 医者 じゃない

きれい　です　→　きれい　だ
きれい　じゃありません　→　きれい　じゃない

おもしろい　です　→　おもしろい
おもしろく　ありません　→　おもしろく　ない

食べ　ます　→　食べる
食べ　ません　→　食べない

1) かぜ　です　→
かぜ　じゃありません　→
2) 用事　です　→
用事　じゃありません　→
3) 元気　です　→
元気　じゃありません　→
4) 休みます　→
休みません　→
5) わかります　→
わかりません　→
6) いります　→
いりません　→
7) します　→
しません　→
8) 出(で)ます　→
出(で)ません　→
9) 痛(いた)い　です　→
痛(いた)く　ありません　→
10) ほしい　です　→
ほしく　ありません　→
11) あります　→
ありません　→
12) います
いません　→

4-2 Explanatory statements

例(れい)) きっぷ、出(で)ません　→　きっぷ　が　出(で)ない　(の / ん) です。

1) (わたし)、きょう、宿題、ありません　→
2) (わたし)、今度　の　日曜日(にちようび)、海(うみ)、行きます　→
3) リーさん、きょう、クラス、出(で)ません　→
4) (わたし)、コーヒー、飲みません　→
5) 飛行機(ひこうき)　の　きっぷ、あまり、高く　ありません　→

ドリル

I Expressing desire

A：何　が　ほしい　です　か。

B：そう　です　ね。わたし　は
コンパクト　な　ワープロ　が　ほしい
です。

新しい	服(ふく)　くつ　ぼうし
やさしい	友だち
いい	辞書(じしょ)　ステレオ　CD

Ⅱ Expressing hopes for your future

A：将来(しょうらい)、何　に　なりたい　です　か。

B：医者(いしゃ)　に　なりたい　です。

医者(いしゃ)	大学　の　先生	英語(えいご)　の　先生	べんごし

Ⅲ Explaining the situation

A：どう　した　ん　です　か。

B：きっぷ　が　出(で)ない　ん　です。

駅

きっぷ	が	出(で)ません
おつり	が	出(で)ません
漢字(かんじ)	が	わかりません
さいふ	が	ありません

クリニック

ちょっと	頭(あたま)	が	痛(いた)い	です
ちょっと	おなか	が	痛(いた)い	です
ちょっと	気分	が	悪(わる)い	です
ちょっと	気持(きも)ち	が	悪(わる)い	です

Ⅳ

A：あした　休みたい　ん　です　が……。

B：なぜ　です　か。

A：用事(ようじ)　が　ある　ん　です。

医者(いしゃ)　に　行きます
両親(りょうしん)　が　来ます
スピーチコンテスト　に　出(で)ます

Ⅴ Inviting, accepting/declining an invitation

A：今度　の　日曜日(にちようび)　に　友だち　と　海(うみ)　に　行く　ん　です　が、
　　Bさん　も　いっしょ　に　行きません　か。

B：ええ、ぜひ　行きたい　です。

B：すみません。その　日　は　用事　が
　　ある　ん　です。ざんねん　です。

Inviting

山　へ　行きます	新宿(しんじゅく)　に　行きます
テニス　を　します	美術館(びじゅつかん)　に　行きます

Declining

予定
アルバイト
勉強(べんきょう)

Ⅵ Deciding what you are going to have

A：食事(しょくじ)　でも　しません　か。

B：そう　です　ね。

A：何　が　いい　です　か。

B：わたし　は　やきとり　が　食べたい　です。　Aさん　は　何　に　します　か。

A：わたし　は　てんぷら　に　します。

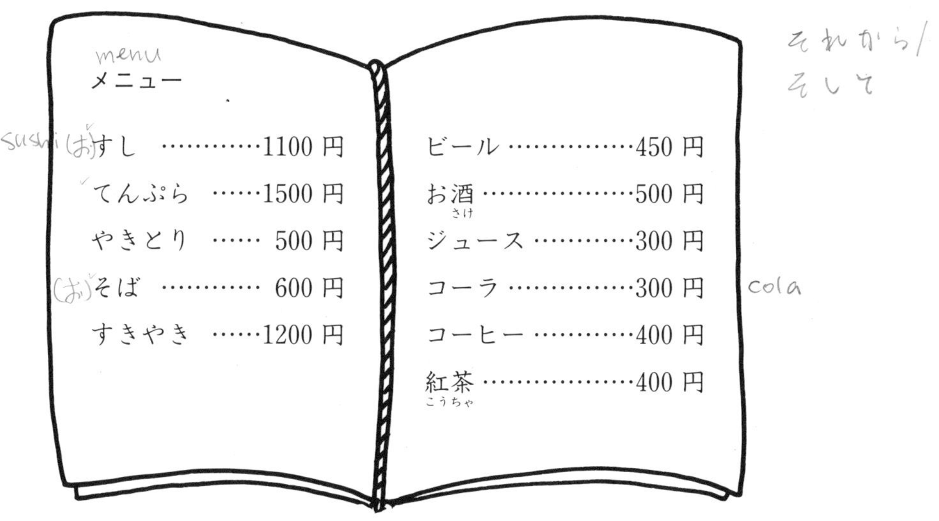

ロールプレイ

CARD A
I　Declining an invitation You ask a friend to go to Shinjuku on Saturday.

CARD B
I　Declining an invitation You are asked to go to Shinjuku, but unfortunately you have something else to do. Show appreciation but politely decline the invitation.

CARD A
II　Ordering a meal at a restaurant You go into a restaurant and order a meal.

CARD B
II　Ordering a meal at a restaurant You are a waiter/waitress at a restaurant. Serve the customer.

GRAMMAR NOTES

1. Become

	Nに		
N が	ANに	なります	N becomes N / Adj
	Adj-く		

The verb なる corresponds to the English 'become' or 'get'. When a noun or an adjectival noun precedes なる, it is followed by に, and when an adjective precedes なる, it appears in the -く form.

わたし は 先生(せんせい) に なります。	I will become a teacher.
町(まち) が きれい に なりました。	The city became clean.
コーヒー が 冷(つめ)たく なりました。	The coffee got cold.

2. Want (1)

1) (わたしは) N が ほしい です — I want N

The adjective ほしい 'want' is used to express the speaker's desire for something. The desired thing, a noun or noun phrase, is marked with the particle が. If the desirer is mentioned (and it can only be the speaker in a statement or the hearer in a question), he/she can be marked with the topic marker は.

何(なに) が ほしい です か。	What do you want?
いい 辞書(じしょ) が ほしい です。	I want a good dictionary.
わたし は ワープロ が ほしい です。	I want a word processer.

2) (わたしは) N は ほしく ありません / ないです — I don't want N

This is the negative form of GN2.1 above. The undesired thing is normally marked with は in negative sentences (L6 GN). If が is used, it lays a special emphasis on the thing and means 'It is N that I don't want'.

車(くるま) は ほしく ありません。　I don't want a car.
ワープロ が ほしい です。　I want a word processor.
いい 辞書(じしょ) が ほしい です。 でも、小(ち)さい の は ほしく ないです。
I want a good dictionary. But I don't want a small one.

3. Want (2)

The Japanese language distinguishes the speaker's desire to possess something from the desire to do something. The former is expressed with ほしい 'want N' as shown above, and the latter with V-たい 'want to V'.

(わたしは)	V-たい　です			I want to V
(わたしは)	N	が を	V-たい　です	I want to V N

To express the speaker's desire to do something, the verb has the suffix -たい attached to its -ます stem. The suffix -たい is inflected like adjectives.

Vowel verbs

見(み)たい	mi-tai	want to see, want to look, want to watch
起(お)きたい	oki-tai	want to get up
寝(ね)たい	ne-tai	want to go to sleep／bed
食(た)べたい	tabe-tai	want to eat

Consonant verbs

聞(き)きたい	kiki-tai	want to hear, want to listen
泳(およ)ぎたい	oyogi-tai	want to swim
話(はな)したい	hanashi-tai	want to talk
待(ま)ちたい	machi-tai	want to wait
帰(かえ)りたい	kaeri-tai	want to go home
買(か)いたい	kai-tai	want to buy
遊(あそ)びたい	asobi-tai	want to play
読(よ)みたい	yomi-tai	want to read
死(し)にたい	shini-tai	want to die

Irregular verbs

したい	shi-tai	want to do
来たい	ki-tai	want to come

For those who prefer the kana syllabary table for ascertaining the conjugation of verbs, the table below is for consonant verbs. From this it can be seen that the stem of consonant verbs to which -たい is attached comes in the [i] row.

w-	r-	m-	b-	n-	t-	s-	g-	k-	
わ	ら	ま	ば	な	た	さ	が	か	a
い	り	み	び	に	ち	し	ぎ	き	i
う	る	む	ぶ	ぬ	つ	す	ぐ	く	u
え	れ	め	べ	ね	て	せ	げ	け	e
を	ろ	も	ぼ	の	と	そ	ご	こ	o

The noun preceding the verb can be marked by が since the verb is suffixed with -たい, which is adjectival, and like ほしい it allows a ～は～が construction (L5 GN8). But since the noun can also be considered the object of the verb, the particle を can also be used (L3 GN4).

何が したい です か。／何を したい です か。	What do you want to do?
泳ぎたい です。	I want to swim.
レストラン へ 行きたい です。	I want to go to a restaurant.
音楽 が 聞きたい です。／音楽 を 聞きたい です。	I want to listen to music.
せ が 高く なりたい です。	I want to become tall.
医者 に なりたい です。	I want to become a doctor.
元気 に なりたい です。	I want to become healthy.

Note that the V-たい form is always understood to have the same subject as the verb from which it is formed; that is to say, the person who is doing the wanting and the person who is doing the action must be the same person. Thus, this form cannot be used in a Japanese sentence corresponding to a sentence like 'I want Mary to go', in which the 'I' who wants and the 'Mary' who goes are different people. To see how this type of sentence is phrased in Japanese, see Lesson 9 GN2.3.

(わたしは)	V-たく ありません V-たく ないです	I don't want to V
(わたしは)	N は/を V たく ありません N は/を V-たく ないです	I don't want to V N

There are two negative forms for the V-たい predicate when it behaves as an adjective. The two forms were introduced in Lesson 5 GN2. More detail on plain forms of adjectives and adjectival nouns will be given in GN4 below. The noun preceding V-たく　ありません or V-たく　ないです is generally marked by は instead of が because it has usually already been mentioned in context or contrasted to something else (L6 GN2).

食(た)べたく　ありません。　I do not want to eat.

わたし　は　帰(かえ)りたく　ありません。　I do not want to go home.

その　本(ほん)　は　読(よ)みたい　です。でも、買(か)いたく　ありません。

I want to read the book. But I do not want to buy it.

なっとう　は　食(た)べたく　ない　です　が、　やきとり　は　食(た)べたい　です。

I do not want to eat natto ('fermented beans'), but I do want to eat yakitori.

Note that, as explained in Lesson 6, the topic/contrastive marker は may be used with noun phrases other than those used as the object of the verb (L6 GN2). Note the following examples.

わたし　は　先生(せんせい)　には　なりたく　ありません。

I do not want to become a teacher.

東京(とうきょう)　へは　行(い)きたく　ありません。

I do not want to go to Tokyo.

4. Plain predicate forms

Following is an overview of plain predicate forms for verbs, adjectives, adjectival nouns, and nouns. One of the outstanding features of plain forms is their use in sentences which are embedded in the main sentence, as shown in GN5 below.

1) Affirmative forms

Verbs:	V-(r)u	V
Adjectives:	Adj-い	is Adj
Adjectival nouns:	AN だ	is Adj
Nouns:	N だ	is N

Verbs ending in -(r)u are in the so-called dictionary or plain non-past affirmative form. Vowel verbs are followed by -る and consonant verbs by one of the kana in the [u] row of the table in Lesson 3 GN1.1.

The -い form is the plain non-past affirmative form of adjectives. The non-past affirmative form of adjectival nouns is made by adding the copula だ, just as with nouns. In other words, the copula だ is necessary to form a noun or adjectival noun predicate, but unnecessary to form an adjective predicate.

Verb	見(み)る	see, look, watch
	聞(き)く	hear, listen
Adj	高(たか)い	is high, expensive
	大(おお)きい	is big
AN	きれいだ	is clean, pretty
	静(しず)かだ	is quiet
N	コーヒーだ	is coffee
	学生(がくせい)だ	is a student

The copula forms だ, です, and でした, which serve to make predicates out of nouns (including adjectival nouns), are contracted forms of the particle で with the verb ある.

である → だ
であります → です
でありました → でした

2) Negative forms

Verbs:	V-(a)-ない	does not V
Adjectives:	Adj-く　ない	is not Adj
Adjectival nouns:	AN じゃない	is not Adj
Nouns:	N じゃない	is not N

The plain non-past negative predicate forms of vowel verbs consist of the root form + ない, and that of consonant verbs consist of the root + [a] + ない, or an [a] row syllable + ない. The plain non-past negative form of ある 'exist' is ない.

The plain non-past negative predicate forms of adjectives consist of the -く form + ない, and those of adjectival nouns consist of the adjectival noun plus じゃない, as is the case with nouns. As was explained in Lesson 1, じゃ is a contracted form of では (pronounced [dewa]).

Vowel verbs	見ない	mi-nai	does not see, look, watch
	食べない	tabe-nai	does not eat
Consonant verbs	聞かない	kik-a-nai	does not hear, listen
	泳がない	oyog-a-nai	does not swim
	話さない	hanas-a-nai	does not speak
	待たない	mat-a-nai	does not wait
	帰らない	kaer-a-nai	does not return
	買わない	kaw-a-nai	does not buy
	遊ばない	asob-a-nai	does not play
	死なない	shin-a-nai	does not die
Irregular verbs	しない	shi-nai	does not do
	来ない	ko-nai	does not come
Adjectives	高くない		is not high, expensive
	大きくない		is not big
Adjectival nouns	きれいじゃない		is not clean, pretty
	静かじゃない		is not quiet
Nouns	コーヒーじゃない		is not coffee
	学生じゃない		is not a student

Uncontracted forms using では［dewa］are used in certain contexts, such as expository writing, formal speech, etc.

では → じゃ

5. Stating reasons or explanations: ～のです／～んです

It is (just) that S

Plain forms of predicates

V	non-past	V-る		
Adj	non-past	Adj-い		
AN	non-past	AN だ	→	AN な
N	non-past	N だ	→	N な

A sentence with a plain form predicate followed by の です (a nominalizer + polite copula) corresponds to the English construction 'it's (just) that...', and is used to elicit or offer explanations or reasons for some situation, often implicit. The nominalizer

の is often reduced to ん in conversation ([no]→[n]). Note that when the sentence preceding の ends with the copula だ (i.e., in the case of nouns and adjectival nouns followed by だ), だ changes to な. The past form of these predicates will be introduced in Lesson 10.

どう　した　ん　です　か。
What's the matter?

きっぷ　が　出(で)ない　ん　です。
(It's just that) the ticket won't come out (of the machine).

あした　テスト　が　ある　ん　です。
There's a test tomorrow. (It's just that there is a test tomorrow.)

たくさん　漢字(かんじ)　を　書(か)きました　ね。
You've written a lot of kanji, haven't you?

好(す)き　な　ん　です。
Oh, I like them. (It's just that I like them.)

リーさん　は　きょう　休(やす)みです　か。
Is Lee absent today?

ええ、　かぜ　な　ん　です。
Yes, he has a cold. (It's just that he's got a cold.)

いつも　あの　スーパー　へ　行(い)く　ん　です　か。
Do you always go to that supermarket? (Is it that you always go to that supermarket?)

ええ、あそこは　(物(もの)　が)　安(やす)い　ん　です。
Yes, because things are cheaper there.

Very often in informal speech among friends, the です of のです is omitted, so that the sentence ends with の. This happens both in declarative and interrogative sentences. Note, however, that in such abbreviated forms stress, intonation, tone of voice, etc. play an important role in expressing nuance, which is especially difficult for beginning students of Japanese to capture. (Compare the many ways of saying 'Thank you' in English, for example.) To avoid unnecessary misunderstandings, students are urged to be particularly careful in using these forms.

どう　した　の?
[The question mark indicates a rising intonation.]　What's the matter?

お金(かね)　が　ない　の。
I don't have any money.

きょう　大学(だいがく)　へ　行(い)く　の?
Are you going to the university today?

うん、テスト　が　ある　の。
Yeah, there's a test.

Another informal form of のです used among friends, hence one you will hear often, is んだ, which is a combination of the contracted form ん and the plain non-past copula だ. This is mostly used in declarative sentences. Care should be exercised in using this form, also.

> 歌(うた) じょうず だ ね。
>
> You're good at (singing) songs.
>
> いやあ。でも、好(す)き な ん だ。
>
> No. But I like (singing).

READING

A Student Composition

んで京都へ行きます。日本人の友だちといっしょに行きます。大阪にイギリス人の友だちもいますから、大阪へも行きたいです。そのイギリス人の友だちに会いたいです。それから、広島へも行きたいです。でも、お金がありません。八月のおわりに国へかえります。
国へかえってから、大学院へ行きます。ほうりつをべんきょうして、しょうらいはべんごしになりたいです。

おわる	V	to finish
北海道（ほっかいどう）	PN	Hokkaido
京都（きょうと）	PN	Kyoto
大阪（おおさか）	PN	Osaka
広島（ひろしま）	PN	Hiroshima
大学院（だいがくいん）	N	graduate school
ほうりつ	N	law

マイク・ジョンソン

　わたしは九月にイギリスから来ました。来年の八月までICUで日本語と日本のせいじをべんきょうします。インテンシブ・コースは来年の六月におわりますが、七月十日から八月十五日までサマー・コースでべんきょうします。

　サマー・コースがおわってから、旅行をしたいです。北海道へ行きたいですが、ひこうきのきっぷは高いです。それで、しんかんせ

□ Before Reading

1. あなたは日本で何をしたいですか。

□ Comprehension Check

1. マイクさんは日本で何をべんきょうしますか。
2. マイクさんはいつまで日本でべんきょうしますか。
3. マイクさんはべんきょうがおわってから、何をしますか。
4. マイクさんはいつイギリスへかえりますか。
5. マイクさんは国へかえってから何をしますか。
6. マイクさんはしょうらい何をしますか。

□ Writing Activity

1. 夏(なつ)休みの予定
2. しょうらいの予定

WRITING
[KANJI]

読み方を覚えましょう

両親（りょうしん）: parents
宿題（しゅくだい）: homework
予定（よてい）: plan
今度（こんど）: next time, this time
交通（こうつう）: traffic
用事（ようじ）: business, errand

新しい漢字

58

ことば	れんしゅう	子
1 子（こ）・2 子（こ）ども・3 お子（こ）さん	子 子	くん: こ / おん: し
		いみ: a child
		かきじゅん: フ 了 子
1 a child 2 a child 3 your/someone's child		

59

ことば	れんしゅう	友
1 友（とも）だち	友 友	くん: とも / おん:
		いみ: a friend
		かきじゅん: 一 ナ 方 友
1 a friend		

60

ことば	れんしゅう	元
1 元気（げんき）	元 元	くん: / おん: げん
		いみ: origin
		かきじゅん: 一 二 テ 元
1 healthy		

61

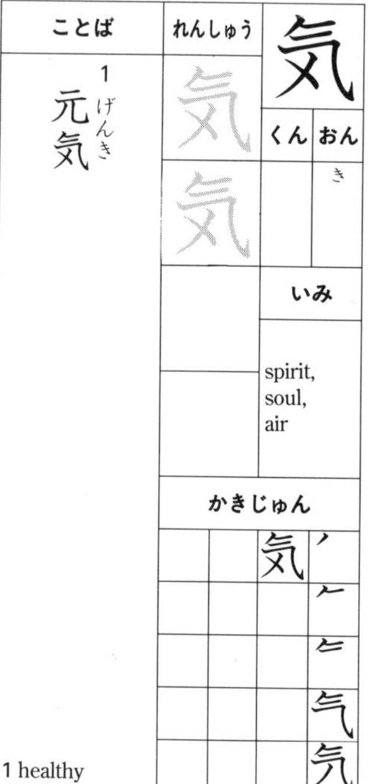

ことば	れんしゅう	気
1 元気（げんき）		くん: — / おん: き
		いみ: spirit, soul, air
1 healthy		

62

ことば	れんしゅう	外
1 外（そと）・2 外国（がいこく）		くん: そと / おん: がい
		いみ: outside
1 outside 2 a foreign country		

63

ことば	れんしゅう	休
1 休む（やすむ）・2 休み（やすみ）		くん: やす(む)・やす(み) / おん: —
		いみ: to rest, to be absent
1 to take a rest, to be absent 2 a rest, a break, a holiday		

64

ことば	れんしゅう	会
1 会う（あう）・2 会話（かいわ）		くん: あ(う) / おん: かい
		いみ: to see, to meet, a meeting
1 to meet, to see 2 a conversation		

65

ことば	れんしゅう	語
1 日本語（にほんご）・2 中国語（ちゅうごくご）		くん: — / おん: ご
		いみ: a language, a word, to tell
1 Japanese language 2 Chinese language		

書く練習(れんしゅう)

一、□(とも)だちと□(そと)で□(あ)いました。

二、□(やす)みに□国(がいこく)へ旅□(こう)します。

三、わたしは□□(げんき)です。

四、□(こ)どもが□□(さんにん)います。

五、□国□(がいこくじん)の□(とも)だちと□□□(にほんご)で□(はな)します。

六、□(こ)どもは□(そと)で遊(あそ)びます。

七、仕事を□(やす)みたいです。

八、□□(やまかわ)さんは□□(げんき)ですか。

九、□(とも)だちに、□□□(にほんご)で手紙(てがみ)を□(か)きました。

十、□国(がいこく)で□□(せんせい)に□(あ)います。

読む練習(れんしゅう)

一、わたしの両親は元気です。

二、今、外国(こく)にいます。

三、今度の休みの予定は何ですか。

四、週末は用事がありません。

五、東京は交通が便利です。

六、今晩は予定がありません。宿題をします。

七、友だちと会います。

八、子どもは外で遊(あそ)びます。

九、日本語で手紙(てがみ)を書きます。

十、今度の休みに外国(こく)へ旅行します。

LESSON 9 第九課

LISTENING AND SPEAKING

Objectives

Inquiring about the location of someplace in town
Understanding explanations of apartment or dormitory regulations

Points

- giving directions
- pointing out locations
- inquiring about locations
- offering/accepting help

Sentences

1 まど を 開けましょう か。

2 と を 閉めて ください。

と を 閉めないで ください。

3 （わたし は） お金 が ない から、（わたし は） 買い物 に 行きません。

4 電話 は つくえ の 横 に あります。

5 電話 は つくえ の 横 です。

Expressions

1 じゃ、お願い します。 Yes, please. （ドリル III）

2 いいえ、けっこう です。　　No, that's fine. （ドリル III）

3 気 を つける こと は どんな こと です か。

What kind of things (rules) should I be careful about? （ドリル IV）

4 はい、わかりました。　　O.K. I understand. （ドリル IV）

5 どうも すみません でした。　　Thanks very much. （ドリル VI）

フォーメーション

1 Shall I ～

例) まど を 開ける → まど を 開けましょう か。

1) 電気 を 消す →

2) コピー を とる →

3) 先生 を よぶ →

4) 部屋 を そうじ する →

2-1 Verbs in て/ないで form

例) 食べる → 食べて
→ 食べないで

1) 行く →
→

2) 書く →
→

3) 話す →
→

4) 待つ →
→

5) 死ぬ →
→

6) 読む →
→

7) 乗る →
→

8) 買う →
→

9) 泳ぐ →
→

10) よぶ →
→

11) つける →
→

12) する →
→

13) 来る →
→

2-2 Please ～

例) と を 閉める → と を 閉めて ください。

1) この 漢字 を 教える →

2) テレビ を つける →

3) 日本語 で 手紙 を 書く →

4) (車 を) 運転 する →

2-3 Please don't ～

例) 先生、(その　こと)、言う　→　先生　に　(その　こと　を)　言わないで　ください。

1) ここ、コーヒー、飲む　→

2) 部屋、料理、する　→

3) たくさん、コピー、取る　→

4) 時計、忘れる　→

3 Reasons

例) お金　が　ありません

→　(わたし　は)　お金　が　ない　から、(わたし　は)　うち　に　います。

1) いそがしい　です　→

2) 友だち　が　来ます　→

3) 試験　が　あります　→

4) 勉強　します　→

4-1 Phrases stating locations

例) つくえの上

例) 上

1) 下

2) 中

3) 横

4) 前

5) 後ろ

6) 右

7) 左

8) 間

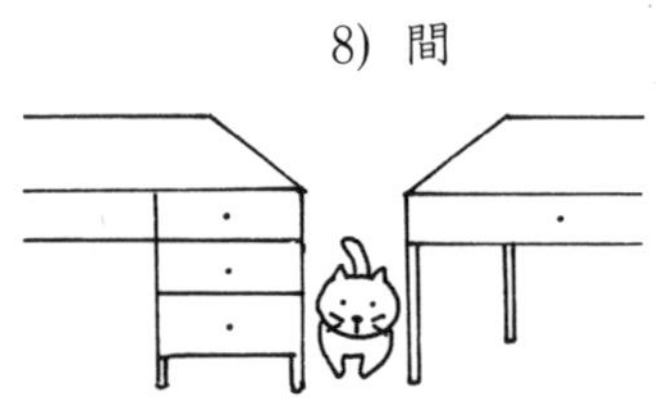

4-2 Locations (1)

例(れい)) 電話、つくえ、横 → 電話 は つくえ の 横 に あります。

1) 明子(あきこ)さん、かおるさん の 左 →
2) CD プレーヤー、本ばこ の 上 →
3) 時計(とけい)、かばん の 中 →
4) かおるさん、明子(あきこ)さん と けんさん の 間 →
5) 薬局(やっきょく)、すし屋 の 前 →

5 Locations (2) (〜は〜です)

例(れい)) デパート、駅、向こう → デパート は 駅 の 向こう です。

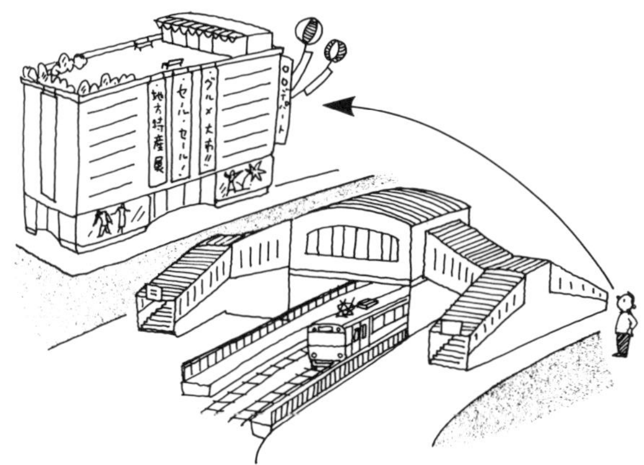

1) 映画館、この ビル、向こう →

2) 寮(りょう)、図書館(としょかん)、向こう→

3) 寮(りょう)、食堂(しょくどう)、そば →

4) 薬局(やっきょく)、駅、そば →

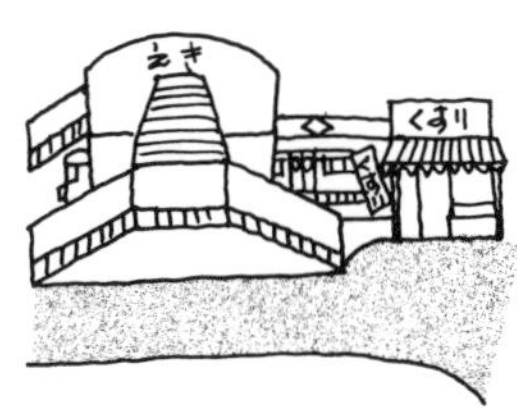

ドリル

I　Telling where someone is

A：リーさん　は　どこ　に　います　か。

B：リーさん　は　ホワイトさん　の　右　に　います。

II　Offering/Accepting/Declining help

A：まど　を　開(あ)けましょう　か。

B：ええ、開(あ)けて　ください。　B：いいえ、寒(さむ)いから、開(あ)けないで　ください。

	reasons
テレビ　を　つける	うるさい　です
電気　を　消す	暗(くら)い　です
と　を　閉(し)める	暑(あつ)い　です
電話　を　かける	おそい　です

III　Offering/Accepting/Declining help

A：わたし　が　しましょう　か。

B：そう　です　か。じゃ　お願(ねが)い　します。

B：いいえ、けっこう　です。自分(じぶん)　で　します　から。

手紙(てがみ)　を　書く、コピー　を　取る、郵便局(ゆうびんきょく)　へ　行く
手紙(てがみ)　を　出(だ)す、連絡(れんらく)　する

IV　Explaining apartment regulations　(A: Tenant　B: Landlord)

A：気　を　つける　こと　は　どんな　こと　です　か。

B：そう　です　ね。きちん　と　そうじ　を　して　ください。

A：はい、わかりました。

して　ください	しないで　ください
夜(よる)　かぎ　を　かける	大きな　声(こえ)　で　話す
火　に　気　を　つける	夜(よる)　おそく　テレビ　を　見る
家賃(やちん)　を　25日　に　払(はら)う	ペット　を　かう
ごみ　を　月曜日(げつようび)　に　出(だ)す	夜(よる)　おそく　せんたく　する

V　Giving directions

A：テーブル　は　どこ　に　おきましょう　か。

B：部屋　の　真ん中(まんなか)　に　おいて　ください。

A

① CDプレーヤー	⑥ ふとん
② テレビ	⑦ カレンダー
③ テーブル	⑧ え
④ スピーカー	⑨ 時計(とけい)
⑤ 本ばこ	⑩ ストーブ

B

VI　Inquiring about locations

A：すみません。この　あたり　に　銀行　が　あります　か。

B：ええ。銀行　は　郵便局(ゆうびんきょく)　の　となり　です。

A：どうも　すみません　でした。

B：この　あたり　には　銀行　は　ありません。

A

郵便局(ゆうびんきょく)	薬局(やっきょく)
スーパー	ぶんぼうぐ屋
カメラ屋	パン屋
せんとう	レコード屋
ガソリンスタンド	病院
とこ屋	

B

ロールプレイ

CARD A

I Asking the way

You are going to visit a friend's house and are lost. Show your friend's address to a passerby and ask for directions.

CARD B

I Asking the way

On the street a foreign student stops you and asks directions to a friend's house. Show him/her the way, pointing out landmarks.

CARD A

II Explaining the rules

At an apartment house:
You are a foreign student. Ask the manager of the apartment a few things you have to know concerning the rules for garbage collection, cleaning the building, etc.

CARD B

II Explaining the rules

At an apartment house:
You are the manager of an apartment house. Explain a few rules that a foreign student should know about garbage collection, cleaning the building, etc.

GRAMMAR NOTES

1. Offering help

（わたし　が）　V-ましょう　か	Shall I V?

The form V-ましょう followed by the question marker か is used for offering help to the person one is talking to. It corresponds to the English 'Shall I...?'

Regarding the formation of V-ましょう, refer to L4 GN5.

まど　を　開(あ)けましょう　か。　Shall I open the window?

テーブル　は　どこ　に　おきましょう　か。　As for the table, where shall I place it?

わたし　が（郵便局(ゆうびんきょく)　に）行(い)きましょう　か。　Shall I go to (the post office)?

2. Requesting

1)

V-て　ください	Please V

This expression is used for politely requesting someone to do something, and it consists of the -て form of verbs and the auxiliary ください 'give it to me'.

V-て is a conjugated form of verbs, adjectives, and the copula です (following either nouns or adjectival nouns). Syntactically the V-て form has two important functions: 1) it connects predicates (sentences) and 2) produces various expressions (e.g., V-てください) when immediately followed by an auxiliary verb.

The -て form is made from the dictionary form in the following way:

① Vowel verbs: Replace the last sound -[ru] of verbs with -[te] (-て).

開(あ)け-る	開(あ)け-て	open (a door)
つけ-る	つけ-て	turn on (a light)
起(お)き-る	起(お)き-て	get up

見(み)-る	見(み)-て	see, look

② Consonant verbs: According to the last sound (-く, -ぐ, -す, -つ, -ぬ, -ぶ, -む, -う, or -る) of the dictionary form, five types of changes in the pronunciation of the word occur. The last sound of the dictionary form is replaced by the appropriate variant among the five types, as shown below.

Verbs ending with -[k] (く): Replace the last sound -[k] (く) with -[i-te], -い-て.

書(か)-く	書(か)-い -て	write
聞(き)-く	聞(き)-い -て	listen

Note, however, that the verb 行(い)く is an exception to this rule: the -て form of 行(い)く is 行(い)って.

Verbs ending with -[g] (ぐ): Replace the last sound -[g] (ぐ) with -[i-de], -い-で.

泳(およ)-ぐ	泳(およ)-い-で	swim
こ-ぐ	こ-い-で	row (a boat)

Verbs ending with -[s] (す): Replace the last sound -[s] (す) with -[shi-te], -し-て.

話(はな)-す	話(はな)-し-て	speak, talk
わた-す	わた-し-て	hand (something) to somebody

Verbs ending with -[(w)] (う), -[ts] (つ), or -[r] (る): Replace the last sound -[(w)] (う), -[ts] (つ), or -[r] (る) with -[t-te], -っ-て.

買(か)-う	買(か)-っ-て	buy
立(た)-つ	立(た)-っ-て	stand up
帰(かえ)-る	帰(かえ)-っ-て	return

Verbs ending with -[b] (ぶ), -[m] (む), or -[n] (ぬ): Replace the last sound -[b] (ぶ), -[m] (む), or -[n] (ぬ) with -[n-de], -ん-で.

よ-ぶ	よ-ん-で	call
飲(の)-む	飲(の)-ん-で	drink
死(し)-ぬ	死(し)-ん-で	die

③ Irregular verbs: There is no set rule to follow for these irregularly conjugated verbs, so they have to be remembered as they are.

来(く)る	来(き)て	come
する	して	do

と を 閉(し)めて ください。

Please close the door.

（車(くるま)　を）　運転(うんてん)　して　ください。
Drive the car, please.

テレビ　を　つけて　ください。
Please turn on the TV.

In casual speech, ください may be omitted.

と　を　開(あ)けて。
Open the door, please.

（車(くるま)　を）　運転(うんてん)　して。
Drive the car, please.

テレビ　（を）　つけて。
Turn on the TV, please.

2) | V-ないで　ください | Please don't V

This expression is the negative counterpart of V-てください, and is used to politely request the hearer(s) not to do something.

The form V-ないで is the corresponding negative form of V-て. It is made by attaching -で to V-ない, the plain non-past negative form of a verb (L8 GN4).

① Vowel verbs:

Dictionary Form plain non-past affirmative	V-ない plain non-past negative	V-ない-で
開(あ)ける	開(あ)けない	開(あ)けないで
つける	つけない	つけないで
起(お)きる	起(お)きない	起(お)きないで
見(み)る	見(み)ない	見(み)ないで

② Consonant verbs:

書(か)く	書(か)かない	書(か)かないで
泳(およ)ぐ	泳(およ)がない	泳(およ)がないで
話(はな)す	話(はな)さない	話(はな)さないで
買(か)う	買(か)わない	買(か)わないで
立(た)つ	立(た)たない	立(た)たないで
帰(かえ)る	帰(かえ)らない	帰(かえ)らないで
よぶ	よばない	よばないで
死(し)ぬ	死(し)なない	死(し)なないで
飲(の)む	飲(の)まない	飲(の)まないで

③ Irregular verbs:

来(く)る	来(こ)ない	来(こ)ないで
する	しない	しないで

ここ で コーヒー を 飲(の)まないで ください。
Please don't drink coffee here.

部屋(へや) で 料理(りょうり) を しないで ください。
Please don't cook in your room.

学生(がくせい) は この 部屋(へや) に 入(はい)らないで ください。
As for students, don't enter this room, please.

3) In order to express 'I want you/someone to V', 「〜に〜てほしい (です)」 can be used. However, 「〜てください」 is more polite.

ジョンさん に 行(い)って ほしい (です。)
I want John to go.

この ケーキ は あなた に 食(た)べて ほしい (です。)
As for this cake, I want you to eat it.

だれ (に)も この 部屋(へや) に 入(はい)らないで ほしい (です。)
I don't want anyone to enter this room.

ここ に 自転車(じてんしゃ) を 止(と)めないで ほしい (です。)
I don't want them to park their bicycles here.

3. Locative expressions (2)

THING	は	N	の	LOCATIVE WORD	に	あります
PERSON						います
ANIMAL						

As for THING/PERSON/ANIMAL, it exists LOCATION

As explained in L6 GN, this pattern is used to express the location of the thing or person which was referred to in a preceding context. In addition to the ones already introduced in L6 GN1.3, more locative words are introduced here. These locative words can be used in the location phrase N の LOCATIVE WORD に.

Locative Words

上(うえ)	on, above	下(した)	under, below
中(なか)	in	左(ひだり)	left
横(よこ)	side	間(あいだ)	in between

後ろ(うしろ)　behind　　向こう(むこう)　beyond, over
右(みぎ)　right

電話(でんわ)　は　つくえ　の　上(うえ)　に　あります。
As for the phone, it is on the desk. / The phone is on the desk.

デパート　は　駅(えき)　の　向こう(むこう)　に　あります。
As for the department store, it is beyond the station.

明子(あきこ)さん　は　かおるさん　の　左(ひだり)　に　います。
As for Akiko, she is on the left of Kaoru.

In this pattern, に　あります/ に　います may be replaced by です without changing the meaning denoted by the pattern.

電話(でんわ)　は　つくえ　の　上(うえ)　です。
As for the phone, it is on the desk.

デパート　は　駅(えき)　の　向こう(むこう)　です。
As for the department store, it is beyond the station.

明子(あきこ)さん　は　かおるさん　の　左(ひだり)　です。
As for Akiko, she is on the left of Kaoru.

In the same way, other verbs may be replaced by です when the original meaning is understood from context.

銀行(ぎんこう)　は　午前(ごぜん)9時(じ)　から　午後(ごご)3時(じ)　まで　です。
Banks are open from 9:00 A.M. to 3:00 P.M.

At a restaurant
A：何(なに)　に　します　か。　What would you like to eat?
B：わたし　は　ステーキ　です。　I'll eat steak. (As for me, it is steak.)

4. Sentence connectives (3): Reasons

S_1 から、	S_2
REASON	CONSEQUENCE
CAUSE	RESULT

Because S_1, S_2

This pattern is used to express reasons/causes and their consequences/results. The sentence connective から ('from') means 'because, since' in English when it is attached to S_1. Note that it is S_1 which states reasons/causes. The predicate of S_1 is generally in the plain form, although it can be in the polite form, depending on the formality of the situation.

時間(じかん) が ない から、 わたし は タクシー で 行(い)きます。
Because I don't have time, I will go by taxi.

友(とも)だち が 来(く)る から、 きょう は うち に います。
Since a friend is coming, I will be at home today.

あの店(みせ) は 安(やす)い から、 お客(きゃく)さん が よく 入(はい)る。
That shop is cheap, so many people go there. (That shop is cheap, so customers often enter.)

ひま だ から、 友(とも)だち に 手紙(てがみ) を 書(か)きます。
Because I have free time, I'll write a letter to my friend.

先生(せんせい): あした は 試験(しけん) が あります から、勉強(べんきょう)して ください。
Teacher/Professor: You have an examination tomorrow. Therefore, please study.

In the spoken language, it often happens that the order of S_1 + から and S_2 is reversed: the sentence giving consequences/results (S_2) is stated first, followed by the sentence giving reasons/causes (S_1 + から)。

A：わたし が しましょう か。
Shall I do it?

B：いいえ、けっこう です。 自分(じぶん) で します から。
No, thank you, because I'll do it myself.

(A, a friend of B, is about to open the window.)

B：あっ、開(あ)けないで。 寒(さむ)い から。
Oh, don't open it, because I am cold.

READING

Going to the *Sentoo*

スミス：　田(た)中さん、今度、せんとうに行きたいんですが、このあたりにありますか。

田中：　せんとうですか。そうですねえ。わたしは分かりませんから、山川さんに聞(き)いてください。

————————————————————

スミス：　山川さん、このあたりにせんとうがありますか。

山川：　せんとうですか。ええ、ありますよ。

スミス：　どこですか。

山川：　白山公園の右にスーパーと病院がありますね。

スミス：　ええ。

山川：　そのスーパーと病院の間です。名(な)前は「みたか湯」です。

スミス：　ああ、そうですか。どうもありがとう。山川さんもいっしょに行きませんか。

山川：　わたし？　そうですねえ。じつは、せんとうのお湯はちょっとあついんです。すみません。

せんとう	N	public bath
白山（しろやま）	N	Shiroyama
湯（ゆ）	N	hot water

□ 読む前に

あなたはせんとうに行きますか。

□ 質問（しつもん）

1. スミスさんは、どこに行きたいですか。
2. それはどこにありますか。
3. 山川さんも行きますか。

□ 書きましょう

1. あなたのまちの病院はどこにありますか。
2. あなたのまちの映画館はどこにありますか。

□ 話しましょう

WRITING
[KANJI]

読み方を覚えましょう

向こう（むこう）: beyond, the opposite side
横（よこ）: beside, next to
取る（とる）: to take
消す（けす）: to put out, extinguish
病院（びょういん）: hospital
〜屋（〜や）: store, shop

新しい漢字

66

ことば	れんしゅう	上
上（うえ[1]）・上げる（あげる[2]）・上がる（あがる[3]）	上 上	くん: うえ・うわ・あ(げる)あ(がる) おん: じょう
		いみ: up, on, to rise, to raise
1 the top 2 to raise 3 to rise		かきじゅん: 丨 ⺊ 上

67

ことば	れんしゅう	下
下（した[1]）	下 下	くん: した・くだ(さる) おん: か
		いみ: down, under, to fall
1 the bottom		かきじゅん: 一 丅 下

68

ことば	れんしゅう	左
左（ひだり[1]）	左 左	くん: ひだり おん:
		いみ: left
1 left		かきじゅん: 一 ナ 左 左 左

69

ことば	れんしゅう	右
1 右（みぎ）	右 右	くん: みぎ / おん: —
		いみ: right
1 right		かきじゅん: ノ ナ ナ 右 右

70

ことば	れんしゅう	間
1 間（あいだ）・2 時間（じかん）・3 六時間（ろくじかん）	間 間	くん: あいだ・ま / おん: かん
		いみ: between, among
1 between 2 time, hour(s) 3 six hours		かきじゅん: 丨 冂 冂 冂 門 門 門 門 門 間 間

71

ことば	れんしゅう	雨
1 雨（あめ）	雨 雨	くん: あめ / おん: —
		いみ: rain
1 rain		かきじゅん: 一 一 冂 币 币 雨 雨 雨

72

ことば	れんしゅう	電
1 電気（でんき）・2 電話（でんわ）	電 電	くん: — / おん: でん
		いみ: electricity
1 electricity 2 a telephone		かきじゅん: 一 冖 亠 币 币 币 币 雨 雫 雫 雪 雪 電

73

ことば	れんしゅう	車
1 車（くるま）・2 電車（でんしゃ）	車 車	くん: くるま / おん: しゃ
		いみ: a car, a wheel
1 a car 2 a train		かきじゅん: 一 厂 冂 百 亘 亘 車

WRITING LESSON 9 第九課

書く練習(れんしゅう)

一、□(くるま)の□(した)にねこがいます。

二、テーブルの□(うえ)に□□(でんわ)があります。

三、□□(でんしゃ)の□(なか)で□(とも)だちに□(あ)いました。

四、□(ほん)屋の□(ひだり)に映画館があります。

五、東京駅から□□(でんしゃ)に乗って□(やま)に□(い)きました。

六、□(あめ)が□□(ときどき)降(ふ)ります。

七、□□(せんせい)の□(みぎ)にわたしの□(とも)だちがいます。

八、駅と□□(だいがく)の□(あいだ)に公園があります。

九、両親と□□□(いちじかん)□□(でんわ)で□(はな)しました。

十、□(こ)どもは□(あめ)の□(なか)で遊(あそ)びます。

読む練習(れんしゅう)

一、テレビの右に本があります。

二、つくえの上に宿題があります。

三、郵(ゆう)便局と銀行の間に病院があります。 四、電気を消します。

五、公園の向こうに本屋があります。

六、駅の横の映画館に行きました。

七、三時間、電車に乗りました。

八、テーブルの上の電話の左に新聞(ぶん)があります。

九、その本の下のノートを取ってください。 十、雨が降(ふ)ります。

LISTENING AND SPEAKING

Objectives

Maintaining a conversation about vacations and free-time activities
Stating impressions of places and scenery

Points

- telling about sequential activities
- telling about past events
- stating impressions and opinions
- giving reasons for not doing something
- describing things, people, and places
- asking for someone's opinion
- expressing feelings of regret

Sentences

1 きのう　は　(あなた　は)　いそがしかった　です　か。

はい／ええ、(きのう　は　わたし　は)　いそがしかった　です。

いいえ、(きのう　は　わたし　は)　いそがしく　ありません　でした。

2 その　店(みせ)　は　サービス　が　よかった　でしょう。

3 (わたし　は)　レポート　で　いそがしい　です。

4 この ワープロ は 新しくて、(この ワープロ は) デザイン が いい です。

(わたし は) いそがしくて、(わたし は) パーティー に 行きません でした。

5 わたし は 飲み物 を 買って から、パーティー に 行きました。

フォーメーション

1-1 Past polite forms of adjectival nouns, adjectives, and verbs

例) 静か → 静か でした → 静か じゃありません でした

赤い → 赤かった です → (赤く ありません でした / 赤く なかった です)

出る → 出ました → 出ません でした

1) いい →
2) 長い →
3) まずい →
4) すばらしい →
5) 短い →
6) きれい →
7) せいかく →
8) にぎやか →
9) しんせん →
10) いんしょうてき →
11) 見る →
12) 泳ぐ →
13) 遊ぶ →
14) 休む →
15) 降る →
16) 教える →

1-2 Past plain forms of adjectival nouns, adjectives, and verbs

例) 静か → 静か だった → 静か じゃなかった

赤い → 赤かった → 赤く なかった

書く → 書いた → 書かなかった

☆Use the cues in 1-1.

1-3

例) その 町、静か

→ その 町 は 静か でした か。

はい/ええ、(その 町 は) 静か でした。

いいえ、(その 町 は) 静か じゃありません でした。

(あなた)、きのう、いそがしい

→ (あなた は) きのう いそがしかった です か。

はい／ええ、(わたし は きのう) いそがしかった です。

いいえ、(わたし は きのう) いそがしく なかった です。

1) その 町、きれい →

2) 食堂 の 食べ物、おいしい →

3) バス、時間、せいかく →

4) その レストラン、サービス、いい (よい) →

5) (あなた)、先週 の 週末、ひま →

2 ～でしょう

例) その 店 は サービス が よかった です

→ その 店 は サービス が よかった でしょう。

1) きょう の テスト は むずかしく ありません でした →

2) (あなた は) 3月1日 から 3週間 タイ へ 旅行 しました →

3) 山 は きれい でした →

4) その けしき は あまり いんしょうてき じゃありません でした →

5) (あなた は) 先週 は アルバイト を ぜんぜん しません でした →

3 ～で (the reason)

例) レポート：(わたし)、いそがしい → (わたし は) レポート で いそがしい です。

1) かぜ：きのう、(わたし)、学校、休む →

2) 用事：あした、(わたし)、大阪、行く →

3) 仕事：きょう、(わたし)、帰り、おそく なる →

4) 試験：あした、授業、ない →

5) 用事：リーさん、うち、帰る →

4-1 Adjectival nouns, adjectives in て form and なくて form

例) にぎやか → にぎやか で

→ にぎやか じゃなくて

いそがしい → いそがしくて

→ いそがしく なくて

1) 多い → 2) いい →

3) すばらしい　→　　　　7) きれい　→

4) まずい　→　　　　8) いんしょうてき→

5) 少ない　→　　　　9) しんせん　→

6) ひま　→　　　　10) 安全(あんぜん)　→

4-2 Joining adjectival clauses

例(れい)) この　ワープロ　は　新しい　です：この　ワープロ　は　デザイン　が　いい　です

→　このワープロは新しくて、(このワープロは)デザインがいいです。

1) この　ホテル　は　安(やす)い　です：(この　ホテル　は)　サービス　が　いい　です　→

2) 食べ物(たべもの)　は　しんせん　でした：(食べ物(たべもの)　は)　おいしかった　です　→

3) バス　は　時間　が　せいかく　です：(バス　は)　速い　です　→

4) その　レストラン　は　まずかった　です：(その　レストラン　は)　高かった　です　→

5) 田中(たなか)さん　の　部屋　は　広(ひろ)い　です：(田中(たなか)さん　の　部屋　は)きれい　です　→

4-3 Stating the reason implicitly

例(れい)) (わたし　は)　いそがしかった　です：(わたし　は)　パーティー　に　行きません　でした

→　いそがしくて、(わたし　は)　パーティー　に　行きません　でした。

1) 天気　が　よく　なかった　です：(わたし　は)　ざんねん　でした　→

2) いなか　は　けしき　が　きれい　でした：(いなか　は)　いんしょうてき　でした　→

3) 食べ物(たべもの)　が　しんせん　じゃありません　でした：(食べ物(たべもの)　は)　まずかったです　→

4) 今週(こんしゅう)　は　レポート　が　多い　です：(わたし　は)　いそがしい　です　→

5 Talking about sequential activities

例(れい)) (わたし　は)　飲み物(のみもの)　を　買いました：(わたし　は)　パーティー　に　行きました

→　(わたし　は)　飲み物(のみもの)　を　買って　から、パーティー　に　行きました。

1) (わたしたち　は)　昼ご飯(ひるごはん)　を　食べました：わたしたち　は　映画　を　見ました　→

2) (子ども　は)　北海道(ほっかいどう)　に　来ました：子ども　は　元気　に　なりました　→

3) (わたし　は)　少し　休みました：(わたし　は)　テニス　を　しました　→

ドリル

I　Talking about past events

A：パーティー　は　楽(たの)しかった　です　か。

B：ええ、楽(たの)しかった　です。　　B：いいえ、楽(たの)しく　{ありません　でした。／なかった　です。}

きのう	いそがしい
昼(ひる)ご飯(はん)	おいしい
今週(こんしゅう)	暑(あつ)い
映画	いい
あの　店(みせ)	高い
テスト	むずかしい
旅行	おもしろい

II　Describing past events

A：Bさん、横浜(よこはま)　は　どう　でした　か。

B：食(た)べ物(もの)　が　おいしかった　です。
　それ　に、海(うみ)　も　きれい　でした。

A：それ　は　よかった　です　ね。

B：ええ。

B：それ　が、用事　で　行きません　でした。

A：それ　は　ざんねん　でした　ね。

B：ええ。

	予定	went or not	どう　でした　か	理由
1	海(うみ)	×		雨　が　降(ふ)りました
2	京都(きょうと)	○	にわ　が　きれい おてら　が　いんしょうてき	
3	パーティー	○	にぎやか 食(た)べ物(もの)　が　おいしい	
4	山	×		レポート　が　ありました
5	北海道(ほっかいどう)	○	おんせん　が　いい けしき　が　いい	

Ⅲ Making a few comments (in one sentence)

A：日本 の 食(た)べ物(もの) は どう です か。

B：おいしくて、 安(やす)い です。　　　B：おいしい です が、 高い です。

A	B
新しい ワープロ	デザイン が いい／悪(わる)い
授業(じゅぎょう)	大きい／小さい
食堂(しょくどう)	高い／安(やす)い
東京	おいしい／おいしく ない
～さん の { テレビ	きれい／きれい じゃない
～さん の { 自転車(じてんしゃ)	軽い／重い
～さん の { 車	宿題 が 多い／少ない
	便利／不便
	むずかしい／やさしい

Ⅳ Suggesting ideas for a series of activities

A：クラス が 終(お)わって から 何 を しましょう か。

B：少し 休みましょう。

A：それから、何 を しましょう か。

B：そう です ね。少し 休んで から テニス を しましょう か。

運動(うんどう) する	晩(ばん)ご飯(はん) を 食べる	コーヒー を 飲む
テレビ を 見る	シャワー を あびる	テニス を する
新聞 を 読む	少し 休む	さんぽ を する
電話 する	次の日 の 準備(じゅんび) を する	

LISTENING AND SPEAKING

LESSON 10 第十課

ロールプレイ

CARD A

I Asking/telling impressions

You are on a weekend homestay and talking to your host mother/father. You will be asked your impressions of your life here.

CARD B

I Asking/telling impressions

A foreign student is staying with you over the weekend. Ask the student his/her impressions of life here. Topics should include college life, meals, the university dining hall, and study of the Japanese language.

CARD A

II Talking about past events

You ask a foreign student how he/she spent the holidays. Ask his/her impression of where he or she went.

CARD B

II Talking about past events

You are a foreign student. A Japanese person asks you how your holidays were. Unfortunately you could not do something that you had planned owing to urgent business.

CARD A

III Describing daily life

You and a friend talk about college life (i.e., the campus, the dormitory, classes, homework, the cafeteria).

CARD B

III Describing daily life

You and a friend talk about college life (i.e., the campus, the dormitory, classes, homework, the cafeteria).

GRAMMAR NOTES

1. Past tense of adjectives

1) Plain | Adj-かった | was Adj

Polite | Adj-かった　です | was Adj

The plain past form of adjectives is formed by adding -かった to the stem in place of -い; as with non-past forms, the polite past forms add です.

いそがしい	is busy
いそがしい　です	is busy
いそがしかった	was busy
いそがしかった　です	was busy

The stem of the adjective いい 'good' is よ- in all forms other than the non-past affirmative. (See GN1.2 below for negative forms.)

いい	is good
いい　です	is good
よかった	was good
よかった　です	was good

食堂(しょくどう)の　食べ物(たもの)は　おいしかった　です。
The food at the dining hall was tasty.

その 店(みせ)　は　サービス　が　よかった　です。
As for that store, the service was good.

2) Plain negative

Adj-く　なかった

was not Adj

Polite negative

Adj-く　ありません　でした なかった　です

was not Adj

The plain negative past form of adjectives is formed by adding -なかった (the past form of -ない 'not') to the -く form of the adjective.

With the polite negative form, the past form of the copula でした is added to ありません. It is also possible to use the plain negative past form of adjectives -なかった followed by です.

いそがしく ない	is not busy
いそがしく ない　です	is not busy
いそがしく ありません	is not busy
いそがしく なかった	was not busy
いそがしく ありません でした	was not busy
いそがしく なかった です	was not busy

Here are some negative forms of the adjective いい 'good', using the alternate stem よ-.

よく ない	is not good
よく ない です	is not good
よく ありません	is not good
よく なかった	was not good
よく なかった です	was not good

きょう の テスト は　むずかしく　ありません でした。
Today's test was not difficult.

その レストラン は　高(たか)く なかった です。
The restaurant was not expensive.

2. Past tense forms of adjectival nouns

1) Plain

AN　だった

was Adj

Polite

AN　でした

was Adj

The affirmative past form of adjectival nouns is formed by adding the past forms of the copula, which are the plain だった and the polite でした.

きれい だ	is clean/pretty
きれい です	is clean/pretty
きれい だった	was clean/pretty
きれい でした	was clean/pretty

その 町 は 静か だった。
That town was quiet.

バス は 時間 が せいかく でした。
The bus was punctual. (lit., As for the bus, its time was accurate.)

2)

Plain negative	AN じゃなかった	was not Adj
Polite negative	AN じゃありません でした	was not Adj

The negative forms of adjectival nouns are made by adding the negative forms of the copula, which are the plain じゃなかった and the polite じゃありませんでした. There are alternative forms for the polite form: ではありませんでした, which is used in writing (and formal speech), and the less common form based on plain negatives: じゃなかったです.

きれい じゃない	is not clean/pretty
きれい じゃありません	is not clean/pretty
きれい じゃなかった	was not clean/pretty
きれい じゃありません でした	was not clean/pretty
きれい ではありません でした	was not clean/pretty
きれい じゃなかった です	was not clean/pretty

駅 の 向こう は 便利 じゃなかった。
The other side of the station was not convenient.

きのう の パーティー は にぎやか じゃありません でした。

Yesterday's party was not lively.

3. Past tense forms of noun predicates

The past tense form of noun predicates is formed by adding the past tense forms of the copula to nouns. Thus, their forms are the same as those of adjectival nouns.

Plain past	N だった	was N

Polite past	N　でした	was N
Plain negative past	N　じゃなかった	was not N
Polite negative past	N　じゃありません　でした	was not N

スパゲッティ　だった	was spaghetti
スパゲッティ　でした	was spaghetti
スパゲッティ　じゃなかった	was not spaghetti
スパゲッティ　じゃありません　でした	was not spaghetti
スパゲッティ　じゃなかったです	was not spaghetti

4. Plain past tense form of verbs

The plain past tense form of verbs is made by adding the suffix -た to the stem of verbs. The formation rules are parallel to those of the -て form of verbs (L9 GN2, -て forms).

Vowel verbs	mi-ru（見る）	mi-ta（見た）	saw
	oki-ru（起きる）	oki-ta（起きた）	got up; happened
	ne-ru（寝る）	ne-ta（寝た）	went to bed
	tabe-ru（食べる）	tabe-ta（食べた）	ate
Consonant verbs	kak-u（書く）	kai-ta（書いた）	wrote
	oyog-u（泳ぐ）	oyoi-da（泳いだ）	swam
	kas-u（貸す）	kashi-ta（貸した）	lent
	mats-u（待つ）	mat-ta（待った）	waited
	ur-u（売る）	ut-ta（売った）	sold
	ka(w)-u（買う）	kat-ta（買った）	bought
	yob-u（よぶ）	yon-da（よんだ）	called
	yom-u（読む）	yon-da（読んだ）	read
	shin-u（死ぬ）	shin-da（死んだ）	died
Irregular verbs	su-ru（する）	shi-ta（した）	did
	ku-ru（来る）	ki-ta（来た）	came

Summary of Predicate Forms

			Verb	Adjective	Adj. Noun	Noun
Plain	Non-past	Affirmative	～る	～い	～だ	～だ
		Negative	～ない	～くない	～じゃない	～じゃない
	Past	Affirmative	～た	～かった	～だった	～だった
		Negative	～なかった	～くなかった	～じゃなかった	～じゃなかった
Polite	Non-past	Affirmative	～ます	～いです	～です	～です
		Negative	～ません	～くありません ～くないです	～じゃありません	～じゃありません
	Past	Affirmative	～ました	～かったです	～でした	～でした
		Negative	～ませんでした	～くありませんでした ～くなかったです	～じゃありませんでした	～じゃありませんでした

5. -て forms of adjectives, adjectival nouns, and nouns

When two or more adjectives and adjectival nouns are connected, the -て form (connective form) is used.

1) Adjectives

Adj-くて	Adj and ～

The connective form of adjectives is formed by adding -て to the -く form.

高(たか)くて おいしい　　expensive and delicious

高(たか)くて 大(おお)きくて 重(おも)い　　expensive, big, and heavy

2) Adjectival nouns

AN で	Adj and ～

The -て form of adjectival nouns is formed by adding で (the connective form of the copula).

きれい で 静(しず)か　　clean/pretty and quiet

静(しず)か で 便利(べんり) で 安全(あんぜん)　　quiet, convenient and safe

3) Nouns

N で　N and ～

GRAMMAR NOTES

LESSON 10

第十課

Noun predicates also have a connective form, which is made by adding で, as in the case of adjectival nouns.

男(おとこ) で 19さい　　male and 19 years old

この ケーキ は 安(やす)くて おいしい です。
This cake is cheap and delicious.

あの ワープロ は 軽(かる)くて 便利(べんり) です。
That word processor is light and convenient.

わたし の アパート は 静(しず)か で きれい です。
My apartment is quiet and clean.

バス は 時間(じかん) が せいかく で 速(はや)い です。
The buses are punctual and fast. (lit., As for the buses, their time is accurate and they are fast.)

あの 人(ひと) は アメリカ人(じん) で、英語(えいご) の 先生(せんせい) です。
He is an American and an English teacher.

4) The -て form of ない is なくて. Thus the negative connective form of adjectives and adjectival nouns is as follows:

Adjectives　　**Adj-く なくて**　　not Adj and/but ～

おいしく なくて 高(たか)い　　it's not delicious and (it's) expensive
高(たか)く なくて おいしい　　it's not expensive but/and (it's) delicious

Adjectival nouns　　**AN じゃなくて**　　not Adj and/but ～

しんせん じゃなくて まずい　　it's not fresh and (it) tastes awful
不便(ふべん) じゃなくて 安(やす)い　　it's not inconvenient and (it's) cheap

Nouns　　**N じゃなくて**　　not N and/but ～

えんぴつ じゃなくて ボールペン　　it's not a pencil but a ballpoint pen
アメリカ人(じん) じゃなくて カナダ人(じん)　　he's not an American but a Canadian

Note that, as in English, conjoined adjectival expressions should belong to the same general class; otherwise, a contrastive connective (such as が or けれども) is more appropriate. (Inappropriate examples below are marked with a *.)

この 部屋(へや) は きたなくて 不便(ふべん) です。
This room is dirty and inconvenient.

＊この 部屋(へや) は きたなくて 便利(べんり) です。
＊ This room is dirty and convenient.

この 部屋(へや) は きたない です が、便利(べんり) です。
This room is dirty but convenient.

この 部屋(へや) は きたない です。けれども、便利(べんり) です。
This room is dirty. But it is convenient.

5) When the cause and effect relation is obvious, the -て form may be used to give a reason or explanation implicitly. (See also GN6 immediately below.)

わたし は いそがしくて パーティー に 行(い)きません でした。
I was busy and didn't go to the party.

パーティー は にぎやか で 楽(たの)しかった です。
The party was lively and I enjoyed it.

用事(ようじ) が あって 行(い)きません でした。
I had something to do and I didn't go.

6. Reason

Nで	with N / by means of N

わたし は きのう かぜ で 休(やす)みました。
Yesterday I didn't attend because of a cold.

7. Talking about sequential activities

V-て から	after V

A sentence with the -て form of a verb followed by から expresses a time sequence and corresponds to the English 'then' or 'after'.

わたしたち が 山(やま) へ 行(い)って から、天気(てんき) が よく なりました。
We went to the mountains and then the weather got better.

少(すこ)し 休(やす)んで から、テニス を しました。
I rested a little and then played tennis. / After resting a little, I played tennis.

Note that the form with -てから expresses clearly that the activities are sequential. The form without the から (i.e., the -て form alone) may indicate sequential activities depending on the situation.

きょう は、新宿 へ 行って、食事 を して、映画 を 見ます。
Today, I will go to Shinjuku, eat, and see a movie.

宿題 を して 寝ました。
I did my homework and went to bed.

8. Asking for agreement: でしょう

S plain でしょう (⤴)	Isn't it that S?

でしょう, spoken with rising intonation (indicated by the arrow) and attached to a plain form predicate, indicates that the speaker is asking for the hearer's agreement. でしょう is the conjectural form of です (L2 GN9). Here it is used to make the sentence sound polite. The tone of voice plays an important role. Take care to avoid sounding unnecessarily accusatory by using a flat or falling intonation.

行く でしょう。(⤴)
You are going, aren't you?

これ、いい でしょう。(⤴)
This is nice, isn't it? (Isn't this nice?)

その 店 は サービス が よかった でしょう。(⤴)
As for that store, their service must have been good, (am I) right?

3月 に タイ へ 旅行した でしょう。(⤴)
You traveled to Thailand in March, didn't you?

先週 は アルバイト を ぜんぜん しなかった でしょう。(⤴)
You didn't do any part-time work last week, (am I) right?

あなた は 学生 でしょう。(⤴)
You are a student, aren't you?

READING

'My Experience at the Sentoo' (from a Student Newspaper)

せんとう

私は先週初めてせんとうに行きました。せんとうのふろはとてもひろいです。それから、ふろの上にきれいなえがありました。ふじ山とうみのえでした。日本のデザインですね。

せんとうでいろいろな人に会いました。会社の人、おすし屋さん、学生、それから、八十さいのおじいさんにも会いました。そして、日本語で話しました。せんとうは日本語のいい「じゅぎょう」です。とてもおもしろかったです。

せんとうのおゆはすこしあつかったから、おふろからすぐ出たかったんです。でも、そのおじいさんとおふろの中で三十分話しました。

せんとうからかえってから、つめたいビールを飲みました。とてもおいしかったです。（トム・スミス）

(お)ふろ	N	bath(tub)	会社(かいしゃ)	N	company
ふじ山(さん)	PN	Mt. Fuji	〜さい	N	〜 years old
うみ	N	sea, ocean	おじいさん	N	an old man
デザイン	N	design			

□ 読む前に

あなたはどこでいろいろな日本人と会いますか。

□ 質問(しつもん)

1. スミスさんはどこに行きましたか。
2. そこに何がありますか。
3. スミスさんはそこでだれに会いましたか。

□ 書きましょう

1. おもしろい日本の場所(ばしょ)／建物(たてもの)
2. 日本のデザイン

□ 話しましょう

WRITING
[KANJI]

読み方を覚えましょう

速い（はやい）: fast
軽い（かるい）: light
初めて（はじめて）: for the first time
次（つぎ）: next
理由（りゆう）: a reason
低い（ひくい）: low
太い（ふとい）: thick, fat

新しい漢字

74 天

ことば	くん	おん	いみ	かきじゅん
1 天気（てんき）		てん	heaven	一 二 チ 天

1 the weather

75 出

ことば	くん	おん	いみ	かきじゅん
1 出る（でる）・2 出す（だす）・3 出かける（でかける）	で(る)・だ(す)	しゅつ・しゅっ	to go out, to put out	丨 屮 屮 出 出

1 to go out
2 to take out, to hand in
3 to go out

76 事

ことば	くん	おん	いみ	かきじゅん
1 食事する（しょくじする）・2 火事（かじ）	こと・ごと	じ	thing (abstract), affair	一 丅 万 百 写 亘 亘 事

1 to have a meal
2 a fire

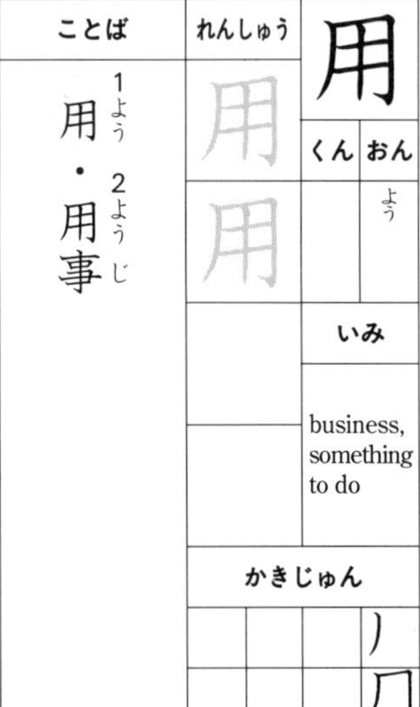

77

用

ことば	れんしゅう	くん	おん
1 用(よう)・2 用事(ようじ)	用 用		よう

いみ: business, something to do

かきじゅん: ノ 冂 月 月 用

1 business, something to do
2 business, something to do

78

仕

ことば	れんしゅう	くん	おん
1 仕事(しごと)	仕 仕		し

いみ: to serve

かきじゅん: ノ イ 亻一 什 仕

1 work

79

社

ことば	れんしゅう	くん	おん
1 会社(かいしゃ)	社 社		しゃ

いみ: society, a company

かきじゅん: ` ラ ネ ネ ネ一 ネ十 社

1 a company

80

重

ことば	れんしゅう	くん	おん
1 重い(おもい)	重 重	おも(い)	

いみ: heavy

かきじゅん: 一 二 亍 亓 亩 盲 重 重 重

1 heavy

81

聞

ことば	れんしゅう	くん	おん
1 聞く(きく)・2 聞こえる(きこえる)・3 新聞(しんぶん)	聞 聞	き(く)・き(こえる)	ぶん

いみ: to hear, to listen to

かきじゅん: 丨 ㄏ ㄏ ㄏ 門 門 門 門 門 聞 聞 聞 聞 聞

1 to hear, to ask
2 can hear, to be audible
3 a newspaper

書く練習（れんしゅう）

一、あしたの□（てんき）は□（あめ）です。

二、□（こん）晩、□（そと）で□（しょくじ）します。

三、□（げつ）曜から□（きん）曜まで□（かいしゃ）で□（しごと）します。

四、週末は、□（なに）も□（ようじ）がありません。

五、□（やす）みの□（ひ）は音楽を□（き）きます。

六、□（にほんご）の□（しんぶん）を□（よ）みます。

七、□（か）曜□（び）に宿題を□（だ）します。

八、この□（おお）きいかばんは□（おも）いです。

九、とてもいい□（てんき）です。

十、□（しごと）の□（あと）で、□（とも）だちと□（しょくじ）しました。

読む練習（れんしゅう）

一、今度の休みは用事があります。

二、この電車はとても速いです。

三、この小さいかばんは軽いです。あの大きいかばんは重いです。

四、先生は学生に理由を聞きました。

五、初めて会社で仕事しました。

六、高い山と低い山があります。

七、次の電車は何時何分ですか。

八、川の横に太い木があります。

九、きのうは天気がよかったです。外で食事しました。

十、駅を出て右へ行きました。

APPENDICES

ROLEPLAYS

第(だい)1課(か)　Lesson 1

I

A：はじめまして[1]。(わたし　は)　○○　です。 どうぞ　よろしく[2]。

B：(わたし　は)　△△　です。どうぞ　よろしく。

A：△△さん　は　アメリカ　の　人(ひと)　です　か。

B：ええ、そう　です。 ○○さん　は？

A：わたし　は　韓国人(かんこくじん)　です。

B：ああ、そう　です　か[3]。 学生(がくせい)　です　か。

A：ええ、そう　です。 △△さん　も　学生(がくせい)　です　か。

B：はい、そう　です。

II

A：すみません[4]。あれ　は　何(なん)　ですか。

B：どれ　ですか。

A：あれ　です。

B：あ[5]、あれ　は　図書館(としょかん)　です。

A：ああ、そう　です　か。 どうも　ありがとう　ございました[6]。

B：どう　いたしまして[7]。

☆★☆

A：ね、あれ、何(なに)？

B：どれ？

A：あれ。

B：あ、あれ　は　図書館(としょかん)。

A：ああ、そう。どうも　ありがとう。

B：いいえ[7]。

III

A：あのう[8]、これ　は　日本語(にほんご)　で　何(なん)　です　か。
B：どれ　です　か。
A：これ　です。
B：それ　は　「○○○」　です。
A：○○○　です　か。どうも　ありがとう　ございました。

IV

（わたし　の　名前(なまえ)　は）　○○　です。わたし　の　国(くに)　は　アメリカ　です。わたし　は　学生(がくせい)　です。専攻(せんこう)　は　経済(けいざい)　です。どうぞ　よろしく。

Expressions

1	はじめまして。	How do you do?
2	どうぞ　よろしく。	Pleased to meet you.
3	ああ、そう　です　か。	Oh, is that so?
4	すみません。	Excuse me.
5	あ、あれ　は　図書館(としょかん)　です。	Ah, that's the library.
6	どうも　ありがとう　ございました。	Thank you very much.
7	どう　いたしまして。／いいえ。	Not at all.
8	あのう、これ　は　日本語(にほんご)　で　何(なん)　です　か。	Uh (excuse me)..., what is this in Japanese?

Vocabulary

韓国人	かんこくじん	N	South Korean (person)
名前	なまえ	N	name

第2課(だいにか)　Lesson 2

I

A：すみません。図書館(としょかん)　は　何時(なんじ)　から　何時(なんじ)　まで　です　か。
B：午前(ごぜん)　8時半(じはん)　から　午後(ごご)　10時(じ)　まで　です。日曜日(にちようび)　は　休(やす)み　です。

A：午前(ごぜん) 8時半(じはん) から 午後(ごご) 10時(じ) まで。日曜日(にちようび) は 休み(やす) です ね。
B：はい、そう です。
A：どうも ありがとう ございました。

☆★☆

A：ね、図書館(としょかん) は 何時(なんじ) から 何時(なんじ) まで？
B：午前(ごぜん) 8時半(じはん) から 午後(ごご) 10時(じ) まで。日曜日(にちようび) は 休み(やす)。
A：午前(ごぜん) 8時半(じはん) から 午後(ごご) 10時(じ) まで。日曜日(にちようび) は 休み(やす) ね。
B：そう。
A：どうも ありがとう。

II

A：すみません。この 新聞(しんぶん) は いくら です か。
B：○○円(えん) です。
A：あ、その ざっし も お願い(ねが) します[1]。いくら です か。
B：○○円(えん) です。ありがとう ございました。

III

A：あのう、すみません。○○ まで いくら です か。
B：○○？ ○○ まで は・・・ ○○円(えん) です よ。
A：○○円(えん) です ね。どうも。

IV

A：ハンバーガー 1つ、ポテトフライ、コーラ の ラージ を ください。
B：ハンバーガー 1つ、ポテトフライ、コーラ の ラージ です ね。○○円(えん) です。

Expressions

1 あ、その ざっし も お願い(ねが) します。 Uh, I'll take that magazine, too.

Vocabulary

ね ね Exp attention-getter (*coll.*): hey

よ	よ	P	sentence-ending emphatic
ハンバーガー	ハンバーガー	N	hamburger
ポテトフライ	ポテトフライ	N	French-fried potatoes
コーラ	コーラ	N	cola
ラージ	ラージ	N	large

第3課(だいさんか) Lesson 3

I

A：いつも　何時(なんじ)　に　起(お)きます　か。
B：6時(じ)　です。
A：それから、朝(あさ)ご飯(はん)　を　食(た)べます　か。
B：ええ。パン　を　食(た)べます。ジュース　を　飲(の)みます。
A：何時(なんじ)　に　大学(だいがく)　に　来(き)ます　か。
B：いつも　8時(じ)　15分(ふん)　に　来(き)ます。
A：歩(ある)いて　来(き)ます　か。
B：いいえ、自転車(じてんしゃ)　で　来(き)ます。
A：そう　です　か。

☆★☆

A：いつも　何時(なんじ)　に　起(お)きる？
B：6時(じ)。
A：それから、朝(あさ)ご飯(はん)　を　食(た)べる？
B：ええ／うん。パン　を　食(た)べる　わ／食(た)べる　よ。ジュース　を　飲(の)む　わ／飲(の)む　よ。
A：何時(なんじ)　に　大学(だいがく)　に　来(く)る？
B：いつも　8時(じ)　15分(ふん)　に　来(く)る　わ／来(く)る　よ。
A：歩(ある)いて　来(く)る？
B：ううん／いや、自転車(じてんしゃ)　で　来(く)る　わ／来(く)る　よ。
A：そう[1]。

II

A：日曜日(にちようび)　は　何(なん)　を　しました　か。
B：あさ、10時(じ)　ごろ　起(お)きました。それから、朝(あさ)ご飯(はん)　を　食(た)べました。
A：それから？

B：それから　地下鉄(ちかてつ)　で　新宿(しんじゅく)　に　行(い)きました。
A：新宿(しんじゅく)　で　何(なに)　を　しました　か。
B：映画(えいが)　を　見(み)ました。それから　喫茶店(きっさてん)　で　コーヒー　を　飲(の)みました。
A：そう　です　か。何時(なんじ)　に　うち　に　帰(かえ)りました　か。
B：6時(じ)　に　帰(かえ)りました。

Expressions

1	そう。	Oh, I see.

Vocabulary

それから	それから	Conj	and then
うん	うん		an affirmative (*coll.*): yeah
わ	わ	P	the sentence-ending emphatic particle characteristic of women's speech
ううん	ううん		a negative (*coll.*): no
いや	いや		no
～ごろ	ごろ	Suf	at about (*time*)
地下鉄	ちかてつ	N	subway

第4課(だいか)　Lesson 4

I

A：今度(こんど)　の　土曜日(どようび)　は　ひま　です　か。
B：ええ、ひま　です　けど[1]・・・。
A：じゃ、いっしょ　に　テニス　を　しません　か。
B：いい　です　ね。何時(なんじ)　から？
A：9時(じ)　から　どう　です　か[2]。
B：いい　です　よ[3]。じゃ、9時(じ)　に　テニスコート　で　会(あ)いましょう。

☆★☆

A：今度(こんど)　の　土曜日(どようび)　ひま？
B：ん、ひま　だ　けど・・・。
A：じゃ、いっしょ　に　テニス　しない？
B：いい　わ　ね／いい　ね。何時(なんじ)　から？

A：9時 から どう？

B：いい わ よ／いい よ。じゃ、9時 に テニスコート で 会いましょう／会おう。

II

A：何 か 飲みません か。

B：そう です ね。ジュース を お願い します。

A：オレンジジュース を 飲みます か。りんごジュース を 飲みます か。

B：りんごジュース を お願い します。

A：はい、どうぞ[4]。

B：どうも ありがとう ございます[5]。

III

A：きのう は 何 か しました か。

B：いいえ、何 も しません でした。Aさん は どこ か へ 行きました か。

A：いいえ、どこ へ も 行きません でした。

B：そう です か。じゃ、今度 の 休み に いっしょ に 何 か しません か。

A：いい です ね。

B：もう 『○○○』 を 見ました か。

A：いいえ、まだ です。

B：じゃ、いっしょ に 見ません か。

A：ええ。

Expressions

1	ええ、 ひま です けど・・・。	I'm free... (what do you have in mind?)
2	9時 から どう です か。	How about 9 o'clock?
3	いい です よ。	O.K. / Fine.
4	どうぞ。	Here you are.
5	どうも ありがとうございます。	Thank you very much.

Vocabulary

今度	こんど	N	this/next
けど	けど	Conj	but

ひま	ひま	N, AN	free (time)
テニスコート	テニスコート	N	tennis court
オレンジジュース	オレンジジュース	N	orange juice
りんごジュース	りんごジュース	N	apple juice

第5課(だいごか) Lesson 5

I

A：いつ　日本(にほん)　に　来(き)ました　か。
B：7月(がつ)　に　来(き)ました。
A：そう　です　か。日本(にほん)　は　どう　です　か。
B：食(た)べ物(もの)　が　高(たか)い　です。それに　乗(の)り物(もの)　が　高(たか)い　です。でも　楽(たの)しい　です。
A：そう　です　か。

II

A：お国(くに)　は　どちら　です　か。
B：オーストラリア　です。
A：オーストラリア　は　どんな　国(くに)　です　か。
B：そう　です　ね[1]。大(おお)きい　国(くに)　です。　それに　空気(くうき)　も　きれい　です。
A：そう　です　か。　いい　です　ね[2]。

☆★☆

A：国(くに)　は、どこ？
B：オーストラリア。
A：オーストラリア　は　どんな　国(くに)？
A：そう　ね。／そう　だ　ね[1]。　大(おお)きい　国(くに)。それに　空気(くうき)　も　きれい。
B：そう。いい　わ　ね[2]／いい　ね。

III

［A　は　店員(てんいん)　B　は　客(きゃく)］
A：いらっしゃいませ[3]。
B：あの　セーター　は　いくら　です　か。
A：35000円(えん)　です。
B：35000円(えん)？　高(たか)い　です　ね。

A：では、これ　は　いかが　です　か[4]。

B：いい　です　ね。いくら　です　か。
A：12000円（えん）　です。
B：じゃ、これ　を　ください。
A：ありがとう　ございます。

B：そう　です　ねえ。また　来（き）ます。
A：はい、ありがとう　ございました。

Expressions

1	そう　です　ね。／そう　ね。／そうだ　ね。	Let me see ...
2	いい　です　ね。／いい　ね。	How nice.
3	いらっしゃいませ。	May I help you?
4	これは　いかが　です　か。	How about this one?

Vocabulary

楽しい	たのしい	Adj	pleasant, happy, delightful
お（国）	お（くに）	Pref	*honorific prefix* (your country)
どちら	どちら	N	where (*polite form of* どこ)
オーストラリア	オーストラリア	N	Australia
店員	てんいん	N	shop clerk
客	きゃく	N	customer
セーター	セーター	N	sweater
では	では	Conj	well then ...
いかが	いかが	Adv	how (*polite form of* どう)
また	また	Adv	again

第6課（だいか）　Lesson 6

I

A：すみません。フィルム　は　あります　か。
B：あります　よ。24枚（まい）　と　36枚（まい）　が　あります。
A：24枚（まい）　の　を　2本（ほん）　ください。
B：1050円（えん）　です。

II

A：すみません。この　あたり　に　郵便局(ゆうびんきょく)　が　あります　か。

B：ええ、あります。あそこ　に　スーパー　が　あります　ね。その　そば[1]　に　あります。

A：どうも　ありがとう　ございました。

B：いいえ、どう　いたしまして。

☆★☆

A：すみません。この　あたり　に　郵便局(ゆうびんきょく)　が　あります　か。

B：ある　わ　よ／ある　よ。あそこ　に　スーパー　が　ある　でしょ／だろ。その　そば。

A：どうも　ありがとう　ございます。

III

A：すみません。50円(えん)　の　切手(きって)　を　5枚(まい)　と　80円(えん)　の　切手(きって)　を　3枚(まい)　ください。

B：はい。

A：それから、はがき　を　2枚(まい)　お願(ねが)い　します。

B：はい。全部(ぜんぶ)　で[2]　○○円(えん)　です。

Expressions

1　その　そば　に　あります。　　It is next to that.

2　全部(ぜんぶ)　で　○○円(えん)　です。　　In all, it comes to ○○ yen.

Vocabulary

あたり	あたり	N	vicinity

第7課(だいか)　Lesson 7

I

A：Bさん　は　よく　水泳(すいえい)　を　します　か。

B：そう　です　ね。1週間(しゅうかん)　に　1回(かい)　くらい　です。あまり　時間(じかん)　が　ありません。Aさん　は？

A：わたし は 見(み)る の は 好(す)き です が、しません。

☆★☆

A：Bさん、よく 水泳(すいえい) する？

B：そう ね／そう だ ね。1週間(しゅうかん) に 1回(かい) ぐらい。あまり 時間(じかん) が ない。Aさん は？

A：わたし／ぼく は 見(み)る の は 好(す)き だ けど、しない わ／しない ね。

II

A：週末(しゅうまつ) に 何(なに) を します か。

B：たいてい テニス を します。Aさん は テニス を します か。

A：ぼく は しません。スポーツ は にがて です。

B：じゃ、週末(しゅうまつ) に 何(なに) を します か。

A：ぼく は 本(ほん) を 読(よ)みます。本(ほん) を 読(よ)む の が 好(す)き です。

B：どんな 本(ほん) を 読(よ)みます か。

A：たいてい しょうせつ を 読(よ)みます。『○○』が 好(す)き です。Bさん は 本(ほん) が 好(す)き です か。

B：わたし は 本(ほん) は あまり 読(よ)みません。ざっし は 時々(ときどき) 読(よ)みます。

A：そう です か。Bさん、音楽(おんがく) は 好(す)き です か。

B：ええ。ジャズ が 大好(だいす)き です。Aさん は？

A：ぼく は クラシック が 好(す)き です。

Vocabulary

ぼく	ぼく	N	I, me (male)
しょうせつ	しょうせつ	N	novel
ジャズ	ジャズ	N	jazz
大好き	だいすき	AN	like very much
クラシック	クラシック	N	classical

第(だい)8課(か) Lesson 8

I

A：今度(こんど) の 土曜日(どようび) に 友(とも)だち と 新宿(しんじゅく) に 行(い)く ん です が、いっしょ に 行(い)きません か。

B：新宿(しんじゅく) です か。いい です ね。いっしょ に 行(い)きたい ん です が、今度(こんど)

の 土曜日 は 用事 が ある ん です。

A：そう です か。ざんねん です ね。じゃ、また 今度 いっしょ に 行きま しょう。

B：ええ、また さそって ください。

☆★☆

A：今度 の 土曜日 に 友だち と 新宿 に 行く ん だ けど、いっしょに 行かない？

B：いい わ ね／いい ね。いっしょに 行きたい けど、今度 の 土曜日 は 用事 が ある の／ある ん だ。

A：そう。ざんねん ね／ざんねん だ ね。じゃ、また 今度[1]。

II

W：いらっしゃいませ。こちら へ どうぞ[2]。メニュー を どうぞ。

A：ステーキ を お願い します。それから サラダ を ください。

W：ステーキ と サラダ です ね。パン と ライス は どちら に します か。

A：ライス に します。

W：お飲み物 は？

A：オレンジジュース を ください。

W：はい、かしこまりました[3]。

Expressions

1	じゃ、また 今度。	Maybe next time.
2	こちら へ どうぞ。	This way, please.
3	はい、かしこまりました。	Yes, ma'am/sir.

Vocabulary

さそう	さそう	CV	to invite someone to do something
の	の		*coll. form of* のです, *often used by women.* See L8 GN5.
ん だ	ん だ		*coll. form of* のです, *often used by men.* See L8 GN5.

こちら	こちら	Dem. Pro.	this way
メニュー	メニュー	N	menu
ステーキ	ステーキ	N	steak
サラダ	サラダ	N	salad
ライス	ライス	N	rice
飲み物	のみもの	N	drink, beverage
オレンジジュース	オレンジジュース	N	orange juice

第9課 Lesson 9

I

A：すみません。 この　アパート　は　どこ　です　か。

B：2丁目　3番地　の　8、グリーンハイツ　です　か。 ああ、この　アパート　は　あの　ガソリンスタンド　の　横　です[1]。 ほら、あれ　です[2]。

A：ああ、あの　みどり　の　建物　です　か。

B：そう　です。

A：どうも、ありがとう　ございました。

☆★☆

A：すみません。 この　アパート　は　どこ　です　か。

B：2丁目　3番地　の　8、グリーンハイツ？　ああ、この　アパート　は、あの　ガソリン　スタンド　の　横　よ／横　だよ。 ほら、あれ。

A：ああ、あの　みどり　の　建物　です　か。

B：そう。

A：どうも　ありがとう　ございました。

II

A：すみません。アパート　の　ごみ　です　が・・・。

B：もえる　ごみ　は　月曜日、水曜日、金曜日　の　朝　出して　ください。

A：もえる　ごみ？　何　です　か。

B：野菜　や　紙　です。それから、プラスチック　や　ガラス　や　ビン　は　木曜日　に　出して　ください。

A：木曜日　です　ね。

B：そう　です。 それから、新聞　や　かん　は　リサイクル　します　から、　毎月　第3　土曜日　に　出して　ください。

A：毎月 1回 です ね。
B：そう です。

Expressions

1 ああ、この アパート は あの ガソリンスタンド の 横 です。 — Oh, yeah ...
2 ほら、 あれ です。 — See, ...

Vocabulary

～丁目	ちょうめ	Suf	choome, a district within a town
～番地	ばんち	Suf	division within a choome
グリーンハイツ	グリーンハイツ	N	*pn*: Green Heights (*name of apartment*)
みどり	みどり	N	green
もえるごみ	もえるごみ	N	burnable garbage
プラスチック	プラスチック	N	plastic
ガラス	ガラス	N	glass
ビン	ビン	N	bottle
かん	かん	N	can
リサイクル(する)	リサイクル(する)	N, V	recycle (to recycle)
毎月	まいつき	Adv	every month
第～ ～曜日	だい～ ～ようび	N	the (first, second, etc.) day of the month

第10課 Lesson 10

I-1

A：○○ は どう でした か。
B：すばらしかった です よ。
A：どこ が よかった です か。
B：○○ です ね。それに 旅館 も おもしろかった です。
A：よかった です ね[1]。

☆★☆

A：○○ は どう だった？

ROLEPLAYS

APPENDICES

B：すばらしかった。

A：どこ　が　よかった？

B：○○。それに、旅館（りょかん）　も　おもしろかった。

A：よかった　ね[1]。

I-2

A：○○　は　どう　でした　か。

B：それ　が[2]、用事（ようじ）　で　行（い）きません　でした。

A：そう　です　か。ざんねん　でした　ね[3]。

II

A：○○　の　生活（せいかつ）　は　どう　です　か。

B：○○　は　広（ひろ）くて、きれい　です。

A：食堂（しょくどう）　は？

B：安（やす）くて　おいしい　です　よ。

A：寮（りょう）　は　どう　です　か。

B：ぼく　の　寮（りょう）　は　古（ふる）くて　暗（くら）い　です。でも　ルームメート　は　親切（しんせつ）　で　おもしろい　です。

A：それ　は　よかった　です　ね。それじゃ、授業（じゅぎょう）　は　どう　です　か。

B：むずかしく　ありません　が、日本語（にほんご）　の　クラス　は　宿題（しゅくだい）　が　多（おお）い　です　ね。

Expressions

1　よかった　です　ね。／よかった　ね。　How nice!

2　それ　が、用事（ようじ）　で　行（い）きません　でした。　Well (what happened was), ...

3　ざんねん　でした　ね。　Oh, that's too bad.

Vocabulary

旅館	りょかん	N	ryokan, inn
ルームメート	ルームメート	N	roommate
それじゃ	それじゃ	Conj	well, then (*coll. form of* それで)

Word Lists

L2 Numbers, from 1 to 10000

1	いち	30	さんじゅう	200	にひゃく
2	に	40	よんじゅう	300	さんびゃく
3	さん	50	ごじゅう	400	よんひゃく
4	し／よん	60	ろくじゅう	500	ごひゃく
5	ご	70	ななじゅう	600	ろっぴゃく
6	ろく	80	はちじゅう	700	ななひゃく
7	しち／なな	90	きゅうじゅう	800	はっぴゃく
8	はち	100	ひゃく	900	きゅうひゃく
9	く／きゅう	101	ひゃくいち	1000	せん
10	じゅう	102	ひゃくに	2000	にせん
11	じゅういち	103	ひゃくさん	3000	さんぜん
12	じゅうに	104	ひゃくし／ひゃくよん	4000	よんせん
13	じゅうさん	105	ひゃくご	5000	ごせん
14	じゅうし／じゅうよん	106	ひゃくろく	6000	ろくせん
15	じゅうご	107	ひゃくしち／ひゃくなな	7000	ななせん
16	じゅうろく	108	ひゃくはち	8000	はっせん
17	じゅうしち／じゅうなな	109	ひゃくきゅう	9000	きゅうせん
18	じゅうはち	110	ひゃくじゅう	10000	いちまん
19	じゅうく／じゅうきゅう				
20	にじゅう				

L2 Time

1時　いちじ	8時　はちじ
2時　にじ	9時　くじ
3時　さんじ	10時　じゅうじ
4時　よじ	11時　じゅういちじ
5時　ごじ	12時　じゅうにじ
6時　ろくじ	1時半　いちじはん
7時　しちじ／ななじ	
何時　なんじ	

L2 Day of the week

Sunday	Monday	Tuesday	Wednesday	Thursday	Friday	Saturday
日曜日	月曜日	火曜日	水曜日	木曜日	金曜日	土曜日

What day of the week
何曜日

L2 Prices

1円　いちえん	10円　じゅうえん
2円　にえん	⋮
3円　さんえん	
4円　よえん	100円　ひゃくえん
5円　ごえん	⋮
6円　ろくえん	1000円　せんえん
7円　ななえん	⋮
8円　はちえん	
9円　きゅうえん	10000円　いちまんえん
何円　なんえん	
いくら	

WORD LISTS

APPENDICES

L 3 Time: Minutes

1分	いっぷん	11分	じゅういっぷん	30分	さんじゅっぷん／さんじっぷん
2分	にふん	12分	じゅうにふん	40分	よんじゅっぷん／よんじっぷん
3分	さんぷん	13分	じゅうさんぷん	50分	ごじゅっぷん／ごじっぷん
4分	よんぷん	14分	じゅうよんぷん	60分	ろくじゅっぷん／ろくじっぷん
5分	ごふん	15分	じゅうごふん		
6分	ろっぷん	16分	じゅうろっぷん		
7分	ななふん	17分	じゅうななふん		
8分	はっぷん／はちふん	18分	じゅうはっぷん／じゅうはちふん		
9分	きゅうふん	19分	じゅうきゅうふん		
10分	じゅっぷん／じっぷん	20分	にじゅっぷん／にじっぷん	何分	なんぷん

L 4 Time Spans

1時間	いちじかん
2時間	にじかん
3時間	さんじかん
4時間	よじかん
5時間	ごじかん
6時間	ろくじかん
7時間	ななじかん／しちじかん
8時間	はちじかん
9時間	くじかん
10時間	じゅうじかん
11時間	じゅういちじかん
12時間	じゅうにじかん
何時間	なんじかん
どのくらい	

L 4 Months

1月	いちがつ
2月	にがつ
3月	さんがつ
4月	しがつ
5月	ごがつ
6月	ろくがつ
7月	しちがつ
8月	はちがつ
9月	くがつ
10月	じゅうがつ
11月	じゅういちがつ
12月	じゅうにがつ
何月	なんがつ

L4 Dates

1日	ついたち	16日	じゅうろくにち
2日	ふつか	17日	じゅうしちにち
3日	みっか	18日	じゅうはちにち
4日	よっか	19日	じゅうくにち
5日	いつか	20日	はつか
6日	むいか	21日	にじゅういちにち
7日	なのか	22日	にじゅうににち
8日	ようか	23日	にじゅうさんにち
9日	ここのか	24日	にじゅうよっか
10日	とおか	25日	にじゅうごにち
11日	じゅういちにち	26日	にじゅうろくにち
12日	じゅうににち	27日	にじゅうしちにち
13日	じゅうさんにち	28日	にじゅうはちにち
14日	じゅうよっか	29日	にじゅうくにち
15日	じゅうごにち	30日	さんじゅうにち
		31日	さんじゅういちにち
何日	なんにち		

L6 Counters-1

	～枚	～台	～人	～さつ	～本	～こ	～ひき	～つ
1	いちまい	いちだい	ひとり	いっさつ	いっぽん	いっこ	いっぴき	ひとつ
2	にまい	にだい	ふたり	にさつ	にほん	にこ	にひき	ふたつ
3	さんまい	さんだい	さんにん	さんさつ	さんぼん	さんこ	さんびき	みっつ
4	よんまい	よんだい	よにん	よんさつ	よんほん	よんこ	よんひき	よっつ
5	ごまい	ごだい	ごにん	ごさつ	ごほん	ごこ	ごひき	いつつ
6	ろくまい	ろくだい	ろくにん	ろくさつ	ろっぽん	ろっこ	ろっぴき	むっつ
7	ななまい	ななだい	ななにん／しちにん	ななさつ	ななほん	ななこ	ななひき	ななつ
8	はちまい	はちだい	はちにん	はっさつ	はっぽん	はっこ	はっぴき	やっつ
9	きゅうまい	きゅうだい	きゅうにん／くにん	きゅうさつ	きゅうほん	きゅうこ	きゅうひき	ここのつ
10	じゅうまい	じゅうだい	じゅうにん	じゅっさつ／じっさつ	じゅっぽん／じっぽん	じゅっこ／じっこ	じゅっぴき／じっぴき	とお
?	なんまい	なんだい	なんにん	なんさつ	なんぼん	なんこ	なんびき	いくつ

WORD LISTS

APPENDICES

L 7 Counters-2

1）days ～日	2）weeks ～週間	3）months ～か月	4）years ～年	5）how often ～回
1 いちにち	いっしゅうかん	いっかげつ	いちねん	いっかい
2	にしゅうかん	にかげつ	にねん	にかい
3	さんしゅうかん	さんかげつ	さんねん	さんかい
4	よんしゅうかん	よんかげつ	よねん	よんかい
5	ごしゅうかん	ごかげつ	ごねん	ごかい
6 the same as days	ろくしゅうかん	ろっかげつ	ろくねん	ろっかい
7 of the month	ななしゅうかん	ななかげつ	しちねん／ななねん	ななかい
8	はっしゅうかん	はっかげつ	はちねん	はっかい
9	きゅうしゅうかん	きゅうかげつ	きゅうねん	きゅうかい
10	じゅっしゅうかん／じっしゅうかん	じゅっかげつ／じっかげつ	じゅうねん	じゅっかい／じっかい
? なんにち	なんしゅうかん	なんかげつ	なんねん	なんかい

L 16 Family Terms

わたしの～ my～	someone's～
父（ちち）	お父さん（おとうさん）
母（はは）	お母さん（おかあさん）
兄（あに）	お兄さん（おにいさん）
姉（あね）	お姉さん（おねえさん）
弟（おとうと）	弟さん
妹（いもうと）	妹さん
おじ	おじさん
おば	おばさん
そふ	おじいさん
そぼ	おばあさん
子ども（こども）	お子さん／子どもさん
むすこ	むすこさん
むすめ	むすめさん
しゅじん／おっと	ごしゅじん
かない／つま	おくさん

New Vocabulary and Expressions

第1課(だい か) Lesson 1

Word	Pronunciation (with accents)	Part of Speech	Meaning
第～	だい～	Pref	the ～st/nd/rd/th
～課	か	Quant	Lesson ～
SENTENCES			
わたし	わたし	N	I
は	は	P	*topic/theme marker, singling something out for contrast*
ジョン	ジョン	N	*pn:* John
スミス	スミス	N	*pn:* Smith
です	です		*see GN*
リー	リー	N	*pn:* Lee
～さん	さん	Suf	Mr., Mrs., Ms.
の	の		*see GN*
国	くに	N	country
中国	ちゅうごく	N	China
パク	パク	N	*pn:* Park
人	ひと	N	person/people
か	か	P	*question marker*
はい	はい	Adv	yes
ええ	ええ	Adv	yes, yeah
そう	そう	Adv	so
いいえ	いいえ	Adv	no
韓国	かんこく	N	South Korea

あれ	あれ	Dem. Pro.	that (*far from both speaker and hearer*)
何	なん←なに	Ques	what
図書館	としょかん	N	library
専攻	せんこう	N	major (field of study)
経済	けいざい	N	economics
も	も	P	also
フォーメーション			
フォーメーション	フォーメーション	N	formation (*our term for structural practice*)
例	れい	N	example
学生	がくせい	N	student(s)
アメリカ	アメリカ	N	*pn*: United States of America
～人	じん	Suf	people from ～
大学	だいがく	N	university
かさ	かさ	N	umbrella(s)
かばん	かばん	N	bag(s)
かぎ	かぎ	N	key(s)
辞書	じしょ	N	dictionary(ies)
本	ほん	N	book(s)
日本	にほん	N	Japan
あなた	あなた	N	you
留学生	りゅうがくせい	N	foreign student(s)
田中	たなか	N	*pn:* Tanaka
先生	せんせい	N	professor, teacher
寮	りょう	N	dormitory(ies)
これ	これ	Dem. Pro.	this (*close to the speaker*)
どれ	どれ	N	which
食堂	しょくどう	N	dining hall

それ	それ	Dem. Pro.	that (*close to the hearer*)
日本語	にほんご	N	Japanese language
ひらがな	ひらがな	N	hiragana
だれ	だれ	N	who
ジョージ	ジョージ	N	*pn:* George

ドリル

ドリル	ドリル	N	drill
文学	ぶんがく	N	literature
で	で	P	in, by (means of)

第2課(だいにか) Lesson 2

SENTENCES

今	いま	N, Adv	now
時間	じかん	N	time
午後	ごご	N, Adv	p.m., afternoon
～時	じ	Quant	～ o'clock
半	はん	N	half
テスト	テスト	N	test, examination
火曜日	かようび	N	Tuesday
～曜日	ようび	Quant	day of the week
おかし	おかし	N	snacks, sweets
～円	えん	Quant	en, yen
この	この	Dem. M	this ～
新聞	しんぶん	N	newspaper
前	まえ	N	before, in front of
～と～	と	P	and
を	を	P	*direct object marker*
午前	ごぜん	N, Adv	a.m., morning
～から	から	P	from
～まで	まで	P	until, to

料金	りょうきん	N	fee
三鷹	みたか	N	*pn:* Mitaka
新宿	しんじゅく	N	*pn:* Shinjuku
でしょう	でしょう		*see GN*
フォーメーション			
何時	なんじ	Ques	what time
日曜日	にちようび	N	Sunday
月曜日	げつようび	N	Monday
水曜日	すいようび	N	Wednesday
木曜日	もくようび	N	Thursday
金曜日	きんようび	N	Friday
土曜日	どようび	N	Saturday
何曜日	なんようび	Ques	what day of the week
いくら	いくら	Ques	how much
ガム	ガム	N	chewing gum
あの	あの	Dem. M	that ～ over there
ざっし	ざっし	N	magazine
フィルム	フィルム	N	(camera) film
その	その	Dem. M	that ～
コンサート	コンサート	N	concert
郵便局	ゆうびんきょく	N	post office
銀行	ぎんこう	N	bank
吉祥寺	きちじょうじ	N	*pn:* Kichijoji
東京	とうきょう	N	*pn:* Tokyo
武蔵境	むさしさかい	N	*pn:* Musashisakai
ICU	アイシーユー	N	International Christian University
イギリス	イギリス	N	*pn:* England, United Kingdom
ドリル			
プール	プール	N	swimming pool
ラボ	ラボ	N	(language) laboratory
会話	かいわ	N	conversation

NEW VOCABULARY

APPENDICES

読み方	よみかた	N	reading
漢字	かんじ	N	kanji
ビデオ	ビデオ	N	video (tape)
作文	さくぶん	N	composition, essay
休み	やすみ	N	holiday
ね	ね	P	*sentence ending: confirming one's understanding*
コーヒー	コーヒー	N	coffee
でんち	でんち	N	battery

第3課（だい　か） Lesson 3

SENTENCES

〜分	ふん／ぷん	Quant	minute(s)
いつも	いつも	Adv	always
に	に	P	*time marker:* at
起きる	おきる	VV : V_i	to get up, wake up
あした	あした、あした	N, Adv	tomorrow
へ	へ	P	*directional marker*
行く	いく	CV : V_i	to go
きのう	きのう、きのう	N, Adv	yesterday
映画	えいが	N	movie
見る	みる	VV : V_t	to see, watch, look at
夜	よる	N	night
で	で	P	*marker for place of action:* at, in, on
バス	バス	N	bus
に	に	P	*destination marker:* to
来る	くる	IV : V_i	to come
朝	あさ	N	morning
〜や〜	や	P	〜 and, 〜 among others
(お) 茶	(お) ちゃ	N	green tea, tea
飲む	のむ	CV : V_t	to drink

フォーメーション			
何分	なんぷん	Ques	how many minutes
書く	かく	CV : V_t	to write
泳ぐ	およぐ	CV : V_i	to swim
話す	はなす	CV : V_t	to speak, talk
待つ	まつ	CV : V_t	to wait
死ぬ	しぬ	CV : V_i	to die
よぶ	よぶ	CV : V_t	to call out to, invite
帰る	かえる	CV : V_t	to go home, return
買う	かう	CV : V_t	to buy
食べる	たべる	VV : V_t	to eat
する	する	IV : V_t	to do
きょう	きょう	N, Adv	today
寝る	ねる	VV : V_i	to go to bed, sleep
今晩	こんばん	N, Adv	this evening
友だち	ともだち	N	friend
うち	うち	N	home
どこ	どこ	N	where
いつ	いつ	Adv	when
読む	よむ	CV : V_t	to read
始まる	はじまる	CV : V_i	to start
昼	ひる	N	noon
昼ご飯	ひるごはん	N	lunch
けさ	けさ	N, Adv	this morning
ラジオ	ラジオ	N	radio
ニュース	ニュース	N	news
聞く	きく	CV : V_t	to listen, hear
レストラン	レストラン	N	restaurant
晩ご飯	ばんごはん	N	supper, dinner
はし	はし	N	chopsticks
フォーク	フォーク	N	fork
手	て	N	hand
ナイフ	ナイフ	N	knife
飛行機	ひこうき	N	airplane

自転車	じてんしゃ	N	bicycle
歩いて	あるいて	Adv	on foot
パン	パン	N	bread

ドリル

朝ご飯	あさごはん	N	breakfast
クラス	クラス	N	class
勉強（する）	べんきょう（する）	N, IV : V_t	studies, to study
テレビ	テレビ	N	television
それから	それから	Conj	and then
何	なに	Ques	what
ご飯	ごはん	N	(cooked) rice, meal
ジュース	ジュース	N	juice
コーラ	コーラ	N	cola
紅茶	こうちゃ	N	black tea
音楽	おんがく	N	music
テープ	テープ	N	audio/video tape
喫茶店	きっさてん	N	coffee shop
デパート	デパート	N	department store
本屋	ほんや	N	bookstore
花屋	はなや	N	flower shop
買い物（する）	かいもの（する）	N, IV : V_i	shopping, to shop
テニス	テニス	N	tennis
花	はな	N	flower
会う	あう	CV : V_i	to see, meet

第4課 (だい か) Lesson 4

SENTENCES

～時間	じかん	Quant	hour
～日	にち／か	Quant	day of the month/for ～ days
に	に	P	*indirect object marker*
家族	かぞく	N	family

写真	しゃしん	N	photograph
見せる	みせる	VV : V_t	to show
いっしょに	いっしょに	Adv	together
来週	らいしゅう	N, Adv	next week
どこか	どこか	N	somewhere
旅行（する）	りょこう（する）	N, IV : V_t	trip, to travel, take a trip
〜ましょう	ましょう		*see GN*
週末	しゅうまつ	N, Adv	weekend
何も（+neg）	なにも		*see GN*
毎日	まいにち	Adv	every day
〜月	がつ	N	month
北海道	ほっかいどう	N	*pn:* Hokkaido
フォーメーション			
何時間	なんじかん	N	how long = how many hours
どのくらい	どのくらい	N, Adv	how many times, how much, how many hours, etc.
何月	なんがつ	N	what month
何日	なんにち	N	what day of the month/how many days
手紙	てがみ	N	letter
貸す	かす	CV : V_t	to lend
子ども	こども	N	child(ren)
英語	えいご	N	English (language)
教える	おしえる	VV : V_t	to teach, tell
えはがき	えはがき	N	picture postcard
送る	おくる	CV : V_t	to send
ジョギング	ジョギング	N	jogging
今週	こんしゅう	N, Adv	this week
アパート	アパート	N	apartment, apartment house
何か	なにか	N	something
作る	つくる	CV : V_t	to make
だれか	だれか	N	someone
道	みち	N	the way, road, street

聞く	きく	CV : V_t	to ask
先週	せんしゅう	N, Adv	last week
どこへも(+neg)	どこへも		*see GN*
部屋	へや	N	room
電車	でんしゃ	N	(electric) train
乗る	のる	CV : V_i	to get on, ride
チェン	チェン	N	*pn:* Chang, Cheng, Chen
秋葉原	あきはばら	N	*pn:* Akihabara
ワープロ	ワープロ	N	word processor(s)
九州	きゅうしゅう	N	*pn:* Kyushu
テープレコーダー	テープレコーダー	N	tape recorder
ドリル			
いい	いい	Adj	good

第5課(だいか) Lesson 5

SENTENCES

広い	ひろい	Adj	spacious, roomy
静か	しずか	AN	quiet
どう	どう	Adv	how
どんな	どんな	Ques	what kind of
赤い	あかい	Adj	red
の(あかいの)	の		*see GN*
新しい	あたらしい	Adj	new
きれい	きれい	AN	pretty, beautiful, clean
それに	それに	conj	also, moreover, besides, what's more
便利	べんり	AN	convenient
でも	でも	Conj	but
高い	たかい	Adj	high, expensive
交通	こうつう	N	traffic, transportation
が	が	P	*subject marker*

フォーメーション			
おもしろい	おもしろい	Adj	interesting
大きい	おおきい	Adj	big
明るい	あかるい	Adj	clear, bright
少ない	すくない	Adj	less, a small amount
かんたん	かんたん	AN	simple, easy
いや	いや	AN	disagreeable, unpleasant, distasteful
親切	しんせつ	AN	kind
安全	あんぜん	AN	safe, secure
仕事	しごと	N	work, job
暑い	あつい	*Adj*	hot (*air, weather*)
タイ語	タイご	N	Thai (language)
むずかしい	むずかしい	Adj	difficult, hard
安い	やすい	Adj	cheap
家賃	やちん	N	rent
つまらない	つまらない	Adj	dull, boring, tedious
空気	くうき	N	air
やさしい	やさしい	Adj	easy, gentle, kind
車	くるま	N	car
小さい	ちいさい	Adj	small
ハンバーガー	ハンバーガー	N	hamburger
おいしい	おいしい	Adj	delicious
食べ物	たべもの	N	food
天気	てんき	N	weather
新幹線	しんかんせん	N	bullet train
乗り物	のりもの	N	means of transportation
電話番号	でんわばんごう	N	telephone number
佐藤	さとう	N	*pn:* Sato
古い	ふるい	Adj	old
せまい	せまい	Adj	small, narrow
暗い	くらい	Adj	dark
建物	たてもの	N	building
まど	まど	N	window

ドリル

白い	しろい	Adj	white
黒い	くろい	Adj	black
とても	とても	Adv	very
生活（する）	せいかつ（する）	N, IV : V_i	life, living, to live
多い	おおい	Adj	many, lots of, much
物	もの	N	things, goods
せが高い	せがたかい	Adj	tall (*of a person*)
せが低い	せがひくい	Adj	short (*of a person*)
低い	ひくい	Adj	low
不便	ふべん	AN	inconvenient
きたない	きたない	Adj	dirty, unclean

第6課(だいかか) Lesson 6

SENTENCES

～枚	まい	Quant	～ sheet(s) of
～台	だい	Quant	*counter for machines (e.g., TV)*
～本	ほん／ぽん／ぼん	Quant	*counter for cylindrical objects*
～人	にん	Quant	*counter for human beings*
～つ	つ	Quant	*counter for small objects*
～こ	こ	Quant	*counter for small objects*
～ひき／ぴき／びき	ひき／ぴき／びき	Quant	*counter for small animals*
～さつ	さつ	Quant	*counter for books*
ここ	ここ	Dem. Pro.	here
に	に	P	*marker showing place of existence:* in, at, on
美術館	びじゅつかん	N	art museum
ある	ある	CV : V_i	to exist (*inanimate*)
いる(学生が)	いる	VV : V_i	to exist (*animate*)
映画館	えいがかん	N	movie theater
店	みせ	N	shop, store, place of business (incl. restaurants)

切手	きって	N	(postage) stamp
はがき	はがき	N	postcard
か	か	P	or
が	が		but, *see GN*
しか（+neg)	しか	P	*with negative predicate:* nothing but

フォーメーション

いくつ	いくつ	Ques	how many
紙	かみ	N	paper
コンピュータ	コンピュータ	N	computer
消しゴム	けしゴム	N	eraser
ねこ	ねこ	N	cat
犬	いぬ	N	dog
えんぴつ	えんぴつ	N	pencil
りんご	りんご	N	apple
公園	こうえん	N	park
町	まち	N	town, city
空港	くうこう	N	airport
外国人	がいこくじん	N	foreigner
クラブ	クラブ	N	club
外国	がいこく	N	foreign country
近所	きんじょ	N	neighborhood
そこ	そこ	Dem. Pro.	that place, there (*by hearer*)
あそこ	あそこ	Dem. Pro.	that place over there
交番	こうばん	N	KOBAN, police box
ハンカチ	ハンカチ	N	handkerchief

ドリル

ボールペン	ボールペン	N	ballpoint pen
～ごろ	ごろ	Suf	at about (*time*)
駅	えき	N	(train) station
すいえい	すいえい	N	swimming
アルバイト(する)	アルバイト（する）	N, IV : V_i	part-time job, to work part-time

スーパー	スーパー	N	supermarket
動物園	どうぶつえん	N	zoo
テーブル	テーブル	N	table
つくえ	つくえ	N	desk
いす	いす	N	chair
ベッド	ベッド	N	bed
れいぞうこ	れいぞうこ	N	refrigerator
カラー	カラー	N	color
白黒	しろくろ	N	black and white
かんコーヒー	かんコーヒー	N	canned coffee drink
あたたかい	あたたかい	Adj	warm
冷たい	つめたい	Adj	cold (*thing*)
青い	あおい	Adj	blue

第7課(だいか) Lesson 7

SENTENCES

～週間	しゅうかん	Quant	～ week(s)
～か月	かげつ	Quant	～ month(s)
～年	ねん	Quant	～ year(s)
～回	かい	Quant	～ time(s)
好き	すき	AN	to like
の	の		*see GN*
時々	ときどき	Adv	sometimes
ドライブ(する)	ドライブ (する)	N, IV : V_i	drive, to go for a drive
に	に	P	per

フォーメーション

野菜	やさい	N	vegetable
きらい	きらい	AN	to dislike
スキー	スキー	N	ski
じょうず	じょうず	AN	good at, skillful
料理 (する)	りょうり (する)	N, IV : V_t	cooking, to cook

へた	へた	AN	bad at
キム	キム	N	*pn*: Kim
とくい	とくい	AN	good at (*about someone's specialty*)
歌	うた	N	song
歌う	うたう	CV : V_t	to sing
鈴木	すずき	N	*pn:* Suzuki
山のぼり	やまのぼり	N	mountain climbing
にがて	にがて	AN	poor at (*about someone's weak point*)
ピアノ	ピアノ	N	piano
ひく	ひく	CV : V_t	to play (*a musical instrument*)
読書（する）	どくしょ（する）	N, IV : V_i	reading, to read (books) for enjoyment
たいてい	たいてい	Adv	usually
あまり（+neg)	あまり	Adv	not very (*with negative predicate*)
ぜんぜん(+neg)	ぜんぜん	Adv	never
時間	じかん	N	time
～ぐらい	ぐらい	P	about

ドリル

よく	よく	Adv	often
スポーツ	スポーツ	N	sport(s)
すし	すし	N	SUSHI, raw fish on rice
ビール	ビール	N	beer
ディスコ	ディスコ	N	disco
もう少し	もうすこし	Adv. phr.	a little bit more
いかが	いかが	Ques	*polite for* どう*:* how
おなか	おなか	N	stomach
いっぱい	いっぱい	AN	full
たくさん	たくさん	Adv	a lot

第8課 Lesson 8

SENTENCES

に	に		*see GN*
なる	なる	CV : V_i	to become
ほしい	ほしい		*see GN*
将来	しょうらい	N, Adv	future
医者	いしゃ	N	doctor
～たい	たい		*see GN*
やきとり	やきとり	N	YAKITORI, grilled chicken on a skewer
きっぷ	きっぷ	N	ticket
出る	でる	VV : V_i	to come out (e.g., ticket(s))

フォーメーション

べんごし	べんごし	N	lawyer
元気	げんき	AN	fine, well, in good spirits
円	えん	N	yen
コンパクト	コンパクト	AN	compact
休む	やすむ	CV : V_t	to rest, to be absent from
遊ぶ	あそぶ	CV : V_i	to enjoy oneself
あつい	あつい	Adj	hot (*thing*)
だ	だ		*see GN*
かぜ	かぜ	N	a cold
用事	ようじ	N	business, affairs, something to do
わかる	わかる	CV : V_i	to understand
いる	いる	CV : V_i	to need
出る	でる	VV : V_i	to attend (class)
痛い	いたい	Adj	to hurt, ache, be sore
宿題	しゅくだい	N	homework, assignment
今度	こんど	N	this/next ～
海	うみ	N	sea, ocean

ドリル

服	ふく	N	clothes
くつ	くつ	N	shoe(s)
ぼうし	ぼうし	N	hat, cap
ステレオ	ステレオ	N	stereo
CD	シーディー	N	CD, compact disc
おつり	おつり	N	change
さいふ	さいふ	N	wallet, purse
クリニック	クリニック	N	clinic
ちょっと	ちょっと	Adv	a little
頭	あたま	N	head
気分	きぶん	N	feeling, mood
気持	きもち	N	feeling
悪い	わるい	Adj	bad
なぜ	なぜ	Adv	why
両親	りょうしん	N	parents
スピーチコンテスト	スピーチコンテスト	N	speech contest(s)
ぜひ	ぜひ	Adv	by all means
日	ひ	N	day
ざんねん	ざんねん	AN	too bad, a pity
山	やま	N	mountain
予定	よてい	N	plan
食事（する）	しょくじ（する）	N, IV : V_i	meal, to dine, eat a meal
でも	でも	P	or something
てんぷら	てんぷら	N	TEMPURA, deep fried fish and vegetables
メニュー	メニュー	N	menu
そば	そば	N	SOBA, Japanese buckwheat noodles
すきやき	すきやき	N	SUKIYAKI, beef and vegetable stew
（お）酒	（お）さけ	N	sake

第9課 (だい か) Lesson 9

SENTENCES

開ける	あける	VV : V_t	to open
と	と	N	door
閉める	しめる	VV : V_t	to close
(お) 金	(お) かね	N	money
から	から		*see GN*
横	よこ	N	beside

フォーメーション

電気	でんき	N	lights, electricity
消す	けす	CV : V_t	to turn off
コピー(する)	コピー (する)	N, IV : V_t	copy, to copy
取る	とる	CV : V_t	to make (a copy)
そうじ(する)	そうじ (する)	N, IV : V_t	cleaning, to clean, vacuum
つける	つける	VV : V_t	to turn on
運転 (する)	うんてん (する)	N, IV : V_t	driving, to drive
こと	こと	N	thing (*abstract*)
言う	いう	CV : V_t	to say
忘れる	わすれる	VV : V_t	to forget, leave behind
時計	とけい	N	watch/clock
いそがしい	いそがしい	Adj	busy
試験 (する)	しけん (する)	N, IV	test, exam, to give a test
上	うえ	N	on, over, above
下	した	N	under, beneath, below
中	なか	N	in, inside of
後ろ	うしろ	N	in back of, behind
右	みぎ	N	right
左	ひだり	N	left
間	あいだ	N	between
明子	あきこ	N	*pn:* Akiko (*female*)
かおる	かおる	N	*pn:* Kaoru (*female*)
CD プレーヤー	シーディープレーヤー	N	CD player

本ばこ	ほんばこ	N	bookcase
けん	けん	N	*pn:* Ken (*male*)
薬局	やっきょく	N	drugstore
すし屋	すしや	N	SUSHI restaurant
向こう	むこう	N	over there, beyond
ビル	ビル	N	building
そば	そば	N	beside, close to

ドリル

ホワイト	ホワイト	N	*pn:* White
寒い	さむい	Adj	cold (*air, weather*)
かける	かける	VV : V_t	to make (a phone call)
うるさい	うるさい	Adj	noisy, pesky, bothersome
おそい	おそい	Adj	late
自分	じぶん	N	oneself
出す	だす	CV : V_t	to post/mail (letter)
連絡（する）	れんらく（する）	N, IV : V_i	contact, to contact
気をつける	きをつける	VV : V_i	to be reminded
きちんと	きちんと	Adv	neatly
かける	かける	VV : V_t	to lock
火	ひ	N	fire
払う	はらう	CV : V_t	to pay
ごみ	ごみ	N	trash
出す	だす	CV : V_t	to put out
声	こえ	N	voice
おそく	おそく	Adv	late
ペット	ペット	N	pet
かう	かう	CV : V_t	to keep (pets)
せんたく（する）	せんたく（する）	N, IV : V_t	laundry, to do laundry
おく	おく	CV : V_t	to put, place
真ん中	まんなか	N	the center
スピーカー	スピーカー	N	speaker
ふとん	ふとん	N	FUTON, Japanese bedding
カレンダー	カレンダー	N	calendar

え	え	N	painting
ストーブ	ストーブ	N	heater
このあたり	このあたり	N, Adv	in this vicinity
となり	となり	N	next door (to)
ぶんぼうぐ屋	ぶんぼうぐや	N	stationer, stationery store
カメラ屋	カメラや	N	camera shop
パン屋	パンや	N	bakery
せんとう	せんとう	N	public bath
レコード屋	レコードや	N	record shop
ガソリン・スタンド	ガソリン・スタンド	N	gas station
病院	びょういん	N	hospital
とこや	とこや	N	barber, barbershop

第10課 Lesson 10

SENTENCES

サービス	サービス	N	service
でしょう(↗)	でしょう		*tag question, said with rising intonation*
で	で		*see GN*
デザイン	デザイン	N	design
パーティー	パーティー	N	party
～てから	てから		*see GN*

フォーメーション

長い	ながい	Adj	long
まずい	まずい	Adj	yucky, bad tasting
すばらしい	すばらしい	Adj	marvelous, wonderful
短い	みじかい	Adj	short, brief
せいかく	せいかく	AN	accurate
にぎやか	にぎやか	AN	lively, bustling
しんせん	しんせん	AN	fresh
いんしょうてき	いんしょうてき	AN	impressive

降る	ふる	CV : V_i	to fall, rain
ひま	ひま	N, AN	free time
タイ	タイ	N	Thailand
けしき	けしき	N	scenery
レポート	レポート	N	report
学校	がっこう	N	school
大阪	おおさか	N	*pn:* Osaka
帰り	かえり	N	return, homecoming
授業	じゅぎょう	N	class
ない	ない		not exist
ホテル	ホテル	N	hotel
速い	はやい	Adj	fast, speedy
いなか	いなか	N	the country (side), hometown
わたしたち	わたしたち	N	we

ドリル

楽しい	たのしい	Adj	pleasant, happy, delightful
横浜	よこはま	N	*pn:* Yokohama
理由	りゆう	N	reason
雨	あめ	N	rain
京都	きょうと	N	*pn:* Kyoto
にわ	にわ	N	garden
（お）てら	（お）てら	N	Buddhist temple
ある	ある	CV : V_i	to have
温泉	おんせん	N	hot spring
軽い	かるい	Adj	light (*weight*)
重い	おもい	Adj	heavy
終わる	おわる	CV : V_i, V_t	to finish
運動（する）	うんどう（する）	N, IV : V_i	exercise, athletics, sports, to exercise
シャワー	シャワー	N	shower
あびる	あびる	VV : V_t	to pour over oneself

次	つぎ	N	next
準備（する）	じゅんび（する）	N, IV : V_t	preparations, to get ready for
さんぽ(する)	さんぽ（する）	N, IV : V_i	walk, stroll, to go for a walk

Vocabulary in Order of Fifty Syllabary

アイシーユー［ICU］International Christian University, L2
あいだ［間］between, L9
あう［会う］to see, meet, L3
あおい［青い］blue, L6
あかい［赤い］red, L5
あかるい［明るい］clear, bright, L5
あきこ［明子］*pn*: Akiko (*female*), L9
あきはばら［秋葉原］*pn*: Akihabara, L4
あける［開ける］to open, L9
あさ［朝］morning, L3
あさごはん［朝ご飯］breakfast, L3
あした tomorrow, L3
あそこ that place over there, L6
あそぶ［遊ぶ］to enjoy oneself, L8
あたたかい warm, L6
あたま［頭］head, L8
あたらしい［新しい］new, L5
あつい［暑い］hot (*air, weather*), L5
あつい hot (*thing*), L8
あなた you, L1
あの that～ over there, L2
アパート apartment, apartment house, L4
あびる to pour over oneself, L10
あまり(＋*neg*) not very (*with negative predicate*), L7
あめ［雨］rain, L10
アメリカ *pn*: U.S.A., L1
ある to exist (*inanimate*), L6
ある to have, L10
あるいて［歩いて］on foot, L3
アルバイト（する） part-time job, to work part-time, L6
あれ that (*far from speaker and hearer*), L1
あんぜん［安全］safe, secure, L5

いい good, L4
いいえ no, L1
いう［言う］to say, L9
いかが *polite for* どう: how, L7
イギリス *pn*: England, U.K., L2
いく［行く］to go, L3
いくつ how many, L6
いくら how much, L2
いしゃ［医者］doctor, L8
いす chair, L6
いそがしい busy, L9
いたい［痛い］to hurt, L8
いつ when, L3
いっしょに together, L4
いっぱい full, L7
いつも always, L3
いなか the country(side), hometown, L10
いぬ［犬］dog, L6
いま［今］now, L2
いや disagreeable, unpleasant, distasteful, L5
いる to exist (*animate*), L6
いる to need, L8
いんしょうてき impressive, L10

うえ［上］on, over, above, L9
うしろ［後ろ］in back of, behind, L9
うた［歌］song, L7
うたう［歌う］to sing, L7
うち home, L3
うみ［海］sea, ocean, L8
うるさい noisy, pesky, bothersome, L9
うんてん（する）［運転（する）］driving, to drive, L9
うんどう（する）［運動（する）］exercise, athletics, sports, to do exercise, L10

え painting, L9

えいが［映画］movie, L3
えいがかん［映画館］movie theater, L6
えいご［英語］English (language), L4
ええ yes, yeah, L1
えき［駅］(train) station, L6
えはがき picture postcard, L4
〜えん［〜円］en, yen, L2
えん［円］yen, L8
えんぴつ pencil, L6

おいしい delicious, L5
おおい［多い］many, lots of, much, L5
おおきい［大きい］big, L5
おおさか［大阪］*pn*: Osaka, L10
おかし snacks, sweets, L2
おきる［起きる］to get up, wake up, L3
おく to put, place, L9
おくる［送る］to send, L4
おしえる［教える］to teach, tell, L4
おそい late, L9
おそく late, L9
おつり change, L8
おなか stomach, L7
おもい［重い］heavy, L10
おもしろい interesting, L5
およぐ［泳ぐ］to swim, L3
おわる［終わる］to finish, L10
おんがく［音楽］music, L3
おんせん［温泉］hot spring, L10

〜か［課］Lesson 〜, L1
か *question marker*, L1
か or, L6
が *subject marker*, L5
が but, *see GN*, L6
〜かい［〜回］〜 time(s), L7
がいこく［外国］foreign country, L6
がいこくじん［外国人］foreigner, L6
かいもの（する）［買い物（する）］shopping, to shop, L3
かいわ［会話］conversation, L2
かう［買う］to buy, L3
かう to keep (pets), L9
かえり［帰り］return, homecoming, L10
かえる［帰る］to go home, return, L3
かおる *pn*: Kaoru (*female*), L9
かぎ key, L1
かく［書く］to write, L3
がくせい［学生］student(s), L1
かける to make (a phone call), L9
かける to lock, L9
〜かげつ［〜か月］〜 month(s), L7
かさ umbrella(s), L1
かす［貸す］to lend, L4
かぜ a cold, L8
かぞく［家族］family, L4
ガソリン・スタンド gas station, L9
〜がつ［〜月］month, L4
がっこう［学校］school, L10
(お)かね［(お)金］money, L9
かばん bag, L1
かみ［紙］paper, L6
ガム chewing gum, L2
カメラや［カメラ屋］camera shop, L9
かようび［火曜日］Tuesday, L2
から from, L2
から *see GN*, L9
カラー color, L6
かるい［軽い］light (*weight*), L10
カレンダー calendar, L9
かんコーヒー canned coffee drink, L6
かんこく［韓国］*pn*: South Korea, L1
かんじ［漢字］kanji, L2
かんたん simple, easy, L5

きく［聞く］to listen, hear, L3
きく［聞く］to ask, L4
きたない dirty, unclean, L5
きちじょうじ［吉祥寺］*pn*: Kichijoji, L2
きちんと neatly, L9
きっさてん［喫茶店］coffee shop, L3
きって［切手］(postage) stamp, L6
きっぷ ticket, L8
きのう yesterday, L3
きぶん［気分］feeling, mood, L8
キム *pn*: Kim, L7
きもち［気持ち］feeling, L8
きゅうしゅう［九州］*pn*: Kyushu, L4
きょう today, L3
きょうと［京都］*pn*: Kyoto, L10
きらい to dislike, L7
きれい pretty, beautiful, clean, L5

きをつける［気をつける］to be careful, L9
きんじょ［近所］neighborhood, L6
きんようび［金曜日］Friday, L2
ぎんこう［銀行］bank, L2

くうき［空気］air, L5
くうこう［空港］airport, L6
くつ shoe(s), L8
くに［国］country, L1
くらい［暗い］dark, L5
ぐらい about, L7
クラス class, L3
クラブ club, L6
クリニック clinic(s), L8
くる［来る］to come, L3
くるま［車］car, L5
くろい［黒い］black, L5

けいざい［経済］economics, L1
けさ this morning, L3
けしき scenery, L10
けしゴム［消しゴム］eraser, L6
けす［消す］to turn off, L9
げつようび［月曜日］Monday, L2
けん *pn*: Ken (*male*), L9
げんき［元気］fine, well, in good spirits, L8

〜こ *counter for small objects*, L6
こうえん［公園］park, L6
こうちゃ［紅茶］black tea, L3
こうつう［交通］traffic, transportation, L5
こうばん［交番］KOBAN, police box, L6
こえ［声］voice, L9
コーヒー coffee, L2
コーラ cola, L3
ここ here, L6
ごご［午後］p.m., afternoon, L2
ごぜん［午前］a.m., morning, L2
こと thing (*abstract*), L9
こども［子ども］child(ren), L4
この this, L2
このあたり in this vicinity, L9
ごはん［ご飯］(cooked) rice, meal, L3
コピー(する) copy, to copy, L9
ごみ trash, L9
これ this (*close to the speaker*), L1
〜ごろ at about (*time*), L6
コンサート concert, L2
こんしゅう［今週］this week, L4
こんど［今度］this/next 〜, L8
こんばん［今晩］this evening, L3
コンパクト compact, L8
コンピュータ computer, L6

サービス service, L10
さいふ wallet, purse, L8
さくぶん［作文］composition, essay, L2
(お)さけ［(お) 酒］sake, L8
〜さつ *counter for books*, L6
ざっし magazine, L2
さとう［佐藤］*pn*: Sato, L5
さむい［寒い］cold (*air, weather*), L9
〜さん Mr./ Mrs./ Ms., L1
ざんねん too bad, a pity, L8
さんぽ（する） walk, stroll, to go for a walk, L10

〜じ［〜時］〜 o'clock, L2
シーディー［ＣＤ］CD, compact disc, L8
シーディープレーヤー［ＣＤプレーヤー］CD player, L9
しか (+*neg*) *with negative predicate*: nothing but, L6
じかん［時間］time, L2
〜じかん［〜時間］hour, L4
じかん［時間（がある）］time, L7
しけん（する）［試験（する）］test, exam, to give a test, L9
しごと（する）［仕事（する）］job, work, to work, L5
じしょ［辞書］dictionary, L1
しずか［静か］quiet, L5
した［下］under, beneath, below, L9
じてんしゃ［自転車］bicycle, L3
しぬ［死ぬ］to die, L3
じぶん［自分］oneself, L9
しめる［閉める］to close, L9
しゃしん［写真］photograph, L4
シャワー shower, L10
〜しゅうかん［〜週間］〜 week(s), L7
ジュース juice, L3
しゅうまつ［週末］weekend, L4

じゅぎょう［授業］class, L10
しゅくだい［宿題］homework, assignment, L8
じゅんび（する）［準備（する）］preparations, to get ready for, L10
じょうず good at, skillful, L7
しょうらい［将来］future, L8
ジョージ *pn*: George, L1
ジョギング jogging, L4
しょくじ（する）［食事（する）］meal, to dine, eat a meal, L8
しょくどう［食堂］dining hall, L1
ジョン *pn*: John, L1
しろい［白い］white, L5
しろくろ［白黒］black and white, L6
しんかんせん［新幹線］bullet train, L5
しんじゅく［新宿］*pn*: Shinjuku, L2
しんせつ［親切］kind, L5
しんせん fresh, L10
しんぶん［新聞］newspaper, L2
～じん［人］people from ～, L1

すいえい［水泳］swimming, L6
すいようび［水曜日］Wednesday, L2
スーパー supermarket, L6
すき［好き］to like, L7
スキー ski, L7
すきやき SUKIYAKI, beef and vegetable stew, L8
すくない［少ない］few, L5
すし SUSHI, raw fish on rice, L7
すしや［すし屋］SUSHI restaurant, L9
すずき［鈴木］*pn*: Suzuki, L7
ステレオ stereo, L8
ストーブ heater, L9
すばらしい marvelous, wonderful, L10
スピーカー speaker, L9
スピーチコンテスト speech contest(s), L8
スポーツ sport(s), L7
スミス *pn*: Smith, L1
する to do, L3

せいかく accurate, L10
せいかつ（する）［生活（する）］life, living, to live, L5
せがたかい［せが高い］tall (*of a person*), L5
せがひくい［せが低い］short (*of a person*), L5
ぜひ by all means, L8
せまい small, narrow, L5
せんこう［専攻］major (field of study), L1
せんしゅう［先週］last week, L4
せんせい［先生］professor, teacher, L1
ぜんぜん (＋*neg*) never, L7
せんたく（する）laundry, to do laundry, L9
せんとう public bath, L9

そう so, L1
そうじ（する） cleaning, to clean, vacuum, L9
そこ that place, there (*by hearer*), L6
その that～, L2
そば beside, close to, L9
そば SOBA, Japanese buckwheat noodles, L8
それ that (*close to the hearer*), L1
それに also, moreover, besides, what's more, L5
それから and then, L3

だ see GN, L8
～たい see GN, L8
タイ *pn*: Thailand, L10
～だい［～台］*counter for machines* (*e.g., TV*), L6
だい～［第～］the ～st/nd/rd/th, L1
だいがく［大学］university, L1
タイご［タイ語］Thai (language), L5
たいてい usually, L7
たかい［高い］high, expensive, L5
たくさん a lot of, L7
だす［出す］to put out, L9
だす［出す］to post/mail (letter), L9
たてもの［建物］building, L5
たなか［田中］*pn*: Tanaka, L1
たのしい［楽しい］pleasant, happy, delightful, L10
たべもの［食べ物］food, L5
たべる［食べる］to eat, L3
だれ who, L1
だれか someone, L4

ちいさい［小さい］small, L5
チェン *pn*: Chang, Cheng, Chen, L4
(お)ちゃ［(お) 茶］green tea, tea, L3
ちゅうごく［中国］*pn*: China, L1
ちょっと a little, L8

〜つ *counter for small objects*, L6
つぎ［次］next, L10
つくえ desk, L6
つくる［作る］to make, L4
つける to turn on, L9
つまらない dull, boring, tedious, L5
つめたい［冷たい］cold (*thing*), L6

て［手］hand, L3
で in, by (means of), L1
で *marker for place of action*: at, in, on, L3
で *see GN*, L10
ディスコ disco, L7
テープ audio/video tape, L3
テーブル table, L6
テープレコーダー tape recorder, L4
てがみ［手紙］letter, L4
〜てから *see GN*, L10
デザイン design, L10
でしょう *see GN*, L2
でしょう (↗) *tag question, said with rising intonation*, L10
です *see GN*, L1
テスト test, examination, L2
テニス tennis, L3
デパート department store, L3
でも but, L5
でも or something, L8
(お)てら Buddhist temple, L10
でる［出る］to come out, L8
でる［出る］to attend (*class*), L8
テレビ television, L3
てんき［天気］weather, L5
でんき［電気］lights, electricity, L9
でんしゃ［電車］(electric) train, L4
でんち battery, L2
てんぷら TEMPURA, deep fried fish and vegetables, L8
でんわ (する)［電話 (する)］telephone, to call, phone, L11
でんわばんごう［電話番号］telephone number, L5

と and, L2
と door, L9
どう how, L5
とうきょう［東京］*pn*: Tokyo, L2
どうぶつえん［動物園］zoo, L6
ときどき［時々］sometimes, L7
とくい good at (*about someone's specialty*), L7
どくしょ(する)［読書(する)］reading, to read (books) for enjoyment, L7
とけい［時計］watch, clock, L9
どこ where, L3
どこか somewhere, L4
どこへも(+*neg*) *see GN*, L4
とこや barber, barbershop, L9
としょかん［図書館］library, L1
とても very, L5
となり next door (to), L9
どのくらい how many times, how much, how many hours, etc., L4
ともだち［友だち］friend, L3
どようび［土曜日］Saturday, L2
ドライブ(する) drive, to go for a drive, L7
ドリル drill, L1
とる［取る］to make (a copy), L9
どれ which, L1
どんな what kind of, L5

ない (ある) *see GN*, L10
ナイフ knife, L3
なか［中］in, L9
ながい［長い］long, L10
なぜ why, L8
なに［何］what, L3
なにか［何か］something, L4
なにも(+*neg*)［何も］*see GN*, L4
なる to become, L8
なん←なに［何］what, L1
なんがつ［何月］what month, L4
なんじ［何時］what time, L2
なんじかん［何時間］how long = how many hours, L4
なんにち［何日］what day of the month/

how many days, L4
なんぷん［何分］how many minutes, L3
なんようび［何曜日］what day of the week, L2

に *time marker*: at, L3
に *destination marker*: to, L3
に *indirect object marker*, L4
に *marker showing place of existence*: in, at, on, L6
に per, L7
に（なる）*see GN*, L8
にがて poor at (*about someone's weak point*), L7
にぎやか lively, bustling, L10
〜にち／か［〜日］day of the month/for 〜 days, L4
にちようび［日曜日］Sunday, L2
にほん［日本］*pn*: Japan, L1
にほんご［日本語］Japanese (language), L1
ニュース news, L3
にわ garden, L10
〜にん［〜人］*counter for human beings*, L6

ね *sentence ending*: *confirming one's understanding*, L2
ねこ cat, L6
ねる［寝る］to go to bed, sleep, L3
〜ねん［〜年］〜 year(s), L7

の *see GN*, L1
の（あかいの） *see GN*, L5
の（きくのがすき） *see GN*, L7
のむ［飲む］to drink, L3
のりもの［乗り物］means of transportation, L5
のる［乗る］to get on, ride, L4

は *topic/theme marker, singling something out for contrast*, L1
パーティー party, L10
はい yes, L1
はがき postcard, L6
パク *pn*: Park, L1
はし chopsticks, L3
はじまる［始まる］to start, L3
バス bus, L3
はな［花］flower, L3
はなす［話す］to speak, talk, L3
はなや［花屋］flower shop, L3
はやい［速い］fast, speedy, L10
はらう［払う］to pay, L9
はん［半］half, L2
パン bread, L3
ハンカチ handkerchief, L6
ばんごはん［晩ご飯］supper, dinner, L3
ハンバーガー hamburger, L5
パンや［パン屋］bakery, L9

ひ［日］day, L8
ひ［火］fire, L9
ピアノ piano, L7
ビール beer, L7
〜ひき／びき／ぴき *counter for small animals*, L6
ひく to play (*a musical instrument*), L7
ひくい［低い］low, L5
ひこうき［飛行機］airplane, L3
びじゅつかん［美術館］art museum, L6
ひだり［左］left, L9
ビデオ video (tape), L2
ひと［人］person/people, L1
ひま free time, L10
びょういん［病院］hospital, L9
ひらがな hiragana, L1
ひる［昼］noon, L3
ビル building, L9
ひるごはん［昼ご飯］lunch, L3
ひろい［広い］spacious, roomy, L5

フィルム (camera) film, L2
プール swimming pool, L2
フォーク fork, L3
フォーメーション formation (*our term for structural practice*), L1
ふく［服］clothes, L8
ふとん FUTON, Japanese bedding, L9
ふべん［不便］inconvenient, L5
ふる［降る］to fall, rain, L10
ふるい［古い］old, L5
〜ふん／ぷん［〜分］minute(s), L3
ぶんがく［文学］literature, L1

ぶんぼうぐや［ぶんぼうぐ屋］stationer, stationery store, L9

へ *directional marker*, L3
へた bad at, L7
ペット pet, L9
ベッド bed, L6
へや［部屋］room, L4
べんきょう(する)［勉強(する)］studies, to study, L3
べんごし lawyer, L8
べんり［便利］convenient, L5

ぼうし hat, cap, L8
ボールペン ballpoint pen, L6
ほしい *see GN*, L8
ほっかいどう［北海道］*pn*: Hokkaido, L4
ホテル hotel, L10
ホワイト *pn*: White, L9
ほん［本］book(s), L1
～ほん／ぼん／ぽん［～本］*counter for cylindrical objects*, L6
ほんばこ［本ばこ］bookcase, L9
ほんや［本屋］bookstore, L3

～まい［～枚］～ sheet(s) of, L6
まいにち［毎日］every day, L4
まえ［前］before, in front of, L2
～ましょう *see GN*, L4
まずい yucky, bad tasting, L10
まだ not yet, L11
まち［町］town, city, L6
まつ［待つ］to wait, L3
まで until, to, L2
まど window, L5
まんなか［真ん中］the center, L9

みぎ［右］right, L9
みじかい［短い］short, brief, L10
みせ［店］shop, store, place of business (incl. restaurants), L6
みせる［見せる］to show, L4
みたか［三鷹］*pn*: Mitaka, L2
みち［道］the way, road, street, L4
みる［見る］to see, watch, look at, L3

むこう［向こう］over there, beyond, L9
むさしさかい［武蔵境］*pn*: Musashisakai, L2
むずかしい difficult, hard, L5
メニュー menu, L8

も also, L1
もう already, L11
もうすこし［もう少し］a little bit more, L7
もくようび［木曜日］Thursday, L2
もの［物］things, goods, L5

や and, among others, L3
やきとり YAKITORI, grilled chicken on a skewer, L8
やさい［野菜］vegetables, L7
やさしい easy, gentle, kind, L5
やすい［安い］cheap, L5
やすみ［休み］holiday, L2
やすむ［休む］to rest, be absent from, L8
やちん［家賃］rent, L5
やっきょく［薬局］drugstore, L9
やま［山］mountain, L8
やまのぼり［山のぼり］mountain climbing, L7

ゆうびんきょく［郵便局］post office, L2

ようじ［用事］business, affairs, something to do, L8
～ようび［曜日］day of the week, L2
よく often, L7
よこ［横］beside, L9
よこはま［横浜］*pn*: Yokohama, L10
よてい［予定］plan, L8
よぶ to call out to, invite, L3
よみかた［読み方］reading, L2
よむ［読む］to read, L3
よる［夜］night, L3

らいしゅう［来週］next week, L4
ラジオ radio, L3
ラボ (language) laboratory, L2

リー *pn*: Lee, L1
りゆう［理由］reason, L10
りゅうがくせい［留学生］foreign student(s), L1

りょう［寮］dormitory, L1
りょうきん［料金］fee, L2
りょうしん［両親］parents, L8
りょうり(する)［料理(する)］cooking, to cook, L7
りょこう(する)［旅行(する)］trip, to travel, take a trip, L4
りんご apple, L6

れい［例］example, L1
れいぞうこ refrigerator, L6
レコードや［レコード屋］record shop, L9
レストラン restaurant, L3
レポート report, L10

れんしゅう(する)［練習(する)］practice, to practice, L11
れんらく(する)［連絡(する)］contact, to contact, L9

ワープロ word processor(s), L4
わかる to understand, L8
わすれる［忘れる］to forget, leave behind, L9
わたし I, L1
わたしたち we, L10
わるい［悪い］bad, L8

を *direct object marker*, L2

KANJI INDEX

This index provides the lesson number in which kanji appear in the「新しい漢字」and「読み方を覚えましょう」sections, a single number indicating the former and a number with an R, the latter. Words in brackets indicate kanji readings which, while standard, do not appear among the controlled readings given in this book.

KANJI INDEX

APPENDICES

KANJI INDEX

APPENDICES

JAPANESE GRAMMATICAL INDEX

ENGLISH GRAMMATICAL INDEX

□著作・編集者
George D.Bedell
Marie J.Bedell
Rebecca L.Copeland
飛田 良文
平田 泉
広瀬 正宜
稲垣 滋子
Mayumi Yuki Johnson
村野 良子
中村 一郎
中村 妙子
根津 真知子(編集責任者)
小川 貴士
尾崎 久美子
鈴木 庸子
田中 真理
山下 早代子
・アルファベット順

イラストレイション：村崎 緑

ICUの日本語(にほんご) 初級(しょきゅう) 1

JAPANESE FOR COLLEGE STUDENTS: Basic Vol. 1

1996年10月11日 第1刷発行
1998年3月6日 第2刷発行

著 者 学校法人(がっこうほうじん) 国際基督教大学(こくさいきりすときょうだいがく)

発行者 野間佐和子

発行所 講談社インターナショナル株式会社
〒112-8652 東京都文京区音羽 1-17-14
電話：03-3944-6493

印刷所 大日本印刷 株式会社

製本所 大日本印刷 株式会社

定価はカバーに表示してあります。

Printed in Japan
ISBN 4-7700-1997-1